PHILOSOPHICAL ARTWORK II

Richard Schain

The emergence of an individual consciousness from the void is, after all, the most amazing fact of human life…"
Hamlin Garland, *A Son of the Middle Border*

"My conception of philosophy is that of an *art form* where the idea *is* the art."
Richard Schain, *Affirmations of Reality*

Philosophical Artwork II

ISBN 978-0-692-91510-3

Γ Π

Garric Press
Glen Ellen, CA

This book is dedicated to Melanie Dreisbach
ever the bright spirit

CONTENTS

AFTERWORD

In retrospect, the overriding aim of my writing life has been to develop and express my own soul—the metaphysical interior self. In the early years, it was an unconscious feeling to which I would have been reluctant to confess as being inadmissible self-indulgence. Beyond that stigma, however, awareness of one's soul has never been easy since the scientific culture of today does not acknowledge the existence of the human soul. The soul exists in a dimension separate from scientific empiricism and is truly the wellspring of *art*, of which philosophy, in my opinion, is the chief literary form. In the past, philosophy was wrongly called the queen of the sciences; it should have really been called the queen of the arts. In the various forms of art, an individual develops his interior self through apprehending and expressing the human condition. This is the proper subject of philosophy as well as art in general. Who knows but that perhaps each human life is destined to add in its own way to some ultimate metaphysical reality? It may seem to be clichés to state that art is created by *inspiration*, not by a display of technical skills or erudition, or to say that an artist obtains fulfillment through the *creation* of his work instead of through societal approval of it. Nevertheless, these concepts form the background upon which this book was written.

There is no greater error than confusing the *logos* or laws common to the material universe with the spiritual *logos* that is unique for every individual human being. This was an error of Heraclitus (whom I otherwise greatly admire) when he advocated the logos, "common to all." Science has universal truths but art has individual expressions. The successes of science have seduced contemporary humanity away from the art of philosophy; if the

i

latter does not recover from this seduction, it has no future worthy of its potential. In my judgment, development of the unique spiritual 'logos' of an individual expressed through the forms of art is the principal route leading one toward personal fulfillment. Those to whom these concepts are without meaning will not find this writing to be worth the effort required to read it.

Philosophical Artwork II is not the outcome of scholarly studies or phenomenological investigations. It derives from the existence-generated *thoughts* developed in the course of thirty-five years of *independent* (non-academic) philosophical activity on my part. They are based on experiences not only of the world and its inhabitants, but also of art, literature—and especially of philosophy. The term *existential* can be attached to my writings (a term that unfortunately has lost much of its meaning in contemporary usage). Existential states—emotions, sentiments, ideas, thoughts, desires—these are who I am and I treasure them dearly. I have tried to express them in a rational manner as befits a philosophical writing. Subjecting them to a dispassionate analysis would be like performing a dissection or analysis on a lifeless brain. The living reality of the expressions would be unavailable. They should be read empathetically or not read at all.

Goethe wrote that he was only interested in work that *enlivened* him, that directly impacted his interior state, and this has come to be my attitude as well. In fact, the development of interior states represents the great events in one's life. This book is a statement of the great events of my life. Poets compose poems; painters create paintings, philosophers give forth philosophy. All these activities act to form one's soul, a metaphysical occurrence clothed in deep mystery.

When I started writing philosophy many years ago, my first books were entitled *Affirmations of Reality* and *Philosophical Artwork*. My basic ideas have little changed since that time. Subsequently, I have thought a great deal more in a philosophical vein and the present writing represents the development of my thoughts. However, I cannot think of a better title than *Philosophical Artwork* so I have retained it for this work, adding the II as acknowledgement of an earlier version. I make no apologies for contradictory features; they represent expansion of my consciousness.

The third part, *Meaning of the Erotic Impulse*, represents a separate essay attached to this book. It is my effort to present *Eros* from a philosophical perspective.

A note about prefaces: This book has six prefaces, two for each of the three parts. It could easily do with a few more because an author's preface—most often really an afterword—may communicate the author's mind more authentically than the body of his writing. Author's prefaces are usually more meaningful than the critiques of litterateurs. It is to be expected that when writings are composed over a long time period, as is the case with the various parts of this book, the author's 'afterword' will undergo alterations. Hence the value of multiple 'prefaces.'

A final note: This is admittedly a long, complicated book that I wouldn't expect anyone except the most dedicated philosophic bibliophile to read in its entirety. But writing it, reviewing it, and preparing it for publication has been an education for myself. This is more than enough justification for its appearance. Besides, I think it contains many original and insightful examples of philosophical artwork.

This book would not have seen the light of day without the dedicated editorial and design work of my wife Melanie Dreisbach. I am eternally grateful to her.

Richard Schain

FIRST PART

AFFIRMATION OF REALITY

CURRENT PREFACE

C The first *Affirmations of Reality* was the product of my youthful enthusiasm for philosophy written in 1981-2 when I first took seriously my role of independent philosopher. I was not young in years, but certainly young as a philosopher. In some ways, I feel that I only wrote it yesterday although some thirty-four years have elapsed since it came into print. Compared to the history of philosophy, this is just a blink of the eye so I think it not inappropriate to revise it and republish it now.

Since then, I have matured much, but the ideas first expressed in it still serve as my guiding lights. However, there is one naïve thought that I want to firmly correct or at least modify. At that time, I had the idealistic idea that I was writing to affect others in a beneficial way. Time has taught me otherwise. The early version was, as they say in the trade, dead on arrival upon publication. Without some kind of status platform for myself, the idea was a hopeless one. "No one knew me," the philosopher Democritus remarked when he visited Athens.

However, that idea has been replaced by ones I believe to be more profound, as well as more realistic. I have altered myself by much the better in writing and rewriting my first books. I cannot imagine myself being whom I am now without having written them and the ones that followed. This is a far more meaningful accomplishment to me than the presumptuous notion of affecting others, especially since few readers would be

1

interested in an abstruse subject like affirmation of reality. A second virtue of having published them is that I can clearly and accurately bring to my present mind the thoughts of the early *Affirmations*. This is a great boon since, in some ways, I was a stronger man then than I am now. The thoughts expressed then might have long since left my consciousness if I did not have the earlier version to remind me. I can communicate with myself across the years. Perhaps years from now (I cannot expect too many) I may have the same pleasurable experience rereading this new version of my early works.

The original version has been much revised so that it is really a new book composed of three parts. I have retained the title *Affirmations of Reality* for the first part. It is to affirm the realities of life and recognize its unreal aspects that I have written this book.

If other individuals should find this writing of interest, I should be pleased; if not, *non importa*, as they say in Italy. However I would hope that anyone peering into my interior life would be respectful of it and refrain from rude remarks.

Well then, a predecessor of mine might have exclaimed! Let the music begin!

ORIGINAL PREFACE

I expect every writer engaged in the art of philosophy should give some account of himself and his motivation for writing, rather than be an unseen presence concealed by pages of print. With this thought in mind, I would like to provide a brief explanation of my motive for publishing a philosophy book, especially one written according to the archaic conception of philosophy as a search for wisdom—or reality, terms that are closely related in meaning.

There are various reasons for publishing a philosophy book. The most common of these, ever since the location of philosophy in university departments, is the desire of the author to obtain academic distinction. There are many professional benefits that follow from this achievement. This reason is not relevant to my motive as I am an independent philosopher unconnected to any academic institution. Another reason of equal importance is the desire for commercial success in the literary marketplace. It would be the height of foolishness for me to be subject to this motivation since my situation makes such an event virtually impossible. Furthermore, having an income adequate to my needs, I would only be unpleasantly burdened by the attentions of a public.

After considerable reflection, I have concluded that the urge to write and publish this book stems from a desire and sense of duty to speak truthfully about the problem of human existence as I see it. This desire has not been fulfilled throughout a lifetime of varied career activities and personal relationships. It may be that in different eras, individuals have been able to speak the truth to chosen listeners who are responsive and participatory; this was the nature of philosophy in ancient Greece. However, this opportunity has not been vouchsafed to me nor is it likely to be ever possible in our role- oriented, soul-denying western culture based on status and technology. Literary expression is the only means I have found for speaking the truth.

I should make it quite clear that I do not write for scholars who bring a different set of values to philosophy. My conception of philosophy is that of an art form dependent upon personal intuition rather than scholarly analysis. My hope for this book is for artistic success, not scholarly virtuosity.

Writers' assessment of the value of their own writings is notoriously unreliable. Stendhal dedicated his novel *Le Rouge et Le Noir* to "those lucky few" who would experience the profundity of his work. On the other extreme is the attitude of Samuel Butler who opined that no sane man would form any opinion about the merit of his own work. I am inclined to think that Butler was closer to the mark than Stendhal; therefore, I would like only to express the wish that those who might read this book may share something of the insights that have come to me through writing it.

DESIRE FOR REALITY

Human beings, it seems to me, remain very mysterious creatures in spite of the clamor about advances in the natural sciences. This is as it should be since humans would be quite remarkable if they were capable of elaborating concepts that explained themselves completely. That which one creates, one can understand and control; the phenomenon of *man* has not been created by men and so remains outside of their comprehension. What is important is that human individuals develop themselves, not understand themselves in an imaginary manner. It is a delusion to think that fulfillment in life can come from turning cognitive faculties upon the self. Fulfillment comes from *experiences* that expand one's interior self and thus develop it. I call such experiences 'real'; those that do not expand the self, I call 'unreal'. This is just a matter of my semantic preferences.

While humans cannot completely understand themselves, they are fully capable of understanding the institutions they have created to sustain their bodies, but which often act to impede their further interior development. Institutions tend to bring false pressures into everyday life. People have a habit of assuming that institutions and the objects associated with them provide a framework of reality and that they, mere individuals, are real beings only insofar as they are associated with these institutions. The beginning of wisdom for individuals is to realize that unreality is built into the fabric of all institutional activities. This is particularly important to grasp with respect to the institutions of technologically based societies since they are built upon 'science', purportedly the great revealer of reality. Nothing could be further from the truth. Neither the physical nor the social sciences fulfill the need of human beings to have real experiences in their lives.

Inhabitants of technological societies are plagued with the problems of living in a world that is unreal to them.

~ ~ ~

It is quite easy to discover the pervasive tensions of life lived in technological societies. In the United States, the epitome of such a society, there is a continuous appearance of writings dealing with the problems of its members. This is a literary vein that has existed since the turn of the nineteenth century and was most exhaustively mined by Lewis Mumford who, more than any other writer, called attention to the dehumanization produced by technology. Prior to this writing, a mass movement against nuclear arms appeared, seemingly inspired by a series of articles entitled *The Fate of the Earth by* Jonathan Schell, a journalist with prior experience writing about the Vietnamese conflict.

Schell described in vivid detail the catastrophic effects of a nuclear strike upon New York City and extrapolated it by analogy to the rest of the nation and the world. His message was that only by forsaking the current situation of militaristic nation states in favor of a nonviolent 'concert of nations' would it be possible for the world to survive. Schell was preoccupied with the fear that human society could forever disappear. Similar arguments were presented by Mumford in his monograph *In The Name Of Sanity*, which in the decade of the 1950s produced only limited public interest.

Journalistic writings usually deal with the surface of events and Schell's was no exception in spite of his frequent references to the works of philosophers. But Schell did not really consider the deeper meaning of such a phenomenon as a nuclear arms race. He ignored the realities of great power political structures that created nuclear arms for the sake of their 'security'. Large nations always feel their security is endangered by other large powers because of the intense competition for resources that is a constant feature of modern technocracies. If it is not nuclear arms, it will be something else. Politicians no more than Schell want a suicidal nuclear conflict but they do want to control the trade and technology of the world as much as they can. It is likely that a measure of safety will continue to be imposed on nuclear weapons, but there is no sign of any controls being imposed on the insatiable appetites of the technocracies occupying the steadily shrinking planet.

A threat greater than nuclear warfare in my opinion is that individuals will be gradually transformed into lesser beings; in fact, this process seems to be already well under way. An antique commentator on the late Roman Empire wrote that it is a land 'where wealth accumulates and men decay.' It is hard not to think a similar judgment could be made of many societies today. There is a continuing momentum in technological societies toward increasing impersonal controls over the general public. The concert of great nations proposed by Schell would be another step toward the anthill society prophesized by George Orwell in his book *1984* written shortly before his death. The vision of Orwell is more likely to be fulfilled than is Schell's nuclear apocalypse.

The control of nuclear weapons can be compared to treating the headache of a brain tumor with narcotics; it ameliorates the immediate problem but in time the underlying disease kills the patient. The underlying basis of the agitation over the risk of nuclear war is the ever-present dread of loss of property and life, which is symbolized by a nuclear holocaust. It is a manifestation of the deep-seated *Angst* that was recognized by Søren Kierkegaard as a consequence of the unreal existence of inhabitants of bourgeois societies. The movement against nuclear weapons for the sake of human survival has arisen in the same society that developed them for the sake of survival; one must ask why these societies feel themselves so continuously threatened. Those who do not share in the affluence of technological societies intuitively realize that the issue is not one that reflects the problems of their own lives.

If a nuclear holocaust should occur, by accident or otherwise, it might be regarded (if there be anyone left to regard it) as only the final denouement of a situation that had been developing for centuries, a final *coup de grace* leveled upon societies that had long since lost their sense of human life's direction. Perhaps we are already living in a near dead world inhabited by zombie-like creatures—ourselves. The extinction of dinosaurs did not come about because they sank into swamps; it occurred because they were no longer suited for life on earth. The nuclear holocaust issue is a diversion from more pressing problems affecting human existence.

~ ~ ~

A person should ask himself at some time or another whether he is interested in these kinds of thoughts or whether he prefers to float along unconsciously on a weak muddy current that is carrying him to who knows where. It may be the nose that is the best instrument for detecting stagnation—i.e., unreality—in one's life. One needs only to sniff a little in everyday living to detect certain odors that offend the sensibilities. Of course, continuous exposure to bad odors deadens sensitivity to them; perhaps this is a necessary accommodation for survival in technological societies.

Nonetheless, it is common for the intellectual person with highly cultivated olfactory sensibilities to sound the alarm that an unpleasant odor is in our midst; as mentioned above, this is a favorite literary theme. People become alarmed but also titillated; bad odors indicate the presence of something rotten in society, which is always of mild prurient interest. However, to truly deal with a rotten condition, one must be familiar with the healthy one, a far from easy task in a situation of widespread decay. The condition of health in societies is a very elusive quality. Still, an effort at recognition must be made and is at least as important as discussions about abolition of nuclear weapons.

Consider these two propositions: 1) the mental health of an individual is determined by his capacity to enlarge his self through significant experiences, and 2) sickness occurs when an individual attempts to do so through directions given to him by his society. It is evident these propositions have to do with the interior self. Those who do not recognize the interior self—the soul or human spirit, if one prefers metaphysical terminology—will not be responsive to these statements. I have no ability to provide insights to those who do not recognize the reality of a metaphysical interior self.

The impulse to transcend or enlarge oneself stems from a desire to experience the *reality* of the external world. For human beings, reality beyond the self is principally to be found in other human beings, although pious individuals may substitute God for other human beings. People may also refer to the experience of the natural world or of the starry skies; this often only indicates the need to escape from the unreality of technological living. Sooner or later, however, the experience of other human beings is sought when nature and the starry skies pale.

It should be unnecessary to state that nothing is as boring— and therefore as potent in arousing the desire for real experience— as vegetative life in all its repetitive monotony. I refer not only to breathing, eating, drinking, excreting, copulating, and other 'natural' functions but also to the societal activities involved in maintaining these functions. Chronic preoccupation with the processes necessary to remain alive leads to a state that is properly regarded as *vegetative* and, therefore, as subhuman. It may be that the desire for transcendental experiences arises solely out of boredom with the immanent. Sentient human beings cannot long bear vegetative life and are subject to the most varied impulses to escape from it.

~ ~ ~

An illusion that people are prone to accept is that the solitariness of self can be transcended through their senses. The essence of naïve faith is to believe that what one sees, hears, touches, tastes, smells provides one with an accurate portrayal of exterior reality. The senses provide information that permits physical survival in a competitive and dangerous world—but no more than that. Sense perceptions tell us no more about the external world than does the wind bringing the sound of men to a deer in the forest tell the deer about human civilization. If philosophy has contributed anything to the world, it is the discovery that reality does not lay in the transitory sensations their senses convey to them. They may obtain pleasure or pain but not the fulfillment that comes from the interior self experiencing reality. Anyone who desires knowledge of himself and the world must learn this ABC of higher knowledge that was set forth long ago by the founders of Greek and Hindu philosophy. It was expressed in the form of perceptual theory by Kant and has been amply confirmed by the discoveries of microphysics.

Although the illusoriness of sense perceptions is widely recognized, there has been only fleeting interest in a second error that is just as prevalent, the illusion that concepts acquired from others possess real value for the individual. This belief involves an inversion of the natural order of mental development; instead of concepts developing subsequent to life's experiences, they are established prior to experience. This is a more serious error than naïve dependence on sense perception. Concepts that are not the outcome of experience have no spiritual substance and are valueless in enriching one's life. There is always a violation of intellectual conscience in permanently holding such concepts. Common examples of this illusion are faith in an inherited religion, automatic acceptance of bourgeois values, and unwavering belief in the value of technology. Those who influence an immature person to form his concepts prior to obtaining his experiences are guilty of corrupting the young. The prevalence of such corruption in no way mitigates its immorality.

~ ~ ~

The desire to expand the self is not the private preserve of philosophers; it is a presence in the life of every human being. Every individual wants to transcend himself in order to overcome the monotony of vegetative existence. Without transcending experiences, life has to be constantly narcotized in order to be bearable. (Nietzsche said the two great narcotics of European life were alcohol and Christianity.) In some individuals, however, the desire to enlarge the self through experience is more intense than in others; these are the ones who have the most difficulty with a society founded on unreal living. One cannot be taught to desire transcending experiences; it is an inborn trait of the personality. But one can be helped to discover the unrealities of societal life and where real experience is to be found.

The key to experiencing reality is not to form a mental representation of the phenomenal world, a representation that is always illusory, but to be *affected* by the world. Reality for a sentient human being is inner experience not external imagery, interior feelings not superficial sensations.

~ ~ ~

While the desire to transcend the self is a mystical urge, the ideas of how one should live in order to fulfill this desire are very much learned from the family and social milieu in which one lives. It would be a utopian existence if one could trust the society into which one is born to provide direction that would help the individual *augment* his reality. It is the recurrent problem of humanity that their societies do not recognize the needs of the individuals within them as paramount. *A basic principle of intelligent living is that one should distrust the society into which he is born.* The childish or naïve trust of one's natal society is the reason behind most failures of individuals to advance their own development.

A perceptive observer has little difficulty noticing how members of societies other than his own are victimized by their societal values. European origin societies have justified their imperialistic tendencies by pointing to the level of superstition, tyranny, brutality, and ignorance that have existed in other areas. This recognition served as moral justification for the waves of European imperialism that engulfed most of the rest of the world. However, Europeans and Americans have not tended to realize that their own societies victimize themselves as well or have conceived of their victimization as the consequence of political or economic circumstances. They have not recognized that the fundamental weakness of their technological culture is its naïve concept of reality for the individual. Thus profound personalities like Kierkegaard or Nietzsche have very little impact on the actual life of European origin societies.

~ ~ ~

The most important aspect of a human life is the values or concepts he or she lives by. "Without a concept of life, men will refuse to live," Dostoevsky wrote; however, it usually does not come to that; men will always find some concepts to live by even if they have to forage through institutionalized trash cans to acquire them. It is well to remember that human beings are the only form of life that have the inborn ability to choose the way in which they will live.

The behavior of other animals is determined biologically according to reflexes, conditioning, and predetermined behavior patterns. Many humans are hardly different from animals; they live according to concepts handed down by their societies, which are analogous to the predetermined behavior patterns of other animal species.

A qualitative change in the lives of *Homo sapiens* occurred when they learned to form concepts from their experiences and to live according to those concepts, known as values. Other animal species have language, some are remarkably intelligent, many develop complex technologies, but the distinctive trait of humans is the ability to formulate values by which they will live. When human beings are healthy and free, the concept they hold most dear is the importance of experiencing the real world in all its dimensions. The search for reality characterizes the behavior of human beings capable of fulfilling themselves. Thus there is a reciprocal dynamic relationship between experience and concept formation.

~ ~ ~

A major difficulty for individuals is to think well enough of themselves to put their energies into their own spiritual development. They are usually taught to regard themselves as unworthy and to require causes outside of themselves that will justify their lives. Respect for the interior self seems to be a hard attitude to engender in human beings. But, as Nietzsche wrote, "the noble soul has reverence for itself." Respect for the interior self is the secret of its development. It is clearly not a biological attribute acquired automatically in the course of life. Witness the primitives of the world who at a moment's notice will give up their own personal dignity for the sake of the glitter of technological civilization. It is rare to find a noble savage who disdains the lure of the technology of 'developed' societies. Reverence for the self is a hard won reward of true culture and even then it only comes to those whose desire to experience reality is a consuming flame. The tendency toward accepting slavery exists at all levels of society. Reverence for self is the fruit of reflection, of learning, of the passion to experience reality in one's own life. The ultimate measure of the value of a society is the frequency with which such individuals appear in it. The 2400-year-old dictum of Protagoras that man is the measure of all things has never been understood in its full import.

One should never feel deprived at not being given meaningful concepts by the society in which one lives, since, after all, the only concepts of real value are those that one acquires from his own experiences. Inheriting concepts is like inheriting wealth; they affect the surface of life but they stand in the way of augmenting the self. Kierkegaard announced a great philosophic truth when he asserted purity of heart is to will one thing, to become an individual, which means to develop the interior self.

Of course, most would agree that it is desirable to become an individual; such an abstraction offends no one. The more difficult question is how shall one live in order to become an individual (which Kierkegaard seemed to misconceive). In order to consider this question, it is obligatory to carefully examine all the concepts one lives by, especially those precious family, social and religious values that have been transmitted to us through our mother's milk or its equivalent.

THE NATURE OF SIGNIFICANT EXPERIENCES

It has already been stated that the most important idea philosophers have contributed to humanity is that there is an illusory element to its perceptions of the world. Plato brought this concept into western thought; the same idea is basic to Hindu and Buddhist scriptures; it is now part of the fundamentals of philosophy (and physics) to realize that things are not as they seem to us.

Immanuel Kant further delineated the illusoriness of human perceptions, extending his analysis to include the human assumption that objects exist in space and in time. Kant demonstrated with great logical force in his *Critique of Pure Reason* that the apprehension of things in space and their persistence in time is a function of our perceptual apparatus, not of things as they really are. What we perceive are the appearance of things, the *phenomena*; the reality of things in themselves, the *noumena* in Kantian terminology, can never be known to an individual as he has no physical means of ascertaining the inner reality of anything. This concept intuited by the atomicists of ancient Greece, logically demonstrated by Kant and confirmed with the tools of modern physics is one of the great intellectual advances of culture. Only the naïve primitive thinks external objects are mirror representations of his perceptions and a darkened sun is extinguished each night by falling into the sea.

Although Kantian thought is buried in the musty archives of university libraries, it has profound meaning for those who are gripped by the desire to experience reality, not unreality, in their lives. No one can be said to have faced reality if he is not familiar with Kantianism or its equivalent. Eastern philosophers have long

14

incorporated their awareness of the illusoriness of sense perceptions into their worldview and have taught that the truth of reality is only to be found in the self. The eastern concept of self lacks the sense of active development of the individual that has been evolved in western culture, giving the former an impersonal quality. The metaphysical legends inherited from Hindu and Buddhist antiquity do not possess human depth or expressiveness by western standards. But eastern philosophy has the great virtue of focusing on the significance of self. It is this traditional awareness of the self as the center of reality that gives eastern thought its superiority over the naïve 'realism' upon which western technological society has been built. The insights of Kant have never been incorporated into western popular culture.

Yet western thought has had a feeling for the compelling urge of humans to enhance their selves through external contact, even though the nature of this contact has been subject to incorrect ideas of all sorts. External reality cannot be physically possessed, this is the bourgeois illusion; it cannot be handled as information, this is the scholar's illusion; it cannot be dominated, this is the scientist's illusion. It certainly cannot be transformed into a deity who tells us his 'will' as theologians would have us believe. But it can be *experienced*; thus when Samuel Johnson sought to disprove the Berkeleian solipsism that asserted the impossibility of knowing an external world, he ignored his gout and, kicking a large rock, exclaimed through clenched teeth, "Thus I prove the rock's existence." He proved it not by logic, but by experiencing the reality of the exquisite pain it caused to his gouty toe.

Johnson did not seek out pain simply in order to experience it; that would be masochism, he used the pain to enhance his own awareness of reality. Experience is a great teacher, it serves to enhance the self; it is *self-serving* in the deepest meaning of the expression. This expression has come to have a pejorative meaning but it is the foundation of individual existence to serve the self. Only when it refers to persons degrading themselves through hypocritical attitudes concealing their true purposes, usually that of object acquisition, is it a reprehensible activity. Much worse than self-serving behavior of any type, however, is the self in the service of imposed concepts. An imposed concept, whatever its nature, reveals the self to be in chains. The naïve self-serving person is undeveloped and can grow to learn where his true interests lie; the one in the grip of an imposed concept has often damaged his self beyond repair.

Human individuals are brought into the world with a destiny to develop themselves. This can only be done through freely experiencing the reality of the world; inherited beliefs inevitably limit this freedom. The commitment of an individual to develop himself is the one attitude necessary for fulfillment of his destiny, since every free person learns, sooner or later, that no one else will honor this commitment for him.

~ ~ ~

It cannot be denied that there are pleasurable feelings produced by conventional beliefs and conventional object possessions. In that repository of philosophical wisdom, Goethe's *Faust*, Mephistopheles sneers that the good doctor is like all other humans; in time he is bound to fall victim to his animal instincts and give up his idealistic search for knowledge. The truth is that we are all oriented to the pleasure principle; it is bred into our bones by the bourgeois society in which we have grown to maturity. Freud built his entire psychology on the desire of humans to experience pleasure, which for him, unlike Epicurus, was not simply the avoidance of pain, but was the gratification of libidinous urges. The recommendation of the Greek philosopher Democritus (acme 420 B.C.) was to allow the self no pleasure unless it was beneficial to the self. This would have seemed absurdly naive to the pessimistic mind of Freud. It is surprising that the desire to experience reality has survived at all in the pervasive pleasure orientation of the contemporary world.

The bourgeois is not merely an economic type as the Russian philosopher Nikolai Berdyaev pointed out; he is a *psychological* type found in all forms of society. The bourgeois stands for the triumph of the pleasure principle over the desire to experience reality and for the abandonment of the values of the interior self for the sake of object possession. The bourgeois spirit of object acquisition—although viewed with contempt by intellectual figures of western culture—seems to have become triumphant in the modern world of technology. However, nothing of value has ever come out of the triumph of the bourgeois mentality; the miracle of our times is that the human spirit still survives in spite of it. But it may not do so forever, and in the apocalyptic images invoked by those who warn of nuclear holocausts may conceal their unconscious fears of the bourgeois way of life.

One may have to compromise with personal weaknesses inherent in bourgeois living but it is silly to parade these weaknesses as progress. Human beings today need some possessions, they need some security of sustenance, they may need help to manage their physical needs as they grow old. It is not necessary to assume that all humans be superhuman in order to have ideals that go beyond human weaknesses. The justification for clinging to some aspects of bourgeois life is a pragmatic one; most people have physical or mental infirmities—brought on in no small measure by societal-induced dependencies—that require supports of various types. Perhaps those who have become habituated to those supports will need them for the remainder of their lives, just as some drug addicts can only survive by continuing to take replacement drugs; there may be no other solution that can preserve their life and sanity. However, one should not pompously proclaim these addictions to be success in life. One should be ashamed of possessions, ashamed of dependence on technology, and ashamed of constrictive relationships if bourgeois lifestyles have brought one to require them for survival. We should educate our young to clearly distinguish between healthful and addictive living.

~ ~ ~

Since experiences and the concepts deriving from them are the means by which individuals expand their interior self beyond the restricted horizon of survival, experiencing reality directly is the key to being alive as a human being instead of as a mere reflexive animal. In German, to live is *leben*, to experience is *erleben;* there is a natural feel for philosophy in the German language. It is easy to lose sight of the reality of direct experiences, fenced about as we are by a world of symbols, techniques and set roles. The substance of human life emerges in the individual's desire to enhance himself through meaningful experiences. This is the essence of it all, the rest are only circus sideshows.

It is undeniable that upbringing has a great deal to do with how a person chooses to experience reality. However, it is only those with a weak character who are completely submissive to societal institutions. Strong personalities resist the mandates of upbringing. If this were not the case, there would be no change in societies of any consequence and they would now all resemble anthills if they had survived at all. It is certain that resistance to one's society is necessary for an individual to develop his fullest potential. But it is also necessary that it be within the limits of human strength to resist the repressive forces in his society.

For some, family loyalties are the primary reality in a complex world. Often family is a continuation of life in the womb well into adult life. Beyond family, the established orders of society try to create their own realities in the mind of a child before he reaches the stage of independence. They try to teach a child how to adapt to societal realities. But humans learn the truth of external reality through experiencing it as individuals, not through instruction or habit. They do not learn about reality as members of a family, citizens of a state, or adherents to a religion; they learn about it functioning as independent individuals.

The strength to embark upon the rocky road toward reality is obtained by absorbing Kierkegaard's dictum that the only question of importance is whether one lives in such a way that he is conscious of being an individual, a *uomo singolare*, as the individualists of the Italian Renaissance expressed it. This is the Archimedean point, the fixed value of human life that distinguishes it from all other forms of life. Whatever does not arise out of the reality of individual experience is uninteresting; that is without experiential value. Falsehood and unreality in human life—and these terms refer to identical phenomena—have interest only from the viewpoint of psychopathology. One's interior self must resonate to these thoughts if individuality is to be possible in a society hostile to it.

~ ~ ~

The truth of many things can be learned through study of their origins. The most striking thing about the infancy of human beings is its instinct for exploration. Any mother of a healthy child will confirm this statement. As soon as control over his legs permits, he travels wherever he can; if he cannot go as fast or as gracefully as other creatures, his determination to explore the world makes up for his awkwardness. Meaningful experience for him is exploring his environment. This drive grows more sophisticated with age so that the youthful individual wants to explore nature, to travel to other lands, to experience how others live. The study of the physical sciences represents the most varied type of scientific explorations of the universe. Historical and archeological studies are retrograde explorations in time, sociological studies explorations of other peoples. All these are continuations of the child's explorations of the universe. Those who have never had these experiences remain parochial beings who do not have a sense of the world that comes with explorations.

However, explorations without physical presence involve considerable limitations of its experiential value; the more distant the vantage point, the more restricted is the experience of reality. In the experiences afforded by exposure to the popular media, the experience is almost entirely illusory, much like experiencing a society by flying over it. The media provide facts that are of no experiential value. Henry David Thoreau once wrote, perhaps with a bit of hyperbole, that he never read any worthwhile news in a newspaper. He regarded all news popularly regarded as mere gossip. One would like to know how he would react to current video news coverage that, at the time of this writing, is said to be scheduled for continuous round-the-clock broadcasting.

~ ~ ~

Travel is one of the greatest forms of acquiring new experiences. The essence of meaningful travel requires complete immersion in the new environment being explored. New functional abilities are developed under these circumstances. When this does not occur, there has been no real experience, only illusory ones. When the efforts and risks of travel are eliminated, as is so often the case today, the experiential value is also eliminated or at least so diluted that it is no longer worth the time and expense. Conversely, those who are forced into a struggle for survival during travel acquire experiences of enduring value. Travel forced by military service comes under this category. The young are usually intuitively aware of this fact; with age, however, may come the delusion that meaningful travel can be engaged in without effort or risk. There is nothing as ridiculous as tourists who completely insulate themselves against the environments they wish to explore. They would be better advised to purchase picture postcards or to view travelogues on the video.

The experience of intimacy with another living being is usually of more experiential value than that of travel. This experience often affords a new dimension to one's life. Aristotle, who had the dispassionate temperament of a scientist, regarded friendship as the most fulfilling form of human experience. Many forms of activity are of value principally as a means of developing friendships. When the activity involves survival, as in the case of war, the friendships established are at a deep level of significance. But other forms of camaraderie, although rarely as intense as wartime relationships, provide some of the most valued experiences in life. Both children and adults often experience relationships with animals as having deep meaning to them; that this applies to philosophers as well is exemplified by Schopenhauer's statement that a relationship with a faithful dog is of greater value than virtually all human relationships.

~ ~ ~

Erotic love is generally not highly regarded by philosophers and there is little in the philosophical literature about it. However, since the days of medieval courtly love, truthful men and women have realized that the most meaningful of human relationships is that of erotic love. The surge of feeling experienced in erotic relationships is unequaled by any other form of human activity; it takes possession of every aspect of the self. The surrounding world disappears as external influences that ordinarily play upon the psyche fade away. One has only to listen to popular music, read popular romances, glance at the motives appealed to by advertisers to realize that the yearning for *Eros* is one of the strongest motive forces in society.

There is good reason for this yearning because through the erotic experience, the self is enhanced in a manner afforded by no other experience in life. A person in the grip of an erotic love relationship is a transformed being; he or she becomes a different person for the same reason that suffering or loss may transform a person, except that it is a joyous transformation instead of a painful one. There is a healing quality in erotic love; the surge of sexual desire intermingled with the idealization of the loved one provides, perhaps for the only time in a person's life, a feeling of fulfillment in which body and mind are harmoniously joined together. This experience of extending the self to include another is as real as anything in life will ever be. It is not for trivial reasons that erotic experience has been regarded as a heavenly gift! The power of erotic love on one's life has been noted equally by the christian Dante and the humanist Goethe, Europe's two greatest poets. Love without sexual desire or sex without feelings of love are only weak imitations of the erotic experience whose uniqueness lies in the fusing of the physical and spiritual elements of existence.

The healing nature of erotic love needs to be more fully understood and lifted out of the crudities of reproductive biology. Perhaps its intensity stems from the biological fact that every cell of one's body bears the mark of sexual gender. The experience of erotic love seems to heal physical and psychical wounds connected to sexual limitation. One of the most remarkable aspects of erotic fulfillment is the peace it brings that "passeth all understanding," albeit such peace may be of brief duration. Neither the experience of isolated copulation or platonic friendship has this healing quality to it. The experience of homosexual relationships is of a different nature than heterosexual erotic love; there is not the merging of sexual opposites, and consequently the impact of homosexuality upon the self is different from that of heterosexual erotic experience.

Yet the inevitable consequence of withdrawal of lovers from the world is that *Eros* does not maintain itself when they are thrust back into society. The fragile flower of erotic love fades upon intrusion of societal life. It was there for a brief instant, out of time and then it is gone; not completely gone, perhaps, for the memory remains. It may be transformed into affection, gratitude, loyalty, compassion, friendship, even hatred; these are all more durable feelings that can stand the test of mundane life. The plunge into the cauldron of societal existence dissipates erotic love more surely than any other event. Lovers must bow to the reality of its evanescence since, as human beings, they cannot survive outside of society. The memory of erotic love survives, however, and has its impact on the personality. These ideas are discussed at greater length in the Third Part, *The Meaning of the Erotic Impulse*.

~ ~ ~

The tortured personalities of many of the greatest western philosophers—Pascal, Kierkegaard, Schopenhauer, Nietzsche, to name but a few—are likely to be in large part due to their inability to experience erotic fulfillment. Genuine philosophers are passionate individuals who are most in need of the healing powers of erotic love. A witty psychoanalyst has claimed that philosophy is one of the sublimations of repressed sexuality; it would have been wiser to state that all forms of artistic expression, including philosophy, are affected by the erotic impulse. I prefer to think that the impact of the philosophers like Kierkegaard or Nietzsche would have been greater with erotic enrichment of their interior selves. Their genius might have soared higher and further if they had experienced the healing powers of *Eros*. Neither was capable of living out a natural life span. Kierkegaard took refuge in his personal brand of Christianity but this did not nurture him indefinitely; his unexplained death at 42 years of age was probably related to his psychic imbalance. Similarly, the tragic flight of Nietzsche into insanity when only a few years older is the clearest sign that his way was not that of the man of the future, a concept that was the great faith of Nietzsche's life.

Brilliant personalities have difficulty with the erotic experience because their matches are not easily found. Their excessively critical attitudes do not provide favorable soil for erotic feelings to develop. The overlooking of limitations that is essential for the flowering of *Eros* does not come easily to them. In the tension between erotic expression and the cold perception of the human condition, a compromise must be struck. The central importance of the erotic experience for personality development requires the willingness and the courage to give oneself completely over to it.

Alexander Pushkin, Russia's greatest poet, understood the significance of timely erotic love. These memorable lines of his should be engraved in the mind of every budding individual:

> To love all ages owe submission.
> To youthful hearts its tempests bring
> the very boon they would petition,
> as fields are blessed by storms of spring.
> The rain of passion is not cruel,
> but bears refreshment and renewal –
> there is a quickening at the root
> that bodes full flowers and honeyed fruit.
> But at the late and sterile season,
> at the sad turning of the years,
> the tread of passion augurs tears;
> thus autumn gusts deal death and treason
> and turn the meadow into a marsh
> and leave the forests gaunt and harsh.
> *Eugene Onegin* (transl. Babette Deutsch)

~ ~ ~

Erotic love, like all life's experiences, suffers a diminishment in proportion to the frequency of its occurrence. One may experience it more than once in a lifetime as one's own personality changes and requires different stimulations for erotic fulfillment. But the obsessive search for erotic encounters is an addiction no different than other addictions. One does not enhance the self from repeated erotic experiences; the meaning of the experience steadily diminishes and becomes trivialized. There are few more pathetic sights than a compulsive Don Juan, ever searching for new love objects. The obsession with erotica found in technological societies stems from the impoverishment of a culture that lacks fulfillment for its members. The stagnating fragments of too many erotic experiences are a sure sign of degeneration of an individual.

~ ~ ~

Every man and every woman has a right to the experience of erotic love and the personal transformations that consequent to it. The society that is so constructed as to result in a significant proportion of its citizenry failing to obtain this experience is a society that has failed its people. The society that depends upon sexual deviations, prostitution, convents, monasteries, drugs, alcohol, or war to substitute for erotic experience is one that is defective and in need of major revision or replacement.

If the United States one day undertakes a revision of the political philosophy underlying its existence as a nation, its Declaration of Independence might be changed to read as follows: "We hold these truths to be self-evident, that all men and women are endowed by their creator with certain inalienable rights, that among these rights are life, liberty, and the experience of erotic love." The pursuit of 'happiness' is a superficial idea that does not deserve to be present in our one valuable national document.

THE EXPERIENCE OF ART

The expressive process called art may have come into the world out of the need of humanity for significant experiences in their life. There is a large literature on theories of art but the only essential idea is that art is a type of activity in which the artist expresses his feelings creatively and the auditor experiences the feelings of the artist through his artwork. This is a mystical process unique to human beings. It is the case for many individuals that without art, life becomes an exercise in boredom. No parade of lovers, no new territories for discovery or exploitation, no fresh accumulation of power or property saves humans from the ennui of repetitive experiences. Art is rejuvenating because it intensifies the experience of reality through contact with the feelings of the artist. There is no end to art just as there is no end to the diversity of the human personality. The person who does not experience art because he has not learned the language of art has been deprived of much of the distinctive quality of human life. And in creating art, one brings his consciousness of reality into concrete existence, an accomplishment that gives a special meaning to one's life.

Although the *sine qua non* of art is the expression of the artist's experience of reality, the value of his artwork may be affected by his conceptual depth, his talent for expression, and the originality of his style. But without that feeling for reality that the artist expresses in his own manner, there is no art. That is why the artist is so intimately involved with the question of reality and how it is distinguished from unreality.

Those concerned with art are often faced with the question of how to separate art from entertainment. It is a problem that defies simple formulation. Somerset Maugham, a literary artist who participated in both types of activities, made the profound observation that the only art of value was art that strengthened character, in other words, strengthened the self. It is natural, therefore, that a person with a concern for self searches for true art, whereas entertainment, which is of no value in developing the self, is ignored as a meaningless activity. But entertainment should not be simply regarded as a harmless diversion relieving the monotony of life; it is rather to be compared to a drug experience that narcotizes the mind. Like all addictive habits, it diverts one from the task—and the fulfillment—of experiencing the reality of the world.

One can distinguish between art and entertainment by sensing the effect that the two forms of experience has upon one's personality. Entertainment amuses, art enhances; entertainment is distinct from the self, art penetrates and enlivens the self; entertainment tranquilizes or stimulates, but art transforms. Art has an expansive effect on the interior self; entertainment has the opposite effect. Much of what is called culture is entertainment; one may divert himself with it but it is self-deceptive to think it is participation in art.

~ ~ ~

Genuine literary, visual, or musical art, meaning artwork created out of the feelings of the artist, can be readily perceived as insignificant by those who do not relate to the artwork. Socrates said he refused to write down his thoughts saying that there was no way to insure against their misuse by ignorant readers. Epicurus refused to give public lectures, presumably for the same reason. In Hindu practices, disciples are not easily accepted by gurus; they have to prove their readiness by long periods of immersion in the study of Hindu scriptures. One cannot grasp the experiences provided by art without entering into the mental set, at least temporarily, of a disciple. This is the only way that great artists such as Beethoven, Gauguin or Nietzsche can be genuinely experienced. Casual exposure to art is of little value; there must be devotion to art by the one experiencing it as well as by the one creating it.

Given the array of technologies available for transforming everything of value into pap, it is not surprising that art itself is often used for background entertainment purposes. Visiting many 'cultured' homes creates the impression that Mozart, Schubert, and Chopin worked themselves to an early death for the dinner tranquillization of the affluent. When Nietzsche said in all seriousness he could not have survived his life without music, we realize that there is a different approach to music than that revealed in its use in restaurants, dental offices, and stockbroker suites. This is the basis for Nietzsche's remark that he reached for his revolver (figuratively) when he heard the word 'culture'. It is the devotees of jazz music and the like who have the artistic approach toward music—it moves their souls.

The plastic and visual arts are likewise easily degraded into background objects to give status to business, medical, or scientific establishments, or to provide affluent homes with evidence, to use Veblen's phrase, of conspicuous consumption. Even literature is transformed into superficial diversions via the lecture podium, CD players, or social book clubs. The works of great artists are pathetically defenseless against every type of inane misuse. They are meant to be experienced wholeheartedly and lose most of their value when utilized for inferior purposes.

~ ~ ~

Art subjected to critical analysis is like a chaste virgin under examination by a police interrogator regarding her virginity. The scholar's approach to art is analytical not experiential; thus the artist and his artwork are examined, not experienced. Repressed aggressive drives of critics are often expressed in their professional work. It is astonishing how many artists attract critics who are hostile to them and unsympathetic to their work. The phenomenon is akin to vultures settling on a dead animal. Often for the critic, the artist is chiefly a source of his own professional advancement. One cannot help feeling that there is sadistic pleasure felt by certain art critics in the denigration of artists who provide them with opportunities for career advancement. There is no need to mention specific cases; every reader familiar with the arts, especially the literary ones, will recognize the phenomenon. The proper interpretation of an artist is given by one whose spirit resonates with his work; others only demean themselves by playing at dissection. The true connoisseur of art knows that responding to an artistic work is a highly personal experience in which one dares not to generalize. Just as there is a lover somewhere for every woman, so somewhere there is an appreciator for every genuine artist.

~ ~ ~

Since art is the expression of the subjective self, it is through art that an individual can have the most intimate contact with another person. One can never exhaust the subjectivity of human beings; therefore, one can never exhaust the experiences available through art. When the erotic life, the life of conquest, the bourgeois life, and all the diverse forms of human relationships have become repetitive and are palling to one's spirit, the world of art offers opportunities for fresh experiences. The worst deception of Christian culture is the myth that love is the permanent saving grace in life. Christian love is at bottom a stereotyped movement away from self, and thus necessarily a limited experience.

The motive for artistic expression remains basically a mystery although, as the poet Edward Arlington Robinson put it, it offers the highest gratification on this side of the grave. Nietzsche in his ironical manner said he wrote out his thoughts because he had found no other way of disposing of them. The philosopher Nikolai Berdyaev confessed that he wrote from a 'physiological' need to do so. There is a quality about artistic self-expression that is basic to human life, perhaps analogous to the animal need for procreation. The intensity felt through creative expression in the arts makes other forms of human activity appear insipid. Unlike erotic experience, the gratification achieved through creative art does not wane as long as one maintains perceptive and expressive powers. It may well be that the unconscious motivating force for artistic activity in an individual is the development of his interior self.

Artists usually view themselves as an elite fraternity in the world but there is no reason to believe that the artistic impulse is any more confined to a favored few than is the erotic impulse.

Inborn talent possessed by individuals is a minor factor in artistic expression. All human beings should develop their expressive artistic self; if it seems to be nonexistent, they should be concerned as to whether there is something seriously wrong with the way they are living their lives. Cultivation of self-expression deserves the highest priority in the life of individuals. Above all, individuals in bourgeois strata of society must resist the temptation to believe that their 'success' in life is measured by the sum total of their possessions and their influence in society. Nor is 'doing good' a counterbalance to bourgeois materialism. One can be an admired do-gooder in the world; still there will be the craving for something more in one's interior being. I think a person should be ashamed of having too many possessions, too much money, too much power, or too many conventional relationships. In our convention-ridden society, these are signs of vulgarity of mind. Only the development of the self through art in one of its many forms leads to the sense of having fulfilled one's task in life.

~ ~ ~

The question of remuneration of the artist contains a fundamental contradiction. The conscious desire of an artist is to *affect* others with his artwork. No artist is free of this desire, he dreams of the person responsive to his art even if it is an unknown, even an unborn person. *"L'art pour l'art"* only means that the artist does not yet know his audience. One may be sure that if the artist were certain his work would be shut up in a cave forever, his creative activity would soon stop. There is no art without an audience anymore then there is thunder without a listener.

However, in conventional bourgeois society, the artist's desire to affect others is quickly transformed into a desire for monetary remuneration, which is a different thing than affecting others. An artist may become resentful if he is not successful on the bourgeois plane of living. This is a dangerous attitude for a creative person as it is only a step away from his transformation into a paid entertainer. It is right that an entertainer be paid since his efforts are motivated by the obligation to entertain his audience, not to engage in personal self-expression. A creative artist cannot expect to be entertaining; the reverse is more likely to be the case as it is impossible to affect someone deeply and entertain them simultaneously.

Nevertheless, the artist must live. It is better for him to have a trade with a stable income even if it is at the cost of some of his energies. This will protect him from the deterioration invariably consequent to artist turned entertainer. This was the view of Leo Tolstoy expressed in his celebrated essay *What is Art*, but his reason was that life lived in conjunction with others for mutual support was more conducive to artistic expression than the traditional social isolation of the artist. Somerset Maugham in his literary self-analysis *The Summing Up* advised struggling artists to obtain government posts because in such work, the artist has the best opportunity to preserve his energies for his principal task. Maugham should have followed his own advice; the need to write popular stories to support his expensive lifestyle led him into avenues that did not tend to fully develop his literary potential. This tendency seems to bedevil literary persons more than other artists. In contemporary American society, one sees the ludicrous spectacle of talented writers grinding out works in order to deal with tax debts or alimony payments.

When institutions, government or otherwise, begin providing for the artist according to their appraisal of his artistic merit or potential, he becomes psychologically crippled. The artist should work against society, not for it; the artist who relies upon patrons or institutions to support him gradually becomes a hired artisan instead of a creative artist whose task it is to reveal reality. This was as true for Michelangelo and Raphael as it was for the socialist realists of our time. Who can say what the talented craftsmen of the Renaissance would have produced if they had not had to answer to a Holy Apostolic Church, *urbem et orbem*, which sets limits to their creative spirit? The judgment of Gauguin sums up the relationship of creative expression with respect to all institutions, "What the state encourages, languishes; what it protects, dies."

The figure of Fyodor Dostoevsky is one of the most striking examples of a writer of genius being compromised by monetary pressures. Dostoevsky himself admitted that much of what he wrote was to meet deadlines in order to support his family. His unique genius for psychological portrayal should not blind one to the fact that he did not develop his capacities, as did a Goethe or a Berdyaev. Dostoevsky the entertainer is never far from Dostoevsky the artist. His conceptual level remained limited; he was obsessed by the figure of Christ while arduously turning out one novel after another depicting the psychopathological characters that it was his special talent to create.

~ ~ ~

The psychology of the artist is a productive area for those interested in human development; it is more relevant to the human condition than are the perennial preoccupations with psychosexual matters or with radical politics. The dream of the artist is to affect others through expression of his feelings in art form. What does this mean "to affect others"? Nietzsche regarded all desire to affect others as a 'will to power', an expression that has given an opportunity for abuse of him by those who dislike Nietzsche. He would have done better to refer to a 'will to affect others'.

The desire to affect others is an unfamiliar concept in society. Western society has recognized the desire to help others, to harm others, to love others, to dominate others—but to 'affect' them is not generally regarded as an important form of human relationships. Nevertheless, one can say with confidence that the artist does not wish to help, harm, love, or dominate his auditor; he wants to *affect* him in a special way. He wants the thoughts and feelings expressed in his artwork to so affect his auditor that the latter's spiritual state is altered. This may be visualized on the level of energetics; the artist has a surplus of psychic perceptions that he wishes to flow into a receptive person. Fulfillment for the artist comes when his perceptions and feelings are assimilated by another, be it only a single individual. The perceptive Heraclitus asserted, "One is worth ten thousand, if he be the best." A vast public is not needed. In the case of writers, painters, or plastic artists, this process may be deferred to posterity, but it must be envisioned as occurring. Otherwise, the artist has expressed himself in vain.

Just as the artist desires to *fulfill* himself by affecting his auditor through his art, so the auditor desires to *develop* himself by experiencing the artist through his artwork. The auditor has as much responsibility as the artist in this process for if he wishes to be affected by the artist, he must dedicate himself to the experience. Serious attention to art is akin to erotic love; one must be ardent toward the loved one. For the perceptions and feelings of the artist to affect the auditor, the latter must embrace the artwork with all the concentrated sentience available to him; he must assume, at least for the moment, the role of disciple.

The experience of art is the highest form of personal development since art is the repository of the highest forms of human expression. Every person should yearn for experiences of art as he yearns for experiences in love; these are the experiences that lead to the enhancement of the self, the *soul*; if this writer be permitted an antiquated term. The person who is unresponsive to art is a *dead soul*; he may function on a physical, intellectual, or emotional plane but he is dead to the uniqueness of his species. I believe that a society that does not prepare its members for the experiences of art is no better than one that does not prepare them to read or write. The recurrent tragedy of the human condition is the death of a person who has lived without *experiencing* art; he cannot be said to have lived humanly, he has only occupied space on a congested planet.

~ ~ ~

If an artist touches the interior self of an auditor, all of his work should be experienced for a meaningful appreciation of his art; his life too should be understood and related to the artwork. It is absurd to think that an artist's life is irrelevant to his art; this is the way of the fundamentalist who believes his revelations come from above. Art is the outcome of the life of the artist; therefore, appreciation of the artist's life and milieu gives depth to appreciation of his work. It is difficult to imagine being fully able to appreciate the works of Dostoevsky, Joyce, Pound, Strindberg, Pessoa, Nietzsche, or any other important literary artists of past eras without familiarity with their lives. The same is true of visual artists. One major difficulty in appreciating contemporary art is the obscurity that usually surrounds the life of artists. An artist who seeks the attention of others should not hesitate to reveal the depths of his life to those who are genuinely interested in his artwork.

Religiosity, nationalism, communism, capitalism, adventurism, bourgeois life—all these styles of living have had their day and are becoming paper tigers unable to command allegiance from human beings. The arena of the world is now occupied by two forces, those of scientific technology and of creative art. It may appear to be an unequal contest between a powerful Goliath and a helpless David, except that art has one powerful ally, the desire of individuals to experience spiritual instead of mechanical reality. Not out of the love of art but out of "the natural tendency of maturing thought toward personal realism," to paraphrase Susanne Langer's profound insight (*Philosophy in a New Key*), will come the breakdown of a dominating technology. Unrestrained capitalism is like a Dionysian rite; it is a denial of the soul in favor of a perverted acquisitiveness.

Human beings ultimately orient themselves, not toward the unreality of impersonal technology, but toward their interior self and the interior self of others. I believe the society of the future will be based on the dominance of art, just as religion has been dominant in the past and technology is dominant in the present. It is only necessary for individuals to maintain their desire for personal reality.

~ ~ ~

A person should periodically consider the plane of existence on which he lives. The physical self of most people functions on a set plane although this can be altered to a certain extent. For example, through rigorous training, an individual can develop his body to a higher level of functioning. This is the case with athletes who train to accomplish exceptional feats of physical prowess; to a lesser degree, all those who maintain regular physical exercise know they enhance their physical abilities in this manner.

Yet even with the severest of training, there are definite limits within which the human body functions. It is surpassed by other animal species in every form of physical activity. In contrast to physical activity, however, there is an enormous range of mental abilities available to humans, both in scope and depth, which is unapproachable by any other species. Mental planes of existence in humans may exhibit differences on a greater scale than the difference in flying range between a sparrow and an eagle. In organized, codified societies, only a very low level of mental activity is required to maintain oneself.

Bourgeois societies, socialist or capitalist, are characterized by an acquisitive plane of existence in which individuals are oriented toward possessions – acquiring them, protecting them, and increasing their monetary value. Orientation to accumulation of possessions is the distinguishing mark of the bourgeois. He may be aware of other planes of existence, but they are subordinate to his orientation toward property and money, and the activities that underlie his acquisitive existence. The bourgeois mind perceives the 'real world' as objects and the money that symbolizes them. He wishes to own this 'real world' to the extent possible for him.

The difficulty of the bourgeois is that his life contains a much smaller portion of reality than he realizes. Ultimately he may come to recognize this. The real world of the bourgeois is actually an unreal world for human beings because it is far distant from the only meaningful reality for them, which is their spiritual reality. The real world of the bourgeois is significant only insofar as it assures his physical survival or the survival of those to whom he is attached. Life on a survival basis is low quality living for human beings, since it is unrelated to the distinctive quality of human life, the cultivation of the interior self. Dissatisfaction, envy, and resentment are the inevitable result of life lived exclusively on the bourgeois plane of existence for, within himself, the bourgeois individual will sooner or later feel the stirrings of an unfulfilled interior self. Adherence to a religion or cult may quiet these stirrings to a certain degree, but it is at the cost of the freedom of his spirit.

The orientation of the individual oriented to his interior self is radically different from the bourgeois orientation. Such a person is sensitive to the value of experiences and their transformation into creative expression. He is involved with bourgeois life only to the extent necessary to provide the material needs of his life and he continuously aims toward their simplification. He intuits that the one thing needful is to attend to the business of significant experiences and comes to realize that unrestrained bourgeois life interferes with these experiences and, therefore, with one's self-development, the principal purpose of human life.

TEMPTATIONS OF TECHNOLOGY

The great problem of modern society is the role of technology. All other problems are relatively minor compared to this one. This situation has been recognized by every astute observer of today's societies from H. D. Thoreau to C. F. Schumacher; no contemporary philosopher is deserving of the name who does not grapple with the influence of technology on the life of individuals. The task of philosophy as an active force in society is not to analyze past philosophers or to lose itself in the games of theories of cognition but to guide individuals to lead fulfilling lives. Human beings are presently threatened by a danger unlike all others in history; they are threatened by a devouring technology that they themselves have created. In former times, nature threatened humanity; now, it is humans who threaten nature and the whole human race insofar as humanity is part of nature.

It is of little value to bemoan present conditions and long for the days when life was simpler and men were purer. In America, there were no better, purer days almost immediately after its revolutionary war. One must remember that it was Thoreau who wrote in the 1840s that most men lived lives of quiet desperation. There has never been any escape from the need to comprehend the impact of scientific technology upon oneself.

Heinrich Heine, a German contemporary of Thoreau, told the fable of the Englishman who created a mechanical robot that looked, acted, and behaved like a human being, an English gentleman to be specific. (England in Heine's day was the fountainhead of technology.) In the course of his human-like life, the robot came to realize he did not have a soul. From that moment on, the mechanical creature tormented his creator with the request for a soul. Night and day, the creature pressed his demand until the

36

distraught Englishman took flight to the continent to escape his creation. However, the robot followed him, gnashing his teeth, and growling with his machinery speech, "Give me a soul! Give me a soul!" But this was the one thing his creator did not know how to do and the two figures to this day, as Heine related it, can be seen rushing about on the highways of Europe (*History of Religion and Philosophy in Germany*). Heine's account resembles the earlier novel *Frankenstein* by Mary Shelley, which expressed a similar theme and may have influenced Heine.

This simple fable reveals Heine's premonition of the problems of a future technological society but it hardly does justice to contemporary realities. The robot has multiplied itself enormously while the creator is nowhere to be found. The machinery has become self-perpetuating. Endowed with tools and apparatus beyond the wildest imagination of people of past centuries, the inhabitants of contemporary technological societies only yearn for souls. What is a soul but the awareness of personal realities in all their dimensions? A great lie envelopes people today—the lie that fulfillment in life is based upon object acquisition and upon obtaining the power and wealth that makes acquisitions possible. The self-satisfied hoarding miser has become virtually an extinct phenomenon—and even more so, Thoreau-like figures who live simpler existences. Today a simple existence simply means poverty, with all the psychological burdens associated with this condition.

The desire for acquisitions has always been present in human societies; the bourgeois type is met everywhere in history. However, it is in the current era with the proliferation of technologies that provide innumerable objects to acquire, that a tendency previously kept in check by limited circumstances is now burgeoning without restraints. The dominant assumption is that object acquisition means expansion of one's self. The desire for reality is now expressed by the impulse toward acquisitions. But there is no more personal reality in object acquisition than there is in religious dogmas; it is only the faith in scientific technology augmented by behaviorist conditioning that motivates individuals to accept the exhausting labors and recurrent anxieties usually necessitated by bourgeois life.

~ ~ ~

The desire of an individual to bring reality into his interior life is a flower that can be beaten to the ground by hostile forces. Besides overwhelming technology, concepts promoted by families, religions, and public leaders stress the reality of the family, of religion, and of community life. The importance of individuality is generally ignored. The wellbeing of the interior self of individuals has rarely been supported by societal institutions. Even worse, the massive indoctrination (brain-washing) exerted by the media today in favor of object acquisition is unique in history. The commercial companies sponsoring the media survive in large part through stimulating people toward ever increasing acquisition of their products—the assumption being that personal wellbeing is thus enhanced, a fateful error.

The idea of projection of self into secular objects instead of into sacred objects was first put forth by Karl Marx when he was still interested in philosophical questions. Yet he probably could not have imagined the gigantic increase in consumerism occasioned by technology that has occurred in the twentieth century. The belief that it is good to acquire and utilize products has taken a place over beliefs in God and country as one of the basic myths in civilized life.

A person cannot continuously project himself in external things and still retain his own strength. The ascetic ideal is not a religious aberration. It is a psychological principle of interior health arising from the experience that continuous projection of self into the world of objects is harmful to the self. There seems to be little awareness today that it is harmful to acquire too many things and that an individual is seriously weakened in an acquisitive, consumption-oriented society.

~ ~ ~

Certain periods of human history are distinctive through evidence of flowering of a culture of individuality. The fountainhead of culture in western civilization appeared in the Greek world during the fifth and fourth centuries B.C. The flourishing of individual philosophers and schools of philosophy during that era represented a unique development in human culture that has not been repeated in any other historical epoch.

A revival of cultural individualism called the Renaissance appeared in Italy during the fourteenth and fifteenth centuries and a similar, even more profound enlightenment occurred during the 18th century in northern Europe, especially France and the German principalities. These episodes were high points in western culture. Goethe remarked toward the end of his long life that he was terrified by the sweeping growth of machinery, which he recognized to be dominating society. "We, with perhaps a very few others," he commented to his confident Eckermann, "are likely to be the last representatives of an epoch that will not soon return." Goethe was right in his forecast even if a few representatives survived a little longer than he had expected. There is no Goethe, Heine, Pushkin, or Kierkegaard in our times. Strindberg, Nietzsche, and Berdyaev were the end of a long line of literary personalities who bestrode their societies rather than hanging upon them or hiding from them.

Profound artists or thinkers have not emerged in recent times in western culture. People now look toward the East for wisdom; a collection of gurus, swamis, and monks are appearing who capitalize on the esotericism of Hindu and Buddhist teachings to dominate the weak, untrained minds of westerners. It is really an absurd idea to think that concepts generated thousands of years ago in the forests of India can help western man out of the technological wilderness in which he is lost. There is nothing to be gained in chanting 'Om', repeating 'Atman is Brahman', or sitting at the feet of costumed charlatans in the hope tranquility will emerge from the smoke of the incense candles. There is a serious element to eastern philosophy; but it is irrelevant to western culture. If our own Christian clerics cannot help us, there is nothing to be gained from Buddhist monks or Hindu swamis. Eastern religion belongs to history; it deteriorated in the east because of its lack of concern with development of individuality. These facts are known to the astute Easterner who may respect his religious traditions, but finds them unsuited for the problems of the present age.

~ ~ ~

The fragility of the spirit of contemporary society is nowhere better exemplified than in the decline of the quality of leadership in the United States since the Revolutionary era. The founding fathers were men with spacious minds who were possessed by a vision of liberty that came to be known as the spirit of '76—a vision of a government that would enhance the personality of its citizens. Inspired by concepts most clearly enunciated in the writings of Thomas Paine, they drew up the Declaration of Independence, one of the world's noblest statements of human aspirations. Yet it is difficult to imagine Washington, Adams, Jefferson, or Madison functioning as political leaders in the United States for more than a generation after the revolution. Henry Adams writing a century later felt the qualities of character that had been bred into his family were long since obsolete. Only empty clichés now connect self-serving political leaders with the radical idealism of the American founding fathers.

Perhaps opening of the frontiers that coincided with the technological explosions of the period were responsible for the unparalleled orientation of Americans toward technology. America became the technological society *par excellence*, with all the material consequences that stem from such an orientation. Ralph Waldo Emerson, the closest that America ever came to producing a Goethe, repeatedly remarks on the ill-considered inclination of his countrymen to blindly accumulate possessions and seek gratification in pointless travel. However, Emerson and his Concord compatriots did not influence America as Goethe did Germany; the flowering of New England, as Van Wyck Brooks called it, was brief, regional, and finally blown away by the tide of technology and the opening of the West. Daniel Boone, Thomas Edison, and Henry Ford were the models for American youth. The suave, commercially oriented Mark Twain, the Walt Disney of his day, became an American literary model. Emerson's writings are now preserved fossils to be gotten through university classes on American literature. (He is completely ignored in academic philosophy.) This may be in part Emerson's fault; he consistently refused to descend from his pedestal of abstractionism. But whatever one thinks of the literary style of Emerson, the failure of his ideas to exert a lasting influence upon American culture was a tragic loss for the American people. Emerson had much to teach Americans—and still does.

~ ~ ~

Since the forces of technology seem to overcome all other influences in the modern world, it is worth trying to uncover the basis for their remarkable power. The origin of technology lies in the instinct of human beings to master nature, which is always threatening them, and to overcome their limitations as part of nature themselves. The first technologies were based on the need to secure food supplies, provide shelter, and ensure protection against the wilderness. The fact that the survival of humans has been long linked to the development of technologies explains at least in part its impact on minds.

Science is the intellectual aspect of technology originating from the discovery that nature can be harnessed best by elucidation of the 'laws' that govern it. This concept of 'natural law' is one of the most powerful ideas ever expounded by the human mind. It is evolved from the reaction to the immensity and complexity of nature—partially out of the instinct for self-preservation, but also out of a will to dominate nature instead of being dominated by it. Much of nature can be controlled once the principle of causality applicable to it is learned. Naturally, the more complex the forms of nature under consideration, the more difficult it is to learn the means to control it. Cancer has proved very difficult to control; flooding of rivers is much easier. However, it is misleading to refer to causality as natural law: it only refers to empirical observations made about common natural events. So-called natural law seems to break down when physicists deal with elementary particles; the work of Planck and Heisenberg has made untenable causality as an invariable principle of nature.

In the present era, the fiction that science is engaged in the study of natural laws has all but been abandoned. It is now generally clear that scientists today are engaged in controlling nature, not understanding it. In retrospect, most of western science can be seen as a violation of nature. It is all quite understandable when science is seen to be in the service of the power struggle of humanity against the forces of nature. The dilemma is that humans are a part of nature also and in violating nature, they find they have violated themselves.

Everyone knows the material aspects of life have been greatly altered by the success of technology in controlling nature. It is often thought that the development of science leads to technology, but the reverse is almost always true; anticipation of useful technology leads to scientific development. From the beginnings of civilization, progress in astronomy and physics were motivated by expectations of improvement in navigation, agriculture, and timekeeping (the last always the *idée fixe* of bourgeois life). Archimedes desired his stable point to improve civil engineering; Copernicus was after a more accurate calendar.

Exceptional scientists are motivated by the spirit of knowledge for its own sake (perhaps such was the case with Darwin and Einstein) but this feeling invariably gives way to the pervasive pressures to master nature for the sake of human needs. Virtually all scientific activity at the present time is 'practical' science; i.e., science directed toward a specific goal deemed desirable by the organization sponsoring it. Modern science is based on high technology, which requires substantial financial investment from sources expecting some return from the science. Technological-based societies depend upon utilitarian scientific research. The gigantic National Institutes of Health in the United States is a prime example of this phenomenon. Pure science has been obsolete for quite a long time.

The problem with the impact of science and technology upon a society is that they exercise a mesmerizing influence upon people everywhere and exert an influence beyond all rationality. Most individuals seem to be incapable of resisting the belief that their life will be enhanced by the products of technology, although this belief usually does not stand up to careful examination. Thoreau gave the example of a friend who said to him he ought to save his money so he could travel to Fitchburg quickly by the new railroad. However, Thoreau reasoned differently; if he went the thirty miles to Fitchburg on foot, he would arrive by nightfall, whereas his friend would have to spend an entire day working to earn the money for the train fare. Moreover, Thoreau would have spent the day walking through the countryside, a pleasurable experience, while his friend would have been at menial labor. In every way, Thoreau's reasoning was superior. Yet Thoreau's ideas were rejected by American society. One can only attribute the consistent triumphs of technology to its magical aura.

Thoreau's type of analysis is much more cogent to the conditions of life today than it was in his era, which now seems wonderfully pastoral to us. Consider the effort and tensions required to sustain life in a technological society; consider what is required from people to maintain the bloated modern home, the expense-ridden automobiles, the mindless gadgetry and endless consumer items that are foisted upon a public, apparently incapable of resisting. The unsuspecting young are under constant media attack to devote their lives toward the trivia of consumerism. The work effort required to maintain a life saddled by technology drains the average person in an inhuman manner. Emerson wrote 150 years ago that things were in the saddle, riding mankind. The situation has only worsened. No wonder the dream of Americans is to become wealthy without labor, to cash in on quick rich schemes, or to be smiled upon by Lady Luck at Las Vegas or Atlantic City.

However, the expectations are all illusions. Even for those who inherit wealth or cash in on clever schemes, the dream that object possession is a means for fulfillment is a cruel hoax. The only benefit that the moneyed may have is relief from the pressures to earn money; while this may be a temporary blessing, it also deprives them of a structure that is necessary for most people to have a sense of purpose in their lives. Furthermore, wealthy people are expected to be 'happy'; when this is not the case, it is more difficult for them to adapt to the reality of their life.

The irrational and illusory belief that object possession— including wealth that is an object surrogate—produces happiness is founded upon the deep-seated human tendency to *project* itself into the world about it. This tendency was first persuasively demonstrated in the nineteenth century by the philosopher Ludwig Feuerbach, who asserted that that the essence of religion is only the projected spirituality of man's intrinsic nature (*Essence of Christianity*). But it is not only religion that receives projections from the active minds of human beings; it is also the object world around them. Humans endow objects with their own attributes; these include feelings, purpose, and functionality. Endowing objects with the qualities of life is known as *animism*; however, instead of a primitive animism postulating imaginary spirits, modern societies have developed an animism based on projection of human qualities into objects.

The young Karl Marx, writing before the compulsion toward changing society overwhelmed him, said that money acts as the "alienated essence of man," dominating him as he worships it (*On the Jewish Question*). We may slightly modify this Feuerbachian thought of Marx (who had read Feuerbach with avid interest) to say that money and the objects money can buy are not only worshipped by contemporary man, but he identifies with them, a more severe degree of psychological aberration. The mental mechanism of projection of one's self into the surrounding world was described by Freud in patients with severe emotional disorders. However, this neurotic mechanism is not limited to those with manifest mental disorders; it is a pervasive trait of individuals who are part of technological societies.

Narcissism is an abnormal state of mind in which the sense of self is confined to the exterior self, the self as an object for others. The narcissistic personality justifies his existence through the approval and attention of other people. This is most obvious in the obsession with physical appearance, but is present in subtler forms among high achievers who are motivated by the desire for recognition of their achievements. Justification of one's existence through the admiration of others is a sign of an undeveloped interior self, incapable of self-enhancement through life's experiences. "The Culture of Narcissism" (title of a book by Christopher Lasch) is a constant tendency in human society; however, in a technological society, there is vastly more opportunity for its development and practice.

~ ~ ~

'Advanced' modern societies operate under the basic tent of Adam Smith expressed in the *Wealth of Nations*—the unacknowledged Bible of technological societies—that "individuals will labor to carry their society to wealth and prosperity if they believe their own condition is bettered in the process." This is the philosophy of entrepreneur-oriented societies whether they designate themselves as free enterprise or socialistic. There are differences between them in methods of administering the economy of the nation, but both claim to be bettering the material conditions of their citizenry. In fact, most societies today are mixtures of the two forms. There are differences in individual freedoms but these are more a matter of national heritage then political theory. Repressive governments are part of the free enterprise world and much free enterprise can be found in socialistic countries. The clichés of their politicians are largely window dressing for maintaining the morale of their people.

It is true that individuals will incessantly labor to better their own condition but it is in the direction of technology only because religions have failed them and they do not know where else to turn. In the words of Dostoevsky's Grand Inquisitor, people are controlled by "magic, miracle, and authority"—and this is how science and technology are experienced by them. There is a strong magical bent to technology; the feelings of awe and respect it inspires are akin to the effect of a Shaman in predicting the death of a sick person. Magic is recourse to hidden natural forces in order to impress an audience. One may concede that a Shaman has prognostic skills but it does not follow that he knows anything else of real value to his followers. Intervention into illnesses was a notorious method of Europeans to gain power over primitive peoples. Mirrors and trinkets were used in a similar manner. But Europeans rarely had goods of substantial value to offer the primitives whom they subsequently enslaved or exterminated.

Much of modern advertising is based on implications that magical qualities reside in objects of production, which can be acquired by their owners. The entire sales strategies of the automobile industry have been based on this approach. Most labor saving apparatus appeals to the emotions, not the mind; then, subsequently, they become necessary fixtures for their owners. Men and women labor for "wealth and prosperity," not from a natural instinct or an outcome of their intelligence, but out of ignorance and conditioning. It is only education that will improve their lot, not vocational education to fit them as cogs into a computer-based technological moonscape, but a meaningful education that will expand their mental horizons.

The desire to experience 'reality' is a universal drive encountered from the beginning of human life. Thoreau said, "rather than love, money, or fame, give me truth". Truth as Thoreau experienced it was not the truth of two plus two is four, but the truth of *interior reality*, the one truth that truly counts. Thoreau spoke not out of dogma or morality, but out of feeling for the meaning of his life. There is no truth in the belief that the value of an individual's life is determined by his wealth or material prosperity; this idea is the destructive illusion underlying technological societies. The object world is unstable; thus recurrent anxiety is the reward of people who center their life upon it. Wealth and material prosperity may have secondary values; yet if there is no primary 'truth' that they serve, they are only harmful preoccupations that divert one from the purpose of their life.

~ ~ ~

Scientists like to believe that they are more than engineers; that they are engaged in the pristine study of the natural world. This is about as true as the belief that churches in Rome or Salt Lake City are purely spiritual institutions. Priests and scientists of our time have one thing in common; they are practical people with utilitarian purposes. One has only to look at the nature of the financial support of contemporary science and the realities become evident. Scientific activity is dependent on big government, big foundations, or big business; there are no other alternatives. No one can seriously maintain that these institutions have any interest in science beyond its technological applications. There is no motivation toward pure science in our times, if one thinks of science as comprehending the nature of the cosmos. Even the most esoteric studies of astrophysics with their apocalyptic theories dream that somehow humanity can control apocalypse. Everything in the modern world is done with an eye toward controlling nature, not comprehending it. The incredibly rapid transformation of molecular genetics into genetic engineering is a recent case in point. Knowledge is converted into power; knowledge *is* power in the minds of many. Epicurus with his atomic theory may have been the last natural philosopher; the prototype scientist of today is a financial broker establishing multi-million dollar enterprises in Silicon Valleys and worrying much about his patents.

The movement of large institutions into sponsoring 'creativity' invariably results in the loss of creativity. Creative science in the United States has been transformed into fee for service engineering projects through large-scale contracts and grants. The major scientific accomplishments of the national government have been the production of nuclear weapons and the ejection of equipment and human beings into outer space. Its accomplishments in the health related fields have been virtually nil in spite of much propaganda to the contrary. The waste of national resources occasioned by these gigantic enterprises along with the explosion of expensive technology into armaments is comparable to the destruction of the economy of Spain in the sixteenth century through its obsession with obtaining precious metals from the New World. It was astonishingly comical to see how the United States and the Soviet Union (before its collapse) vied to outdo each other in worthless feats of military technology much like two great children engaged in a debilitating tug of war.

Most modern scientists are principally oriented toward obtaining institutional grants or contracts. It is their livelihood. They are usually bourgeois types whose values have been formed by the institutions that they serve. More than most other 'educated' individuals, scientists are inclined to value the concrete world of objects. They value science to the extent that their careers are furthered by it. Scientists function in a more subtle manner than businessmen in that they are aware of the psychology of knowledge as power. Of course there are exceptions to these generalities, but they are rare. To a great extent, the excitement of modern science comes from the challenging game of persuading patrons that the scientist is engaged in important activity that makes him deserving of the one reward truly valued by scientists— generous funding of their work. In fact, most scientists are quite unproductive even with respect to advances in technology, accounting for the occupational anxiety of the average scientific entrepreneur.

~ ~ ~

A little recognized but serious problem of science is that the scientists with deeper minds tend to lose interest in their work.

Ultimately, one tires of exploring the universe, whether it be on a cosmic or molecular level, much as one tires of exploring jungles or oceans. There is always more to be unraveled, more distant universes, more minute particles, more variations on themes that have already been established. One even tires of discovering new ways to overcome nature; it is not such a great thing, after all, to dominate the mindless forces of nature. Especially one tires of building larger and more elaborate apparatus, which are only repetitions of golden calves cast in modern molds. It is mental children who are permanently amused by the world of science; to mature minds, it inevitably becomes boring. Kierkegaard wondered how any adult person could devote his intellectual being to scientific pursuits. The shallowness of the phenomenal world of objects is responsible for the boredom experienced by those living the life of science.

Experienced scientists find ways to amuse and stimulate themselves within the confines and limitations of their profession. They engage in little competitions among themselves for priority in discoveries; they fight for high stakes in the form of contracts and grants, they create intricate gadgetry with which they divert themselves. Above all, they travel a great deal; all successful scientists are frequently away from their laboratories participating in the innumerable gatherings throughout the world that is a major part of the life of a scientist. If they are highly successful, they give lectures and write books that may make them wealthy. But the perpetual movement of most scientists reveals the unease that they feel about their labors, which must always be presented as Einstein-like activity to a gullible public.

When many intelligent scientists become bored and restless, it cannot be attributed to a flaw in their personalities; it must be a consequence of the nature of the work that is supposed to give an entrée into a profounder reality than is given by simpler pursuits. In fact, the reverse is true; the life of science and technology plunges the scientist into an unreal world that is unsettling to a person who desires reality in his life. There is nothing real about laboring in a technological world constructed to gratify a society infatuated with technology. Once science relieves the fears of nature, it becomes an exercise in trivial minutiae, a series of diversions like a day in Disneyland. Video games and wristband miniature television demonstrate the computerized face of technological society. When the insulation of humans from nature is complete, the end of humanity will be at hand since human beings, as they are currently constituted, cannot exist apart from the natural world. This threat is closer than is the threat of a nuclear holocaust.

Science as pursuit of knowledge of nature for the sake of deepening man's awareness of reality is as dead as the dodo bird—assuming it ever existed at all.

~ ~ ~

Philosophy was once said to be a matter of dealing with the problem of death. There is no better gauge of a person's soul than his emotions and attitudes vis-à-vis his own mortality. One of the most bizarre features of contemporary American society is what has been labeled by Ernest Becker as the 'Denial of Death' in a book with this title published shortly before his own death by cancer. The denial takes two principal forms, an obsession with detection or cure of illness and a fear of directly confronting death. The obsession with illness has led to the elaboration of a gigantic medical-pharmaceutical-industrial complex to a degree that could have never been envisioned by the pioneers of modern medicine.

The role of medicine in the health of America has been evaluated by scholarly observers like René Dubos (*The Mirage of Health*) and Thomas McKeown (*The Role of Medicine*). They have concluded that the ability of clinical medicine to cure disease is quite limited; most of the significant advances in human health have come through public health measures like safer food and water supplies, preventative steps against certain diseases, better hygiene, and limitation of family size. Care of the sick has played only a minor role in reducing illness. The widespread cure of diseases through medical interventions is largely a myth.

The traditions of western Hippocratic medicine lie mainly in diagnosis and prognosis. The early recognition of diseases and prediction of their natural history permitted a physician to be able to knowledgably deal with them. However, modern medicine has moved away from the Hippocratic tradition; physicians today are expected to cure diseases, the earlier the better. This goal is pursued, albeit usually unsuccessfully, through a fantastic elaboration of medical technology and drugs at astronomical costs. The steeply escalating expenses involved in medical care have become a national emergency in the United States, now that it is well on the way to national health care.

The cathedrals of the medieval era have been replaced by the modern medical center as symbol of the faith of the people. There is a great falling off of the dignity of patients; yet it is dubious whether there has been any real progress in dealing with disease. There are short-term effects produced by surgical or pharmacological treatments, but these rarely translate into long-term health improvement. Ivan Illich took the view of medicine as 'nemesis' (*Medical Nemesis*); he asserted that the fraternity of physicians is a threat to society by breeding ever increasing demands for useless medical care and undermining the ability of the individual to care for his own health. The passage of time has proven Illich to be right—but nothing has changed!

~ ~ ~

The medical scientist is truly the Cagliostro of our day. By implicitly promising prevention or cure of disease through the miracles of science, he attracts huge sums of money from public or private institutions into medical research. The story of polio and tuberculosis is repeated *ad infinitum* to the point of nausea without any regard for the natural variability of prevalence and severity that characterize all infectious diseases. Like his colleagues developing defense, nuclear, and space technologies, the medical scientist is dependent upon institutional support for his expensive activities. However, his task is more bizarre than that of scientists in the physical sciences; he is committed to prolongation of life and eradication of degenerative disorders—goals, which if reached, would certainly create an impossible ecological situation on our planet. Fortunately, there is no sign that this is about to occur through the efforts of medical science; the achievements of technologically-oriented medical research in the United States has been largely limited to minor improvements of the nineteenth century innovation of prevention of diseases with immunizations. One cannot make the case that medical research post-1945 has accomplished more than that prior to World War I when public support of such research was minimal. In general, as McKeown well documented, the achievements of treatment-oriented research tend to be greatly exaggerated. There have been no new breakthroughs for the medical scientist since World War II analogous to the production of nuclear bombs or entry into outer space. The most spectacular advance in recent medical technology has been maintaining severely brain-damaged patients in vegetative states for many years.

But the greatest harm arising from the belief that scientific medicine will take care of disease is not the financial cost; it is the psychological cost both to the community of scientists and to the public. The former must perjure themselves by maintaining a false front of beneficent medical technology while the latter becomes habituated to the idea that they are entitled to access to the miracles of scientific medicine. There is no cultivation of the thought so treasured in antiquity of rising above the circumstances of one's physical state. Illness is obsessively feared and death unconsciously denied. The individual does not form concepts to deal with his inevitable mortality; rather there is a dependence upon science as there was upon religion in former times to escape from feared realities. As Paul Feyerabend pointed out (*Against Method*, 1975), there is an alliance of big government with big science in the twentieth century that creates an irresistible psychological climate of dependency upon science. In no area of science is this dependency as marked as in scientific medicine. All are under the spell of the legions of Cagliostros spawned by the marriage of medicine and technology.

The holistic movements in medical care are an effort at breaking loose from this spell. Yet most people revert to technological medicine when the fear of death or serious illness rises up in them. The degrading death rituals of medical technology have replaced religious death sacraments. One of the most disgraceful features of medical technology is the use referred to above of keeping individuals in vegetative states alive for months or even years before allowing nature to take its course. One is envious of the freedom of wild animals to find a quiet place to retire to in order to end their life with natural dignity and a minimum of disturbance to their fellow creatures.

~ ~ ~

The plight of inhabitants—one is tempted to say inmates—of high technology societies is so ludicrous that there are countless opportunities for comic portrayal by the entertainment industries. The comic strips of newspaper and the sitcoms of television are the best means for learning about the nature of technological society. But satire is not only a thinly veiled contempt of the institutions of a society; it often also reveals a *contempt of self* if one peers below the surface of the satirical wit. Writers are among the most intelligent segments of a society and it is among them that disaffection and loss of values are most evident. Writers who become entertainers, however, rarely have the inner resources to deal with the technological society.

The media create an image of government as Keystone Kops in continuous motion chasing criminals—in this case in order to appease the dissatisfactions of the people who elect it. Taxes are up, taxes are down; defense is up, defense is down; employment is up, employment is down; welfare is up, welfare is down; education is stimulated, education is ignored—on and on goes the perpetual motion machine of government. Foreign affairs are analyzed to the point of distraction. The stock market behaves like a Ouija board moved by invisible spirits. The illusion is fostered that all this is reality for the observer, that somehow it is relevant to the interior condition of the individual.

However, it is all a gigantic deception; the individuals who are the people grow steadily more discontent and they will have their say. There is no fulfillment in societies founded on science and technology; such societies will have to go just as past societies founded on outworn dogmas were transformed or disappeared. It is becoming more and more evident that people are being constantly fed lies, that they are ceaselessly indoctrinated with the false idea that the realities of life are to be found in the products of a lifeless scientific technology. As it becomes clear that this idea is incapable of satisfying the needs of individuals, there tends to be a reaction back to the old panaceas of family relationships and doctrinaire religions. The modern bread and circuses are interlarded with spoonfuls of family and religious feelings by the agile consumer-entertainment industries. But this compounding of the deceptions of consumerism will not work either; the greater aspirations of individuals are not indefinitely satisfied by obsessions with technology, idealization of family relationships, or devotion to religious myths. There are places for these affairs in human life but they are not its final goal. The development of the interior self is that goal; art, not science, provides the means for its realization; until individuals are fully cognizant of the nature of art and the role it should play in their lives, they will remain unfulfilled creatures.

There are many who seem content with what family, religion, and consumerism have to offer. These are the people who are satisfied with the role of paterfamilias or motherhood, with professional or business status, with scientific or community accomplishments. They may appear to be completely satisfied with these traditional forms of social existence. But these are partial people; they are people that society has led into roles that cheat them out of their birthright of full personal development and expression. The ideal of a human society cannot lie in the image projected by the institutionalized personality. The interior self is the first and most important reality; other realities wait upon it; that is the proper state of the human condition. And when one talks of ideals, one reveals a faith that it is through the art of philosophy that an individual will find direction for his personal fulfillment.

RELIGION, PHILOSOPHY & PHILOSOPHERS

Present day discussions of religion and philosophy have a certain other-worldly quality about them since few educated people feel themselves much affected by the tepid influences of contemporary religion and surely not by the esoteric theories of contemporary philosophy. It is more interesting to look into the past at the struggles people have engaged in over rival religious beliefs; there was even a time when philosophical convictions were serious elements in social and political life. That time is long past; there are no Julians or Marcuses on the American intellectual scene.

The inadequacy of western religious beliefs for those dedicated to reality has been dealt with at length by the prodigious thinkers of the nineteenth century. The historically significant and still best books on this topic are Thomas Paine,* *Age of Reason* (1794); Ludwig Feuerbach, *Essence of Christianity* (1841); and, for those who can handle his style, Friedrich Nietzsche, *The Antichrist* (1888). Heinrich Heine in a remarkable passage in his *Religion and Philosophy in Germany* (1833) announced the impending demise of the great Judeo-Christian God Jehovah. Nietzsche's Zarathustra pronounced him dead fifty years later. Schopenhauer, Bakunin, Marx, and Freud heaped scorn on the conventional concept of God. However all these writers were mistaken; the Judeo-Christian God is still alive to a degree in the

---

*The abuse heaped upon Thomas Paine during his lifetime by the inhabitants of the country he helped found is beyond comprehension. The failure of American society to fulfill its early intellectual promise may be considered as retribution for the evil treatment of one of its ablest, boldest, and far-seeing writers.

minds of many people in western society and the Christian religion is even enjoying a fundamentalist revival at the time of this writing. The nineteenth century buriers of God who thought science would destroy belief in Christianity just as Christianity once destroyed pagan religions did not reckon on the inadequacy of science to meet the yearnings of human beings for a deeper reality than the scientific one.

The explanation of the Judeo-Christian illusions, as Feuerbach repeatedly stated, is that individuals project their need for transcendent experience into an external deity and all the trappings associated with this deity. This yearning represents a desire to reach out beyond the individual's sense perceptions toward a transcendental reality. It accounts for the survival of religious beliefs and institutions in an age of science. Religions were founded on the human desire to transcend one's self; they survive and strangely prosper on the same need. The concept of a divinity that cares about them gives human beings a connection to a metaphysical cosmos. In time, traditions develop to hallow the institutions of religion with permanence so that they seem to represent the very essence of reality itself.

However, in spite of the human yearning for transcendence, religions have been undermined by the rise of science. Science asserts a different reality than the religious one; the realties of science are based on observations, measurements, and verification. Persistence of historical religious beliefs do not establish their realty; if that were so, the myths of the Australian aborigines or the stone age forest dwellers of Mindanao would reign supreme as they go back far beyond western religions. The opposite is true and the believers in stone-age myths rush to exchange them as soon as they learn about the more persuasive realities of modern science. In all places and eras, concepts thought to be more in accord with reality are prized over those that are less so. Most educated people are no longer capable of devoutly believing the dogmatic assertions of religion even if their 'metaphysical' needs are not satisfied by science.

Schopenhauer sardonically called religion the 'metaphysics of the people', whom he felt to be ignorant and incapable of evolving their own concepts of human existence. His attitude represented Schopenhauer's elitism that is no longer tenable; the majority of people in developed societies are educated in the principles of science and are well aware of the nature of the universe. They are not of a mind to say, "*Credo quia absurdum*," (I believe what is absurd) unless they are professional theologians who have a vested interest in the idea. Those who maintain religious convictions for traditional or societal reasons are forced into the position of alleging beliefs that they doubt in the secret recesses of their minds; they exhibit weakness of intellectual conscience. Lying to oneself is not without its consequences. Thomas Paine stated the situation with his usual forthrightness, "It is impossible to calculate the moral mischief that mental lying [vis-à-vis religion] has produced in society. When a man has so far corrupted and prostituted the chastity of his mind so as to subscribe his professional belief to things he does not believe in, he has prepared himself for the commission of every other crime."

There is a subtler, yet ultimately more destructive manner in which religions interfere with human development beyond simply fostering hypocrisy. Religions preempt one's search for a transcendent reality since they already possess revealed 'truth'; all that remains for the individual is to accept that truth. The intellectual conscience is dealt with authoritatively; one's own intellectual scruples must bow before revealed truth. The presence of religion in a person's mental life is like a millstone around the neck of a mountain climber. It is not possible for one to develop his own sense of interior reality in a manner that is real and fulfilling until he can once and for all dispose of the illusion that there is a transcendent deity whose will is made known through Holy Scripture or through revelations to a self-appointed elite.

~ ~ ~

But there is a meaning to the Christian religion; it lies in fostering the awareness of an interior self; whether one calls this awareness spirituality, soul, faith, or what one wishes, religious awareness refers to one's inner self. The problem of Christianity lies in the concept (inherited from Judaism) of a divinity determining human values and affairs; this concept has been the downfall of western religions. As soon as people begin thinking about God's intentions for them, a process of mental dependency sets in. The founders of religions never have had faith in their adherents; they have always required a God to make plausible the idea of human spiritual development. But the Christian virtues of love and compassion are thoroughly human in nature. Neither an avenging God nor a paternalistic one does anything to promote human spirituality; it is fear and dependency that are promoted. Millennia of dogmatic teachings about the deity have not changed this reality.

The best in the human condition stems from the drive to connect with reality. The best is always the example of a single individual striving to develop his interior self and to express himself in a truthful manner. Jesus implying to his disciples that he was the 'truth' (John 14:6) was the most powerful thing ever said by him and revealed an unprecedented subjectivity that enlarged the possibilities for human development.

God is often just a code word that stands for the hypostasized spirit of the human race. If one substitutes the abstraction 'spirit of man' for the term God in Scriptures, they read just as well and with a higher meaning. The center of gravity of human thought is then placed where it should be, in the self, rather than the self projected into an imaginary cosmic being.

~ ~ ~

The western concept that philosophy ought to be concerned with the state of mind of the individual originated with Socrates (as related by Plato and Xenophon); prior to him, philosophy was mainly concerned about the nature of the cosmos. Thereafter, Greek thought became intensely involved with individual human beings, reaching a high point in the humanistic teachings of Epicurus. The latter baldly asserted that the gods (if they existed) did not concern themselves with humans and the idea of an afterlife was a fiction promoted by priests. But the victory of a Christianity based on dogmas evolved by 'doctors' of their Church resulted in destruction of most of antique philosophy, fragments of which have only survived by accident. The development of the interior self has not been an idea favored by Christianity, except as a means for solidifying Christian dogmas. The Reformation provided a temporary liberating influence by demolishing the authority of the Papacy in Protestant lands, but this was quickly replaced with the authority of 'Holy Scripture'. Protestantism became even more hostile to humanistic influences than had been the Roman church. Not until Thomas Paine did any notable figure in the western world dare to openly challenge Christian pretensions to revelatory truth.

~ ~ ~

If the influence of religion has not been conducive to the development of philosophy, that of the universities has been even worse. Genuine philosophers defined as 'lovers of wisdom' are not to be found in university environments. University professors of 'philosophy' may be scholars, scientists, or historians; but it is a misconception to regard them as philosophers. In the groves of modern academe, one learns about the history of philosophy and the analysis of mental activity—pursuits that never lead to philosophical wisdom. To be a philosopher, one must live according to his conviction of what truth and reality mean for the individual. University scholars are not suited for bold thinking; they are analytically, not intuitionally oriented. If their mind comes to prefer its intuitions, they usually reject or leave university life, as was the case with Spinoza, Nietzsche, and Wittgenstein. This is why university philosophy has had little impact on society; there is very minor public interest in its 'mental science'.

Most of the great thinkers of Europe and America—Descartes, Leibniz, Spinoza, Schopenhauer, Kierkegaard, Emerson, Thoreau, Nietzsche, Berdyaev, Sartre, Wittgenstein, to name some but not all—were not primarily university people. They cared about the human predicament, not about academic distinction. In the twentieth century, university philosophy has given rise to the movement of phenomenology, an activity that is not philosophy in the strict sense, but represents analysis of the structure of thought. Philosophy as it originated in the Greek world represents the 'love of wisdom', i.e., uncovering of reality for the individual, and is committed to development of one's interior self. Philosophy is *metaphysics*, not science. Descriptive or analytic mental science has its own place in intellectual pursuits, but should be distinguished from philosophy.

Contemporary phenomenology originating from the concepts of the German philosopher Edmund Husserl is reminiscent of the German schools of anatomy of the nineteenth century. Husserl himself said of his work that it was 'strict science'. It is characterized by attention to the minutest detail of human thought and experience with the absolute objectivity of the scientist. It is inhuman when applied to the human psyche. Husserl and his followers represent the culmination of German descriptive science directed toward the mind of human beings. It is disappearing for the same reason that the German anatomical style of work has gone out of fashion—the utter pointlessness of such labor and the boredom experienced by those who attempt it. Phenomenology has been a disaster for philosophy; it has had a negative impact on the creative energies of thinkers like Heidegger and Sartre and has provided a self-destructive model for the development of western philosophy in the twentieth century. There have been efforts to amalgamate it with certain esoteric sects of psychoanalysis. The mixture of Freudian psychoanalysis and Husserlian phenomenology is a sure prescription for the spiritual death of any patient.

~ ~ ~

The identification of western philosophy with the universities has been more detrimental to it than its identification with Christianity in the medieval era. Philosophy had its own dark ages during the period of scholastic domination of European thought. All spiritual values were preempted by church authorities; philosophers could only express themselves in a covert manner. Occasionally the church would take action as in the burning of Giordano Bruno. Protestant leaders were just as bad, especially the ones professing Calvinism. Then hardly had philosophy acquired its independence from religious domination than it was subverted in the region in which it had been flowering most of all—Germany, as represented by Prussia and the smaller German principalities. The German states, through establishing university 'chairs of philosophy' and providing state support for occupants of these chairs, transformed philosophy from a personal form of expression into an academic discipline. The consequences of this move were vividly portrayed by Schopenhauer in his well-known essay, 'On Philosophy at the Universities'. However Schopenhauer was and still is regarded as a querulous eccentric and universities around the world have followed Germany's example.

The plight of philosophy can be best visualized if one would imagine university departments of poetry or theater whose faculty members would be regarded as the most important, if not only, representatives of these 'disciplines'. But it is understood that creative activity in the arts does not belong in universities; for some reason, this understanding has not been extended to philosophy. Perhaps the issue is not a significant one at the present time since little of interest is expected from contemporary philosophy at any location and the public is quite willing to let unintelligible 'philosophers' expend their energies in their academic pursuits.

~ ~ ~

Plato conjectured that nothing of real significance can be taught to a person; he can only be reminded of what he already intuits. A philosopher cannot teach an individual the meaning of the terms 'truth' and 'reality' and their equivalence; he can only remind him of their importance in his life. A philosopher cannot teach an individual the significance of Immanuel Kant's dictum that "every rational being is an end unto himself and not a means toward anything else"; he can only remind him that humanity is moving toward acceptance of this statement. In the depths of his soul, every sentient individual knows that he is a unique being whose task on earth is to make himself all that he is capable of becoming. The recurring tragedy of human life is the failure of development of a human potential. This fact is recognized in the case of children whose physical growth is stunted by starvation, but is overlooked in the lives of those whose mental lives are stunted by societal customs.

Besides reminding individuals about truth and reality, philosophers could also teach them the art of self-defense against harmful beliefs. The teaching of mental self-defense could be an important task of philosophers. "Vain is the word of the philosopher by which no [mental] malady of man is healed," said the arch-humanist Epicurus whose memory was blackened and writings lost by an ignorant world. Naturally, in order to teach effectively, philosophers must know which beliefs are harmful and how one defends against them. This knowledge is not found in university courses of philosophy.

~ ~ ~

The figure of Friedrich Nietzsche (1844-1900) exercises a continual fascination for philosophers and literary personalities. Authors who have written books and articles about Nietzsche constitute a virtual Who's Who of twentieth century western literature. Martin Heidegger has written a two-volume work on Nietzsche; Karl Jaspers confined himself to one volume. Essays on Nietzsche have been published by Thomas Mann, Jean- Paul Sartre, Albert Camus, Martin Buber, George Santayana, Carl Jung, Sigmund Freud, Georg Simmel, Andre Gide, George Bernard Shaw, Ernest Hemingway, Paul Tillich, H. L. Mencken, Hermann Hesse, Georges Bataille and Jacques Barzun. I myself have added to the list of books, *The Legend of Nietzsche's Syphilis*. There are undoubtedly others who have escaped my notice. His influence has permeated European culture; evidence exists that it has extended beyond Europe to the Americas.

How does one account for this remarkable interest in a person who, by every conceivable standard, was a failure during his lifetime; a person who was isolated, unrecognized, and impoverished; a person without close relationships or conjugal love and who was devoid of allegiance to family, country, or religion. The last decade of his life was spent in a state of catatonic withdrawal. His philosophic writings are of limited scholarly value. Walter Kaufmann, the Princeton professor who was his most capable translator into English, despaired over his faulty scholarship. His prose style is often obscure, verbose, and redundant, although original and eloquent. *Thus Spoke Zarathustra*, Nietzsche's most famous work, carries on the tradition of German sentimentality and pomposity. Many of Nietzsche's ideas are from acknowledged or unacknowledged sources; in particular, Goethe, Heine, Stirner and Emerson were important providers of Nietzschean concepts. Doctoral dissertations have been easily constructed out of uncovering the origins of Nietzsche's thoughts.

Yet Nietzsche remains the most influential philosopher of modern times and the one whose ideas have had the greatest impact on the literary world. The key to understanding the magnetic attraction of Nietzsche is that he embraced the role of philosopher as creative artist and he understood philosophy to be the expression of the feelings of the philosopher. "I am at all costs going to venture on a description of my feelings" (*Empfindung*), he wrote in the preface to his early work *The Use and Abuse of History* and he never deviated from that purpose. There can never be any doubt on reading Nietzsche that his work is centered on his feelings, that his *own* perceptions and thoughts are the main focus of his writings, that his personal experience is the material upon which his work is based.

The center of gravity of the work of scholars is to be found in historical sources; their own *persona* is subdued for the sake of the scholarship. The mental analysis of cognition is the favored 'scientific' activity; thus the dominance of phenomenology and deconstruction. For theologians, the center of gravity is the sacred documents and traditions handed down to them; the theologian is only the interpreter by which revealed truth is transmitted to the faithful. Scholars and theologians are alike in that they suppress their own selves for the sake of historical and institutional allegiances. But Nietzsche speaks out boldly, he is informed about culture and religion; but he himself is the center of his expressions. He is a creative artist in concepts; it is beneath his dignity to stoop to use the tools of the scholar's trade such as dated citations, references, and footnotes. It is his vocation to transform how the world has affected him into ideas. He will not divert his energies into the minutiae of scholarship or 'deconstruction' of language.

Beyond his style, Nietzsche's power derives from the depth of his insights into worldly institutions and knowledge. Through his elite education, he was steeped in the traditions of western philosophy and religion. He understood the fundamental insight of philosophy that the phenomenal world was not what it appeared to be to the public and that reality dwelt in the depths of one's interior self. These ideas were not just to be used for analytical games; they were beliefs by which he lived his life. Thus, early in his career, he felt the need to abandon his professorship in philology at the University of Basel. He saw it as a constraint upon his vocation as a philosopher.

Nietzsche was handicapped by physical problems that weighed upon him throughout his life. They were not conducive to his development as a philosopher in spite of his counter-phobic assertions that his illnesses stimulated his thought. Still Nietzsche was an authentic artist in a field where there is urgent need for artistic expression. This is why his influence steadily grows in the public at large while that of the academics at the universities fades into oblivion.

~ ~ ~

Or how do the following propositions strike our ears?—that passion is better than stoicism or hypocrisy; that honesty, even in badness, is better than concealing oneself in the morality of tradition; that the free man can be good as well as bad but that the unfree man is a shame to Nature and has no share in the consolation of heaven or earth; finally, that the one who wishes to become free must do so by himself and that no one receives freedom as a miraculous gift that falls in his lap. However harsh and strange these words may sound, they are the sound from a future world *which is in need of art* and which also expects authentic satisfaction from it; they are the voice of nature *restored in man*; they are what I have earlier named as correct perceptions as opposed to the incorrect perceptions that rule today.

Nietzsche: *Richard Wagner in Bayreuth*

~ ~ ~

Nietzsche suffered greatly from his rejection by the German literati and his failure to affect the German people for whom he had had extravagant expectations. As his life progressed with the total absence of recognition, he retreated behind a wall of irony and sarcasm. This trait of the later Nietzsche has offered many opportunities to scholars who have no interest in his thoughts (more often they are contemptuous of them) for playing the academic game of analyzing the obtuse. A similar fate has befallen James Joyce among English-language scholars. In fact, there are great similarities in the psychological and literary development of Joyce and Nietzsche.

A serious problem that developed in Nietzsche was his elitist attitude expressed by his idea that the human race has always consisted of masters and slaves. It is easy to see, in retrospect, that this concept represented his effort at maintaining his self-esteem in the face of the massive rejection of his writings for which he had sacrificed his life to produce. No individual can long live in the modern world with such a concept; there was really no recourse for Nietzsche except the flight into insanity. He had prepared the way; one cannot read all of Nietzsche without realizing the seductive attraction that insanity had for him. These issues are discussed in detail in my book, *The Legend of Nietzsche's Syphilis.*

The most powerful expressions of Nietzsche's mind are in his four *Untimely Reflections.* As he grew older, his later work came to reflect the wrecking of his personality through deprivation of human intercourse, poverty, painful illnesses, and literary rejection. In spite of all, Nietzsche's works are more interesting and insightful about the world than the writings of virtually any other philosopher. It is surprising though that Walter Kaufmann preferred his last writings of 1888 to his earlier works and translated them all while ignoring the *Untimely Reflections.* Kaufmann's ambivalent feelings toward Nietzsche are evident in the voluminous prefaces, notes, and commentaries attached to his translations. The philosopher in Kaufmann was powerfully drawn to Nietzsche as revealed in his cutting attacks on Nietzsche critics. But Kaufmann the academician had an instinctive aversion to his freewheeling style.

The Nazi philosophical hacks who seized upon Nietzsche's work were captivated by his master-slave conception of humanity. However, there is little doubt into which category he would have placed the Nazis. His greatest scorn was reserved for the German tendency to abandon individuality under the whips of nationalism and authoritarianism. He thought Bismarck was a disaster for

Germany. He joked that maps of Europe should show Germany as a white patch analogous to the white patch used to indicate undeveloped, uncivilized central Africa. The 'masters' in the world should be, for Nietzsche, those free thinkers who stood against their societies; the slaves were those who followed a *Führer*. He broke his intense relationship with Richard Wagner over this principle. The obedient Germans were the last people Nietzsche would have designated as the 'master race'; it is absurd beyond belief that the Nazi leadership should have had anything to do with Nietzsche; the only explanation is that they did not read his writings. Nietzsche once wrote ironically that it was his fate to be cast in with the Germans; unfortunately for his reputation and his work, this has remained true throughout two World Wars, the Nazi regime in Germany, and up to the present time.

~ ~ ~

A belief that has gained wide acceptance is that Nietzsche died of general paresis—a late form of syphilitic brain disease. Kaufmann and other scholars gave credence to this view. It is too bad that lawsuits cannot be mounted against defamation of the memory of great men. The evidence that Nietzsche had syphilis is virtually nil. It was based on nonspecific minor and unreliable neurological findings and an allegation of early syphilitic infection given second hand by an unknown person with no details. The whole thing might have been a comical parody of medical diagnosis had it not been taken seriously by Nietzsche critics. His 'diagnosticians' regarded his case as an 'atypical' one, the term usually utilized by physicians to cover their own uncertainties. Laboratory confirmation of syphilis was not available during Nietzsche's lifetime and the term syphilitic paresis was a wastepaper basket one analogous to schizophrenia or Alzheimer's disease at the present time. The crucial points of objective evidence of early infection or later organic dementia were not present; his catastrophic nervous breakdown occurred over a brief period of time and the subsequent course was not characteristic of general paresis. Today he might have been diagnosed as manic-depressive (bipolar) disease and would have been helped to a degree by medications. Yet Nietzsche's reputation continues to be clouded by the implication that his thoughts were the product of a mind deranged by syphilis. Philosophers must beware the hidden rage of envious scholars!

The fact that the work of Nietzsche has survived its association with syphilis and with Nazi ideology is testimony to the yearning individuals have for free philosophical expression and the ability of such expression to affect individuals despite barriers of language and culture.

~ ~ ~

Søren Kierkegaard is easily the most uninhibited artist in philosophy. He even outshines Plato at times in lyricism of expression. He embraced Christianity with a strange Quixotic fervor. I feel his faithfulness to his own version of religion represents a transformation of his devotion to his religiously extremist father; in fact, Kierkegaard says as much in his writings. The flavor of Kierkegaard cannot be conveyed by commentary; he must be read and reread. The following passage from *Repetition*, one of his lesser known works, reveals the existential state of the artist at the height of his powers. He is describing the breakup of a relationship (his own, of course, with Regina, his fiancée):

> I am again myself. This self, which another would not pick up from the road, I possess again. The discord in my nature is resolved. I am again unified…I am again myself, the machinery has been set in motion. The snares in which I was entangled have been hewn asunder, the magic spell which bewitched me so that I could not return to myself has now been broken. There is no one any more who lifts up her hands against me, my liberation is assured, I am born to myself, for so long as Ilithia [goddess of childbirth] folds her hands, one who is in travail cannot bring to birth.

> It is over, my yawl is afloat, the next minute I am where my soul's yearning was, where the ideas foam with elemental rage, where thoughts arise

boisterously like the nations in migration, where at another season there is a stillness like the profound silence of the South Seas, so that one can hear oneself speak even though the movement goes on in one's interior—there where one's every instant stakes one's life, every instant loses it, and wins it again.

I belong to the idea. When that beckons me I follow, when it appoints a tryst I await it day and night, no one calls me at midday, no one awaits me at supper. When the idea calls I forsake everything, or rather I have nothing to forsake, I deceive nobody by being faithful to the idea, my spirit is not grieved by having to grieve another. When I return home no one reads my looks, no one deciphers my countenance, no one extorts from my being an explanation that not even I can give to another, as to whether I am blissful in gladness or despondent in distress, as to whether I have gained life or lost it.

The chalice of inebriation is again held out to me, already I inhale its fragrance, already I am sensible of its foaming music...

translated by Walter Lowrie

Such are the reasons philosophers tend to remain unmarried. Kierkegaard will have an eternal place in the annals of philosophy for his elevation of *individuality* above all other modes of societal existence. He had reverence for his own self; it was the basis upon which he developed his creative philosophy.

~ ~ ~

The distinction between the existential philosophy of Kierkegaard deriving from the interior feelings of the philosopher and the scientific philosophy of Immanuel Kant arising from the analyzing capacities of the mind is clearly revealed by comparing the work of these two philosophers. *The Critique of Pure Reason* was the first great work of scientific phenomenology although Kant did not use the term. It rigorously related man's perceptions of the external world to his fixed '*a priori*' notions of time and space and demonstrates the former to be defined by the latter. This is one of the great milestones of philosophical thought. Kant's concept of the *a priori* meant that he had separated science from art; *a priori* judgments are not based on feelings or ideas generated by the individual; they are unconscious representations of sense data derived from the outer 'phenomenal' world. Science is based on rigorous analysis of 'objective' representations, that is to say the *a priori* representations translated into quantitative or descriptive data. Instruments are more reliable sources of data than human beings since they are not subject to the influence of confounding human variables. As one plods through the relentless analysis of the *Critique*, he feels himself to be in the presence of the true scientific mind—dispassionate, analytical, and unswerving.

However, as it turned out, Kant was not willing to give up completely on philosophy as an existential form of expression. In his preface to the 2nd edition of the *Critique*, he abruptly abandoned his analytical style and revealed his conviction that there are three beliefs humans must hold to for practical employment of their reason. These are belief in a divine being, belief in free will, and belief in the immortality of the soul. One can hardly trust the text, so abrupt is Kant's change of tone. But Kant felt himself to be a feeling person as well as a scientist; he must respond to the external world on a feeling level as well as an analytic level even if he wonders about the origin of his responses and flirts with the role of pragmatic theologian. One has to admit, however, that Kant the artist in philosophy falls well below the stature of Kant the scientific philosopher; his feelings are often mundane and contradictory.

~ ~ ~

The Judeo-Christian belief in a Divine Being is a naïve response to an individual's realization of his infinitesimally minute physical self. It is distressing to realize how insignificant one is in the physical universe; the belief in an almighty God who cares about him soothes man's nervous psyche. The development of scientific technology has enlarged men's physical self-image, lessening the need for a faith in a personal God, but it still remains an understandable response of humans to the awareness of their finitude. However, there are alternative responses to the awareness of finitude. Stoicism and Epicureanism (not to be confused with the modern meaning of 'epicure') were philosophies evolved in the Greco-Roman era that did not depend on an external deity to sustain the dignity of self. The victory of Christianity over these more intelligent ways of thought was a consequence of the philosophical illiteracy that has been the usual condition of multitudes in most eras.

Kant was not a philosophical illiterate; his inclusion of belief in God in his trinity of beliefs was probably more a matter of lack of freedom of expression than of genuine faith; as it was, Kant's work came perilously close to being banned by the Protestant establishment in Prussia. Intellectual perversity and love of tradition may explain the otherwise inexplicable 'faith' of many intellectuals. Discussion of the religious faith of intelligent human beings goes beyond the purposes of this writing.

The belief in the immortality of the soul is akin to belief in God; it is a reaction against the awareness of the eternity in which the individual will not exist. It is especially thinkers of Kant's type who shrink from the idea that their minds will disappear forever upon their death. It is unbearable to them to imagine that their laboriously acquired mental powers will instantaneously vanish upon death of their puny bodies. Perhaps they have reason to disbelieve this apparent fact but immortality is a very long time. It does not warrant faith from individuals with an intellectual conscience.

The heaven-hell eschatology of Christianity is replaced in the east by the concept of metempsychosis in which there is rebirth of one's soul in another body according to the laws of karma. Even Socrates (according to the *Phaedo*) was inclined to find justification in the idea of an after life of the soul. The high-minded Epicurus would have nothing to do with what seemed to him to be a puerile belief. However, the rigorous thinking of Epicurus did not survive the tidal wave of Christianity in the antique world.

~ ~ ~

The concept of free will is a time honored philosophical notion that is in accord with the nature of philosophy as an expressive art. It derives from the universal experience that human beings often wish to free themselves from predetermined or externally imposed behaviors. The awareness of free will would never arise if an individual did not conceive that he could rise above his physiology or influences from his environment. Even fatalism is a form of free will; it is the expression of an individual's choice to accept his fate as in the motto *amor fati* of Nietzsche—love one's fate. It is the rising of the possibility of choice into consciousness that is the manifestation of free will. Whether one chooses passive acceptance of the nature of one's situation (fatalism) or active resistance to it, (rebelliousness) are both the signs of free will.

A philosophy of fatalism can be developed as well as a philosophy of overcoming of fatalism. By and large, eastern philosophies teach fatalism by emphasizing the illusoriness of the phenomenal world; this is the message of the *Bhagavad Gita*, a scripture much valued by devotees of eastern thought. The desire of individuals to act and express themselves according to their individuality is regarded as a negative quality in the *Gita*. Fulfillment for the devout Hindu or Buddhist is never possible until one has extinguished the desire for personal self-expression in his daily life. In fact, Kant was more of a fatalist (conformist) than a free will practitioner as is usually the case with university professors. His idea of free will was based on the Protestant preoccupation with punishment of 'sin', in which the concept makes humans eternally responsible for their sins, as defined by Christian dogmas. The highest form of free will was regarded by Kant to be acceptance of Christian morality. The concept of individual conformity to external constraints of whatever type is a style of mental activity just as is the concept of individual freedom from these constraints. The consequences of mental style are vividly apparent in contemplating the outcome of lives based on these differing concepts.

~ ~ ~

Fundamentally, one must regard Kant as a primitive figure in philosophy in spite of his contributions to it. He was a brilliant phenomenologist but he was not oriented to the expression of feelings, which is the essence of philosophy. He was not interested in human individuality and did not attempt to explore its depths; thus he was a philosophical primitive much like the two dimensional American painters popular at the time of the Revolutionary War. It was left to his successors in German philosophy to more profoundly express the nature of the interior self of human beings.

Ludwig Feuerbach conceived himself as filling the void left by Kant regarding the metaphysical aspects of the self, for which the latter would not do more than provide the label of the 'noumenon'. As mentioned previously, Feuerbach explained how humans *project* their spiritual feelings into fictitious external deities and the trappings of institutionalized religions. As Kant has been deified, so Feuerbach is vilified and ignored as a significant figure in western philosophy. It is amazing that the famous theologian Karl Barth in a virulently hostile preface to the English edition of Feuerbach's *Essence of Christianity* accused him of 'spying' on Christianity because he used Christian phraseology and imagery to elaborate his humanist views. Barth seemed to think that faith, goodness, and spirituality are the private property of the Christian religion. In reading Barth, one cannot help feeling that if Barth had been a Lord Protector when Feuerbach was alive, one would again smell the stench of burning flesh on fagots.

The young Karl Marx was strongly influenced by Feuerbach's writing. Marx had the potential to be a great philosopher; like all budding artists, he wrote poetry as a young man. His initial writings are filled with the spirit of philosophy. I have earlier stated that Marx originated the concept that 'money' is an alienated essence of man's life that dominates him as he worships it, a clear anticipation of the psychoanalytic theory of projective identification, but with a better sense of its relevance to the bourgeois condition. However, Marx's resentment overcame his philosophical values; he lost his belief in philosophy and transformed himself into a doctrinaire revolutionary personality.

It was a tragedy for Europe that Marx did not follow Goethe's example of the artist in political life. Goethe, who served many years in administrative posts, always expressed his valuation of the artist far above the politician and never deluded himself to think that altering economic or social structures could alter the quality of human beings. Yet Marx once wrote words that might bring tears to the eyes of all who have suffered under the oppression of Marxist-Leninism. "What is to be avoided above all is the re-establishing of 'Society' as an abstraction vis-à-vis the individual. *The individual is the social being*" (italics added) (Economic and Philosophical Manuscripts of 1844).

~ ~ ~

In England, logical positivism has long been the dominant style of philosophical thought. British thinkers have been bemused by science in the days of Francis Bacon. British philosophers generally express themselves with fluency and lucidity; they have been trained in the tradition of the great English prose stylists. There is almost a hypnotic quality to the mellifluous prose of Locke and Hume; the pattern has been carried on through Herbert Spencer, Bertrand Russell, and Alfred North Whitehead. It is as though their minds work on syntactical principals undisturbed by inner feelings. It is natural that modern British philosophy has been strongly influenced by mathematics and its culmination has been in a grammar of signs and symbols. But the observation of Heine is still valid; one has difficulty in finding a soul in British philosophy. My impression is that the English turn to religion when they feel the need for deeper modes of expression; thus the apparent turning to Anglo-Catholicism among English intellectuals.

~ ~ ~

Ralph Waldo Emerson was a remarkable philosophical genius whose writings were greatly valued by Nietzsche, a man not inclined to value other philosophers. Emerson's weakness was his inability to project his own self into his writing, a failing that may be the consequence of stemming from an unbroken line of five generations of New England clergymen. Emerson could not descend from his abstract mental pulpit. However, his essays and journal reveal a breadth and depth that is unique in American letters.

What Emerson lacked, Henry David Thoreau possessed—the ability to clearly express his thoughts on a personal level. Thoreau is the single Socratic figure that has appeared in the United States; he is a philosopher because he possessed the one thing needful for a philosopher, the ability to express his interior self in his concepts. Thoreau's 'travelogue' *A Week on the Concord and Merrimack Rivers'*, written during his stay in his cabin on Walden Pond, is filled with original philosophical observations. Equally is it true for *Walden*, his account of his life on the pond. One has to reach back to the Greeks to find philosophers as bold and as integrated in their persona as was Thoreau. However, unlike Greek philosophers such as Socrates, Zeno, and Epicurus, and like his fellow Concordian Emerson, Thoreau has had virtually no philosophical impact on the society in which he lived. He is known as an eccentric moralist who wrote about nature and has been totally ignored by academic philosophy. Thoreau is a prime example of the error in relying upon philosophy professors for guidance in philosophy.

~ ~ ~

Philosophy is the last area in which Great Britain still exercises cultural hegemony over the United States. Consequently, with the exception of Thoreau, we have not been blessed with thinkers committed to philosophy on the ancient Greek model. This is not to say that the United States has not produced thinkers on the British intellectual style of prose masters. There has been Royce, James, Santayana, and Dewey who have made their marks in Euro-American philosophy. William James contributed a distinctive American innovation to philosophy by asserting that reality is what works in practice; his theories have been adopted by lesser minds who think of reality as success in society. I succeed, therefore I am. But of course, this is not philosophy; this is social adaptation.

Since World War II, academic philosophers capable of inspiring readers seem to have become an extinct species. Lewis Mumford, perhaps the most powerful twentieth century commentator on American life, spoke about societies, not individuals. Mumford is the voice of Jeremiah rather than Socrates. Americans seem to be too involved with the institutions of their society to be able to stand aside from them for the sake of deepening the individual's awareness of his reality.

~ ~ ~

The most recent wave of European immigration to America occasioned by two world wars brought a new depth of scholarship to American universities. Nonetheless, scholarliness, no matter how intellectual it may be, is not equivalent to independent philosophy. In addition, to add to the woes of philosophy in America, there has emerged a genre of promoters of eastern metaphysics and religion with swarms of American adherents. These types may have something to contribute to the American melting pot, but they do not represent the commitment to flowering of the interior self that lies at the heart of the Greek philosophical traditions from which western thought emerged. This commitment requires establishing the individual above the constraints of his upbringing and the pretensions of doctrinaire thought.

A recent trend in American intellectual life has been the 'New Age' ways of thought. These have revealed that erudition is essential to philosophy even if it is not identical to it. Unhistorical superficial ideas contribute nothing to philosophy. They are fostered by university extension courses, private institutes, charismatic individuals, and other camp followers of the 'wisdom' industry. Considerable money is to be made by writing trendy books that purport to explain the elusive cosmic questions as well as how to be happy. These are usually along the lines of traditional systematic philosophy, except they are written in an urbane witty style rather than in the arcane prose of academicians. Most commonly, one is provided with the hitherto inscrutable wisdom of the East, dressed up for western consumption. Perhaps an east-west smorgasbord is offered, such as the oneness of the Tao fused with quantum physics. Mathematical field theory may be equated with the oneness of Brahman. Some of the pop philosophers are exceptionally entertaining as befits the satirical style that is the dominant American literary form and to which I fear this chapter is deteriorating.

Satire aside, there is nothing more destructive to philosophy than turning it into a moneymaking enterprise. Philosophy becomes sophistry and philosophers become entertainers. Socrates noted the frequent dishonesty of the Sophists of his day; nothing has occurred since to alter the correctness of his observation. The antique definition of sophistry as an art of making money clarifies the nature of American 'pop' philosophy. Guruism is a profitable business in the western part of the United States.

In essence, the contemporary promoters of popular systematic metaphysics provide a rehash of eastern or western metaphysical ideas of the past. 'Spirituality' is Christianity without Christ and the Christian dogmas or is the ancient metaphysics of a transplanted Hinduism. It is as though Kant had never lived to point out the unreal nature of traditional metaphysics. Philosophy has had its systematizers; it is unlikely that the current crop will improve upon Spinoza, Leibniz, Hegel, or Teilhard de Chardin. Since Kant, one knows that systematizing is only of value as an exercise for the mind. Alan Watts was sophisticated enough to recognize this when he tells his readers that, "the universe is at root a magical illusion and a fabulous game." At best, philosophical systems are forms of mnemonics, handy methods of stringing together large numbers of ideas to suit our causality-oriented mental functions. As a mnemonic, the system of Teilhard de Chardin is the most up to date one presently available; pop philosophers would do well to popularize the intelligent and imaginative Père Teilhard, rather than reconstruct inferior systems that stem from obsolete cultures.

The main point is that all philosophical systems are mental exercises analogous to learning the multiplication tables. The only value in organizing the universe of phenomena on a cognitive level is to make the cosmos appear more manageable; it is a convenience for living just as learning arithmetic is a convenience for commerce. But one must not forget that the goal toward which the human mind should be dedicated is the elaboration of what is inside oneself, not what is outside itself. Toward this goal, no system, popular or classical, is capable of leading an individual.

Jack London and Henry Miller are the closest the United States has come to producing creative philosophical personalities in the twentieth century. Miller expresses many original ideas, if one is not put off by his libidinous obsession. Perhaps he is more of a novelist and essayist than philosopher, but his writings project the image of a powerful independent personality. He understood the need of the creative individual to be free from institutional domination and to be capable of acting and writing in a manner that is expressive of his innermost feelings. Much the same can be said of London who streaked across the American literary scene in the early twentieth century like a meteor and burned himself out at age 40 years. He is still remembered in Europe, although hardly in the United States.

~ ~ ~

The search for authentic independent philosophers is a difficult task. It may be that the Greeks accomplished too much, inhibiting successors who have been prone to wander off into metaphysical abstractions or cognitive science. It was not until the nineteenth century that philosophers appeared to rival Plato and the philosophical schools of Greece. Kierkegaard was a naturally gifted philosophical genius who was diverted from his task by his obsession with his version of Christianity. Nicolai Berdyaev, in my judgment, the greatest philosopher of modern times, exhibited a similar problem although to a lesser degree. Both of these writers were great creative artists in the domain of philosophy; that is to say they experienced life intensely, thought deeply about their experiences, and expressed these thoughts in their work. Kierkegaard had a poetical style of expression while Berdyaev was more akin to a Rodin. It may be that the bulwark of religion was necessary for these two individuals to stand apart from their society. Both of them seemed to have persuaded themselves that belief in God was necessary for man's freedom.

In Arthur Schopenhauer and Friedrich Nietzsche, one comes upon philosophers who stood apart from both society and God. Consequently, their writings reveal the profoundest mental development of any philosopher since Plato. Schopenhauer was the embodiment of the intellectual strongman; he was a man who confronted his solitary existence fearlessly, relying only on his motto *Vitam impendere vero* (life dedicated to truth). Unlike many other independent philosophers, he ran the course of his life firmly until its natural end. More than his philosophy, Schopenhauer's life as an independent philosopher deserves recognition.

Nietzsche has already been discussed. It should be emphasized that he needs to be read slowly and with care, as if one were reading a foreign language, even when reading him in translation, since Nietzsche's depth of discourse goes far beyond everyday thought. The ideas of Nietzsche have not yet been assimilated in their entirety by western culture.

The post-1914 period reveals a falling off from the peak of philosophical heights of the previous century (with the exception of Berdyaev who really belongs in the pre WW I era). The continental phenomenologists and existentialist philosophers—Husserl, Heidegger, Jaspers, Sartre, Maritain, Merleau-Ponty, to name some of the most prominent—were academic, religious or political personalities. They were too bound up with scholarly preoccupations or social activism to represent the 'solitary individual' in the manner of a Kierkegaard or a Nietzsche. Their center of gravity was not in their interior selves but elsewhere, lending a certain unreal quality to their writings, in the sense that I have defined 'reality'.

A SPECIAL ART FORM

A I believe that the main thing to know about philosophy is that it is a form of art. Philosophy is the art of reflection on the realities of the human condition; a philosopher who has not experienced life in its many manifestations is like a composer who has never heard music. The idea is inconceivable. Much of what goes under the name of philosophy today is actually science, theology, mathematics, history, or journalism. Philosophy is none of these; it is an art form whose identifying characteristic is the expression of ideas about the realities experienced by the philosopher. The appreciation of philosophy requires a taste for art that is not greatly different from that required for other art forms. The person whose spirit is not touched at one time or another by music, by painting, by architecture, or by poetry will not be touched by genuine philosophy. Plato, regarded as the founder of discursive western philosophy, was seen as a poet by the scientifically minded Aristotle.

With a little imagination, one can notice that the style of philosophers is often similar to the style of other artists of their locale and time. Thus British philosophy of the 17th and 18th century resembles British landscape painting and portraiture; it is somber and oriented toward the surface of phenomena. One could envision Hobbes, Locke, and Hume as intellectual landscapists. French philosophers of the Enlightenment resemble their country's fiction writers and dramatists; they are clever, light, and full of nuances. Voltaire and Rousseau are like frothy cakes. The French impressionist school of art continued in this vein. In central Europe, however, one finds philosophers in the expressionist style, resembling artists such as Ernst Kirchner, Edvard Munch (Norwegian but worked in Germany), or Franz Marc. The emphasis is on seriousness, depth, and feelings. Kierkegaard and Nietzsche are the foremost examples of Expressionism in philosophy (a better term than Existentialism); both were explicit in their identification with art.

~ ~ ~

At one time, systematic philosophy, which may be regarded as an architectural mode of philosophical expression, was the principal form of philosophy. One can detect a theological spirit in the works of systematizers like Spinoza, Leibniz, and Hegel, except they are founded upon a feeling of intellectual rather than divine revelation. The persecution of philosophers as heretics is explicable as churches' response to rival theologies. Churches rarely burned other types of artists; even the New England Puritans were content to limit their punishment of artistic sinners to a day or two in the stocks. Raphael could include his voluptuous mistress in his *Transfiguration* that now hangs in the Vatican. However, the gentle Spinoza and the harmless Descartes were menaced by their churches, and in Italy, that country's promise of a humanistic philosophy was brought to an end by the Inquisition. Père Teilhard de Chardin, the last European systematizer, had his enlightened conceptions worked out in *Le Phénomène Humain* suppressed by the Vatican. At the present time, systematic philosophy has gone out of fashion, largely as a result of the loss of reputation suffered by all non-empirical cosmologies in a scientific era.

~ ~ ~

The expropriation of the term 'philosophy' by academicians has been catastrophic for this high form of human expression. Genuine philosophy as originated in the ancient Greek world does not exist today. There is philosophy as mathematical science, there is the form of psychological anatomy known as phenomenology, and there is, as always, the history and critique of former philosophers that is the stock in trade of university professors in need of academic advancement. A more recent trend is lucrative popular philosophy that has become a commercial affair of university extensions and other business enterprises.

The prototype modern western philosopher is a person who writes in a scholarly manner, but also with a smooth journalistic touch. He finds his audience within an intellectual elite who enjoys scholarly accounts of happenings on the world's stage. However, the world is in need of *art*, as Nietzsche wrote, not scholarly historians and certainly not journalists. The world needs art because it needs to experience life in newer and more profound ways than in the past; the onslaught of technology has concealed the reality of life from contemporary individuals. It is through experiences that individuals deepen the reality of their lives; it is the purpose of art to provide experiences to those who yearn for them, to both the artist and the auditor of art. Of all the arts that are needful to human beings, the art of philosophy is needed most of all since it is in meaningful concepts that the modern age is most deficient. Technology builds robots everywhere but it cannot provide the inner life needed by living individuals. Concepts that enliven one's soul do not come mechanically from the powers of science any more than they can be handed down by powers on high; they appear during internal 'processing' (for want of a better term) of meaningful experiences. The experience of the feelings of another human being occurs through art; when these feelings are expressed through conceptions of reality, they are called philosophy.

~ ~ ~

Today, the philosopher must be an artist who believes in the value of ideas objectified in literary form and that stand for his life experiences. But the era of a Socrates enchanting his listeners verbally is long over. Now a philosopher is an alchemist who must transform experiences into written language for a reader. His art is judged not by the fluency of his prose, his virtuosity with language, or his gifts of imagery and metaphor. All of these may contribute to his art but are not central to it, any more than accuracy of representation or cleverness in composition is central to the work of a great painter. What is central is the expression of thoughts that represent his own realities, and thereby open the reader's eyes and ears to what he has not previously seen or heard—or perhaps his nose to what he had not smelled! It is the task of the reader to relate to the truth of the philosopher's ideas, not truth as understood scientifically from the viewpoint of acquisition of facts, but a deeper truth in which the reader *experiences* the ideas of the philosopher as they represent his own unformed feelings. The successful encounter of the artist and his auditor is much like falling in love; it is an event clothed in mystery that is impossible to predict or insure. Goethe caught the spirit of philosophical creativity in lines from the prologue to *Faust* in which the Lord is speaking to mankind:

> *Das Werdende, das ewig wirkt und lebt,*
> *umfass euch mit der Liebe holden Schranken,*
> *und was in schwankender Erscheinung schwebt,*
> *befestigt mit dauernden Gedanken!*

> New creation, eternally occurring,
> ye shall contain with love's kind attention,
> and what freely floats, dimly swaying,
> surely shall ye fix with lasting conception!

~ ~ ~

Therefore, the task of the artist-philosopher is to express ideas that affect his readers. He cannot rely on sound, story, rhyme, rhythm, or visual effects to affect them; when he does so, he moves away from his role as a philosopher. It is his ideas that are his central concern and it is their expression that he must rely upon to accomplish his goal—affecting the interior state of his readers. Suzanne Langer defined philosophy as the continual pursuit of meaning; but meanings, of course, can only come from the philosopher's own experiences. Thus the ancient maxim, 'first live, then philosophize'. In his concentration on conceptualizing from the reality of his own experiences, the philosopher is more purely an artist than any other type of creative person since he does not honey his work with sweet glosses. When a philosopher adulterates his work with the attractions of poetic form, drama, or story, he may facilitate attracting an audience, but it is at the price of loss of attention to his ideas. Who takes seriously now the ideas of Shelley, Byron, D. H. Lawrence, Bernard Shaw, or even Thoreau who wove his profound thoughts into his discussions about nature?

Heraclitus was on target when he wrote: "the Sibyl with raving mouth uttering her solemn, unadorned, unperfumed words reaches out with her voice over a thousand years."

Philosophy is not for children any more than Rembrandt or Beethoven is for them. It is not a question of chronological age but of maturity of mind. The majority of people never develop their interior selves sufficiently to be responsive to philosophic thought; for those people, there are other art forms or if all else fails, there are the myths of religion to provide for their needs for transcendence. Still there is an element of pathos felt when a chronologically mature person cannot experience philosophy; it is a form of illiteracy that suggests some cultural impoverishment within a society. A large number of philosophically illiterate individuals indicates cultural impoverishment, akin to reading illiteracy in a society. Such societies are vulnerable to all forms of demagoguery and oppression. Without philosophy, it is difficult to maintain one's dignity into adult life; this may be why philosophically illiterate societies are youth oriented.

~ ~ ~

Scientists impose control on their surroundings through technology; artists influence their surroundings though their art. The faith of the artist is that the feeling or thought he expresses in his art will affect someone, even if it should be just one person. Once this is understood, the nature of philosophy as an art form becomes clear. The difficulty with philosophy arises when the philosopher is deluded into thinking that he transmits universal facts instead of personal expressions. The systematizers, positivists, and phenomenologists do not want to be artists; they want to be scientists. They are frustrated physicists, mathematicians, or cognitive psychologists who try to adapt philosophy to their own purposes. Edmond Husserl famously said philosophy must be 'strict science'.

The urge to be scientists, linguists, or theologians, anything but philosophers, is why philosophers have been prone to disconnect their concepts from their human origins. One then has philosophy as natural law, descriptive science, or revelation from without. Somehow the philosopher has been privileged—how, one is never told—to be given insights into the world beyond ordinary mortals. Ralph Waldo Emerson said that the generalizing urge is felt to be a manifestation of divinity in human beings; this is why a thrill is felt upon creation of every generalization. Emerson was speaking with tongue in cheek, but there is more to be learned from his comment than all the epistemology of logicians. Religions developed out of the desire of men to transform their personal conceptions into eternal truths. This tendency reveals a failure of understanding of the personal nature of conceptions and essentially a lack of respect for the creative process. Philosophy as analytic science is the most recent attempt to place philosophic thought on some absolute platform.

Faith in the power of art is the only faith I know that acknowledges the capacity of human beings to *themselves* transcend their animal being. It is the only faith that does not violate one's intellectual conscience. A clear, well-founded conception of the place of art in human life is the best antidote to religious superstition or scientific domination. The Socrates of the *Phaedo* understood philosophy—the love of wisdom—as the greatest of the *arts* and rejected its transformation into science. There has never been any justification for defacing this greatest of all the human arts, which has been so fruitful in elevating the character of those who have embraced it.

~ ~ ~

The philosopher succeeds by bringing his spirit to life in his writings. He cannot live in a bloodless, abstract world (this was a fault of Emerson); neither should he be primarily concerned with topical issues of morality or politics. He must convey the conceptions deriving from his own experiences, acknowledging that his concepts are his mystical reactions to the surround of phenomena in which he exists. He is a *mystic.* Individuals are often victimized by the thoughts of others; the philosopher is the Good Samaritan who stands up for the interior life of every individual. He creates, using the imagery of Père Teilhard, the beneficent *noosphere* in which the life of the mind can develop as it should.

Voltaire commented that no army can stop an idea whose time has come, but Emerson was more accurate when he said beware when the great God lets loose a thinker upon the planet. The time of an idea arrives because the powerful mind of a human being has allowed its emergence in the minds of others. It might have been better to say that no army can destroy an idea once it has been brought into existence by one seized with the spirit of philosophy.

The faith of the philosopher is that someone else, not all but someone, can feel and think what he feels and thinks. The philosopher is intoxicated with the idea that he has a spiritual brother somewhere in the world. It is only when this intoxication proceeds to forgetfulness of self that he becomes a comical figure. Much worse than this forgetfulness, however, is loss of faith in his vision. The spiritual imperative for philosophers is to act as if their *spiritual perceptions* can be shared by someone else. If this faith flags, as it apparently did in the case of Nietzsche, the philosopher *zugrunde geht*, he perishes.

All art forms have their special type of experience that they offer. The art of the novel is the portrayal of characters; it is axiomatic that ideas that interest the novelist must remain secondary to his characters. A poet transforms his inner state into the rhythms and imagery of his language. The experiences offered by theater, musical, and visual arts are self-evident. There are historical changes in receptivity of styles of expression. For example, long narrative poems and poetry as philosophy went out of fashion long ago—as Robinson Jeffers discovered to his chagrin. However, the interesting prose poem *Das Energi* (sic) by Paul Williams might have been a forerunner of a swing back to Lucretius' use of poetry as a philosophical vehicle. So far, this has not happened.

Philosophical expression as a *literary art form* has not entered the consciousness of the contemporary public. It is by his ability to present his feeling-generated ideas that the philosopher must be judged, not by his journalistic abilities or scholarly expertise. Ideas even more than emotions are capable of affecting an individual because they can take root and grow in his mind. Kierkegaard and Nietzsche, the two modern philosophers who have had the greatest impact on western culture, were quite unscholarly, often exhibited incoherent prose styles, and were not understood at first by many well-educated readers. However, they were artists in philosophy who believed that expression of their feelings took precedence over all other considerations and, ultimately, their thoughts took hold. One should be suspicious of a philosopher whose language flows too easily—it is not likely he is expressing his feelings in a meaningful manner.

Philosophy as an art form is found elsewhere besides western culture. It is evident that the forest thinkers of the Vedic world of Hindu India had mastered the art of philosophy. One must peer between lines of the awkward translations of Sanskrit into English to discover the force and liveliness of the ancient Indian philosophers. The Upanishads were the repository of Vedic wisdom, and, unlike ancient Greek philosophy, have been carefully preserved up to the present time. A fine contemporary means of gaining access to the Hindu world of long ago is to view the remains of Hindu erotic temple art. Those Hindus were people of breadth and depth who understood the relationship of eroticism to wisdom! But like the ancient Greeks, the Vedic wise men are long gone along with the world that produced them. India now eagerly snaps up the technology of the west and exports gurus in exchange.

~ ~ ~

Professors and scholars in the university world of philosophy are in the habit of demanding detailed documentation of scholarly credentials as a requirement for publication in philosophy. This is a characteristic of all areas in which scholarly specialists form a guild. It is a means of maintaining control over their areas. But few creative personalities have the inclination to subject themselves to guild control. Scholars reject the idea that the 'unscholarly' can express themselves philosophically in a manner that deserves serious consideration. This is a dog in the manger attitude since 'philosophers' formed by scholarship cannot themselves create original philosophy. Their skills are appropriate for historical research or cognitive science but are of little value in an independent art form like philosophy. The academic monopoly of western philosophy has resulted in its virtual disappearance as a vital form of expression.

The creation of philosophical writing is not like building an architectural monument, it is more like composing a sonata; there are threads to pursue and themes to work out but they are intermingled, not carved out separately. The reader needs to expand his receptive self to follow the expressions of a philosopher; one cannot read authentic philosophy without this expansion any more than one can appreciate Bach without some experience of classical music. Philosophers do not systematically proceed from one foundation stone to another in laying out the 'truth'. The systematic philosophers have deceived their readers since they have provided illusory logical structures in which the human feelings of the philosopher are no longer discernable. This discovery forms the basis of Kierkegaard's criticism of Hegel. Kierkegaard proposed that Hegel would have been an important thinker if he had acknowledged the comical nature of his philosophy; perhaps Hegel might have compared his complex 'system' to a ten-ring circus in which all the acts interact with one another.

The same kind of objection applies even more to the theologians—Augustine, Aquinas, Luther, and others of a similar ilk. They all bring their own religious prejudices into the philosophical arena, claiming to be the recipient of metaphysical revelations that underpin their own philosophies. In my judgment, they are harmful figures that have impeded philosophical development and constricted the minds of those who trusted them.

The philosopher artist does not follow the 1, 2, 3… infinity steps of logical analysis aiming toward scientific truth. He expresses himself according to a different tempo; here, there, there, here. It is the tempo of the tides rather than that of Kant. Each position in his work is existential, not sequential. Critics who find this approach disorganized, unscholarly, or unhistorical should turn to scholarship or history for their edification. However, a reader should remember that a philosophical exposition that does not project the interior state of the philosopher is like a caress not motivated by love; it leaves one with the unpleasant sense of having been used by the caresser.

As for science, it is the plumbing of humanity. As such, it deserves greater or lesser attention according to one's need for plumbing. Societies are generally not habitable without plumbing of some sort. Nonetheless, few will disagree that when a society gives all its energies to the plumbing, it seems hardly worth the effort to maintain it.

~ ~ ~

I think it important that a philosopher guard against writing too much; gigantic philosophical tomes are like the Pyramids of Egypt—monuments whose impact derives from their size rather than their substance. The length of many contemporary books tends to be based on commercial advantage instead of the writer's instincts. If a philosophical book is too long, the spiritual blood of the philosopher is drained before the book is completed. Nietzsche's *Untimely Reflections* are ideal lengths for works of philosophy; later as Nietzsche grew shriller, his books proliferated until finally there was nothing left of the exhausted philosopher.

The art of stopping writing is fully as important as the art of starting. Books of historical analysis may go on for thousands of pages; extreme examples are provided by Spengler and Toynbee. This is impossible for philosophy that is the outcome of the finite mind of a writer. Kierkegaard's and Nietzsche's early short works are their best because they reflect the natural movements of their minds and one does not sense that either of them strained to complete them. On the other hand, *Concluding Unscientific Postscript* and *Thus Spoke Zarathustra* seem to fade away in their endings.

~ ~ ~

The philosopher who writes with the requirements of success in the market place is akin to a lover who woos for the purpose of sexual copulation. Both are reprehensible since they are not straightforward in their expressions. One promises wisdom, the other promises love, but both only desire conquest. No societal or sexual success is worth the deformation of personality caused by deceitfulness. Socrates maintained that the health of the soul is dependent upon cultivation of truthfulness. It is difficult to think of a worse deception than dishonesty of personal expression. It is in direct opposition to the highest human ideal, that of transmission of one's own inner state to other individuals. If a person lies in personal expression, literary or otherwise, he degrades himself and sets the stage for his spiritual oblivion.

~ ~ ~

The philosopher as an expressive artist lives much of his life removed from the milieu of societal living. It is not that he retires from the world out of disdain for it; in fact, the philosopher is a person who intensely responds to the world. It is rather because he alters his personality so that it functions expressively instead of interactively. The alteration cannot be a superficial one—there is nothing as unrewarding as a superficial philosopher—but must reach into the depths of his being and involve his total life's energies. The effort to function expressively and yet maintain a societal life with relationships and all that goes with them produces a great strain on his personality. This is why philosophers seek solitude and are prone to nervous breakdowns as was both pointed out and exemplified by Nietzsche.

Yet one cannot create philosophy in a state of complete isolation. One may find God in a cave or on a mountain peak but if the philosopher wishes to experience mankind instead of God, that is to say reality instead of illusion, then he must reach out to people—even if only to one other person. Dostoevsky wrote that at least one profound relationship is necessary to justify one's presence on earth. More than that is beyond the abilities of most philosophers.

A DECLINING CULTURE

It seems always to be easy for people to take credit for the accomplishments of their predecessors. For example, freedom is a condition much prized in the United States. We pride ourselves on being the leader of the 'free world' in which a person has the opportunity to read, write, and speak freely, travel as he wishes, worship as he pleases, pick the occupation he prefers, marry whom he chooses, raise his children as he sees fit, and dispose of his possessions when he dies. Not all of these virtues are uniformly present in the free world, but it is the ideal that is important.

Most of the freedoms mentioned are of great value. Without freedom, just as without food or shelter, human development has only limited possibilities. It is right for contemporary Americans to be aware of the importance of these freedoms, but it is inappropriate to cultivate a feeling of pride in possessing them. Pride is justified only in the possession of what one has obtained for oneself, not what has been inherited from vigorous predecessors. The reality is that Americans take freedom for granted, just as they take the air they breathe for granted. One cannot live forever being grateful for the things that make one's life possible.

Nevertheless, ideal conditions for daily living never fulfill the life of individuals. This is quite clear in the free affluent society of America, which is filled with people who are unhappy, resentful, or depressed. It does no good to point to others who are less free or who have less material goods and conclude that we should be happy with our conditions of life. The reverse is the reality, no perceptive observer of the American scene could conclude otherwise. Thoreau's comment about the life of quiet desperation of most Americans—made in the 1840s—has been quoted before. A nagging feeling of ill being is and has been pervasive in American society and there is constant dissatisfaction and suspicion directed toward its institutions. The feeling of isolation from communities leads to paranoia. These are realities that will not dissipate amidst the platitudes of politicians.

Schopenhauer wrote that the illusion of mankind is that they should be happy. The opinion of the great Pessimist is quite clear on that score. Nevertheless, individuals struggle toward the goal, which always seems out of reach. To that end, I say it is impossible for the individual to experience fulfillment without freeing himself from restrictive concepts imposed upon him by his society. Other freedoms do not relieve oneself from this responsibility. This proposition has never been truer than in the societies of our times founded on bourgeois assumptions. It is doubtful whether there are any nation states existent today that cannot be classified as bourgeois technological. There may be exceptions to this generalization but I am not familiar with them.

~ ~ ~

Bourgeois societies consistently damage the souls of their youth. In the United States, the message conveyed to a young person who has completed years of tedious schooling and who stands at the threshold of maturity is that he must devote his full energies to preparing himself for a gainful occupation. The purpose of this 'occupation' is to prepare him to take his place amidst the consumer population of the nation. The more consumption, the healthier is the nation's economy. And when times become relatively less affluent (never impoverished because America has always been one of the wealthiest nations in the world), this message becomes increasing shrill and insistent. The bourgeois illusion is fostered that happiness can come through a gainful occupation leading to a prosperous life. It is only exceptional personalities who can resist this siren song and chart an independent course for themselves, thereby incurring family and societal disapproval. Some who do so are already advanced in years, having wasted the prime period of their lives.

This is the message (if asked) that I would give to a youth preparing for an independent life: "You must acquire a trade to provide the necessities of life for yourself and for any others who may become dependent upon you for their sustenance. But be careful that you do not give your life over to the basics of existence, for then you would be no different than the wild animals who spend their whole lives looking for food and insuring their safety. Be sure you keep in mind the nature of human existence, which is to experience, reflect, and express. Do not sell this birthright, as many do, for a mess of monetary pottage. It is necessary to independently sustain yourself; that is not only a requirement of existence but a valuable experience as well; however, it is even more necessary to develop your interior self and your expressive abilities. Do not under any circumstances ignore your interior self. So find some remunerative trade you can rely upon but do not expect it to fulfill your life. No paid occupation can do that for you. Only meaningful experiences and personal expressions provide fulfillment."

So-called 'higher education' has usually become no more than a type of vocational training. Institutions of higher education have become largely repositories of bourgeois values and therefore are not capable of providing an environment for spiritual development. It is difficult to cultivate one's mind in bourgeois society without experiencing alienation from it. Still, alienation is better than illusion, and aspiration toward development of the interior self is better than the cynicism of despair.

The most evil aspect of the domination of technology in society is the image of man that it generates. When human beings envision apparatus and techniques as the backbone of society, when they value technology above all else—in spite of pious platitudes to the contrary—it is inevitable that the concept of a human being begins to resemble that of a machine. The characteristic feature of a machine is that it *predictably* performs an action when triggered; there is no intermediary independent activity. It is only a question of the organization of the energetics. Computer based technology permits an enormous elaboration of the nature of the triggers and the variety of the actions (programming) but the principle of cause and effect predictability remains the same. Machines that become unpredictable are discarded and even are planned to become so, thus stimulating consumption. The programs, once created, acquire a reality of their own; their creators are forgotten and fade into obscurity.

The high regard in which the machine model is held is why the stimulus-response concepts of behaviorism have become so popular in technological societies. They deal with human beings as biological machines that can be 'conditioned' (programming of animals is called conditioning) to respond in predictable manners. Behaviorism is not limited to psychology laboratories; everywhere one hears the language of the behaviorist: contingencies, cues, positive and negative reinforcers, rewards and so forth. The stimulus-response paradigm extends into every aspect of societal life; we even read that foreign policy is a matter of reinforcing the behaviors we want from other nations—positively or negatively. Reflection on the meaning of life is relegated to religious myths and story-telling—hardly to be taken seriously in today's world— and rewards are the universal means by which people are educated to take their place in society.

However, it is forgotten that concepts of behaviorism, in spite of large-scale applications to humans, are based on experimental work with lower animals, largely laboratory-reared rodents that are convenient for laboratory studies of behavior. They ultimately fail when applied to human beings because they do not take into account human nature and the human personality. Behaviorism succeeds with the poorer caliber of humans, not because behaviorist principles are suited to them, but because their will is too weak to resist its pressures. When individuals respond to behavioral techniques, they have betrayed their human quality, which is to respond to life according to one's own values, not the values imposed upon them. Behaviorism is a form of psychological enslavement based upon psychological rather than physical measures, although the latter is also a crucial component of behaviorist training. George Orwell captured the spirit of behaviorism in his novel *1984*. His predictions were fulfilled in communist societies, but the western 'free' world is not far behind, except more sophisticated methods are used to 'shape' behavior and physical force is not part of the reinforcer repertoire. The 'free enterprise' world relies on a relentless behaviorist promotion of consumerism to achieve its ends.

But it will all be to no avail. Those with a feel for the human personality realize that behaviorism succeeds temporarily, not because of its rewards and punishments, but because of the human tendency to worship those who possess power and who seem to comprehend the secrets of existence. As soon as faith in the powers of the promoters of consumerism wanes and the values they espouse no longer are acceptable to people, the entire system will begin to fall apart. Societies have historically crumbled when faith in the principles upon which they operate disappear. This has been true of many societies known to history; it will also be true of technological societies founded on consumerism. The Roman Empire, in spite of its advanced technologies and military superiority, fell apart when Roman values no longer inspired the citizenry. The contemporary technological empires face a similar fate in the not too distant future.

~ ~ ~

One of the most important facts that individuals living in contemporary bourgeois technological societies should grasp is that they live in a declining culture. It is declining because the concept of the value of technology upon which these societies rest is losing its appeal. There is superficial lip service given to technological advances just as there is lip service given to religions, but thoughtful people no longer stand in awe of technology, just as they are no longer in awe of an all powerful divinity. They have become disillusioned with the siren songs of technology, wealth, and consumerism. Adam Smith is dying in the hearts of modern individuals, particularly young ones. People carry on with old forms by force of habit and because of the absence of other values to live by, but the level of discontent grows higher as the discrepancy between the realities of human existence and the unreality of contemporary values grows ever greater.

The vitality of a society cannot be assessed by the gross national product or the life expectancy of its inhabitants. In hell, long life expectancy is clearly a negative feature; for centuries, devout Christians viewed the eternity of roasting in hellfire as the worst consequence of one's sins. Nor is the literacy rate, the infant mortality, or the per capita income any real judge of the worth of a culture; these indices only measure certain material features of the society. National leaders like to recite these statistics as if they were magical incantations bringing awe into the minds of the population who will then presumably continue to have faith in the technologically advanced ship of state. But statistics based upon individuals lumped together as if they were great globs of protoplasm are the most unreal of all the accoutrements of technological society; they are utterly meaningless for the individual, especially one who is conscious of his frustration and discontent with his life.

When confronted with the vastness and organized bureaucracy of the modern superstate, the vivid image of *Revelation* is brought to mind of "the beast with seven heads and ten horns and upon his horns ten crowns." One can imagine that Christianity grew out of rage against the Roman Empire, the rage of the helpless individual against the meaninglessness of its technologies and imperial domination. The Christian's defiant answer to the power of Rome was to have faith in the absurd. The essential idea of early Christianity was the conviction that individual inwardness was more important than the entire Roman Imperium. This is the aspect of Christianity that Kierkegaard embraced with all the passion of his artist's soul. The credibility of Rome's spiritual values had been damaged by its restriction to a small superannuated elite. Culture is always better off in the depths rather than at the pinnacles of a society.

One may wonder what *credo quia absurdum* lies on the horizons of the modern Romes. Surely not the Christian dogmas; they are the tainted products of past eras, no longer tenable for humans who have passed through the age of science. We can be certain, however, that the new ideologies will be based on the concept of the interiority of the individual, not the exteriority of the society, that there must be a new *humanism,* if one is still permitted to use that archaic term.

~ ~ ~

The way to rate a culture is to consider its highest products; individuals who have distinguished themselves in the various forms of artistic expression. The model of Goethe is one of the great milestones in the history of development of the individual— *Bildung* is the German term, which has no equivalent in English. For generations of Germans, Goethe provided an example of an individual rising above the social and religious influences of his day in order to express himself as a developed personality. Unfortunately for Germany, his influence was overcome by a runaway nationalism of the worst type. Bismarckian nationalism and Marxist state socialism evolved out of the concepts of the philosopher Georg Wilhelm Friedrich Hegel, which had centered on the state instead of the individual as the principal reality. Hegel was a university professor in Berlin, which explains much. "By their fruits ye shall know them" is a saying that applies with special meaning to Goethe and Hegel.

It is difficult to imagine that the twentieth century in the western world will be regarded as a positive time for human development. Aside from the catastrophic effects of two world wars, we seem to be in the midst of a *New Dark Ages*, to use a phrase coined by Berdyaev, where the human creative spirit has been extinguished by the power of technology, which has replaced the power of religion. It is certainly not that craft or opportunity is lacking; technology has provided greater scope for craftsmanship and has freed humans from many of the time-consuming drudgery of daily life. It is a concept of the significance of the self that is missing, since a technological society has no awareness of the interior self, never mind respect for it. Technology in our times is the goal, not the tool; the artist who is part of his society cannot help absorbing this attitude to his own detriment. The precious values of individual consciousness, obtained at so much cost in the past, seem to be fading away.

Paul Gauguin said that government involvement in the arts guarantees the triumph of mediocrity; an entertainment and consumer dominated art produces the same guarantee. Socialist realism and Nazi art were the clearest examples of the disappearance of individual artistic expression in controlled societies. Yet these societies could have easily responded by pointing to the kitsch art and trivial literature of the western 'free' world. The Nazi condemnation of 'degenerate' art was not totally off the mark. Satire is the highest art form in western culture; declining cultures are always dominated by an instinct for parody and the satirical mode of expression. The most popular American writers are masters of satirical wit.

It is worth noting that the absence of culture is easier to deal with than is the decline of a culture. A great deal of armor is needed to sustain one's interior self when surrounded by the paraphernalia of a sick culture. Simplification of life is essential for spiritual survival, as Thoreau never tired of repeating. One marvels at the insightful hyperbole of the Gospels; if one does not hate his father and mother and wife and children and brethren— yes, and his own life also—he cannot arrive at reality. Of course, by his own life, one must understand that Jesus may have meant the habits of living that plagued individuals even in his day.

~ ~ ~

But declining cultures are eventually replaced by new ones and it fortifies one to try to envision what they might be like. New cultures will be built by those who can reject the old and who value the reality of their own souls more highly than they do the apparent stability and security offered by technological society. These will be the ones not afraid to step out boldly in the world rather than to follow the fenced-in pathways of specialization. They will concentrate on acquisition of experience of life rather than security of position in society. They will look upon nine to five, five days a week, retirement oriented employment much as we now look back on slavery or child labor. They will view marriage with caution and family development with even greater caution since they will know that historically, these institutions have served as powerful agents for repression of individual development. This knowledge will be as true for women as for men, as both have suffered equally from sex gender assignments.

These new builders will shun patriotism, professionalism, and religiosity as they would the plagues of former times. They will want to contribute their fair share to the workings of their society, but not at the price of their individuality. They will want only to learn those trades that give them the independence to pursue their own individual development and will not listen to the siren song that working for gain and enhancing the self are tasks that can be coalesced into one. They will regard the development of the individual self to be the ultimate task of an individual and responsibility to themselves will take precedence over all other responsibilities. Then, perhaps, will appear the new heaven and earth of which sacred scriptures have spoken. If not the heaven, at least the earth.

~ ~ ~

I think at least several hours of solitary leisure is required most days to maintain one's mental equilibrium. This is a modest need compared to that of others. Thoreau claimed that a visitor once a week to his cabin was often more than he could tolerate. Nietzsche said it might take him days to recover from a visitor. The state of solitary leisure is the principal requirement that a self-respecting person must demand from his surroundings. Solitude without leisure or leisure without solitude is not sufficient; one must be free to be alone with one's thoughts. This is the time when one washes away the noxious influences of societal life and solidifies the reality of self. It is when the final process of meaningful experience occurs, when the impact of phenomena upon the self is digested and assimilated. Being at solitary leisure is like taking the compass of one's life out of a steel jungle that distorts it and allowing the pointer to settle toward one's own true direction in life. Without solitary leisure, one gradually becomes a programmed robot that responds to the world mechanically instead of personally.

The incapacity to exist in a prolonged state of solitary leisure is a dangerous symptom akin to coughing up blood or experiencing chest pain on exercise. It means there is a serious problem in the mind. The person who does not value solitary leisure in his life, who is bored or restless when alone, who requires constant external stimulation during his waking state, is a person who has lost his spiritual independence. There is no unhappier fate for a human being than to be bereft of this precious quality. A person who finds himself in such a predicament is in need of radically rethinking his orientation to his life. He has become dependent upon 'phenomena' to live; he must somehow learn to free himself from this degrading dependence.

Petrarch's essay on *The Life of Solitude* is an insightful study of the topic that has not lost its value with the centuries. It is worth absorbing by anyone who experiences difficulty with solitary leisure. One should ignore Petrarch's Christianity and concentrate on his humanism. Thoreau, of course, is the greatest advocate of solitary leisure since his whole life represented a commitment to it. *Walden* and the essay *Life Without Principles* are Thoreau's enduring legacies to a society that has yet to appreciate his thoughts.

The basic psychic requirement for existing in a state of solitary leisure is a respect for the self. Those who fear isolation because they feel the values of existence are exterior to them will never be content alone. They will always have to be conversing with someone, loving someone, learning something, reading something, earning something, acquiring something, repairing something, exercising, obtaining a suntan, or engaging in any of the other infinite distractions that permit a person to escape from his self. But for human beings, reality is centered in the self, nowhere else, and thus fulfillment in human life is not possible for the purely outer directed person. He is condemned to the fate of Sisyphus, always pushing the stone of outer life uphill, only to see it always rolling down again.

~ ~ ~

Those who find solitude congenial to their personality will at some time have to confront the temptations of psychosis. The psychotic state is one in which the individual is no longer interested or capable—the one leads to the other—of responding to the external world; it is the mirror image of bourgeois life. It is not what a psychotic person thinks that makes him psychotic—it is the withdrawal of his feelings from the world around him. Highly gifted individuals, feeling themselves alienated and at odds with their environment, may be tempted by psychotic withdrawal. The careers of certain artists clearly reflect their submission to this temptation; this was the case with Hölderlin, Gauguin and Nietzsche. Pushkin said he stayed sane because he could not stand being stared at in an asylum, which sometimes seems as good as any other reason to maintain a connection with the world. August

Strindberg utilized psychosis for his literary purposes and seemed to have slipped in and out of psychosis at will. However, this is a dangerous game, analogous to toying with brain altering drugs for the sake of the experience. One runs the risk of never being able to return to sanity, which was the case for Robert Louis Stevenson's fictional character in *Dr. Jekyll and Mr. Hyde.*

The psychotic state is a petrified existence, devoid of the enhancement that comes from interacting significantly with other individuals. It is a form of mental suicide that abolishes the human potential for development. Sadly, perhaps, one realizes that solitary leisure is not a complete solution to life; it is only an essential ingredient of it. As Nicolai Berdyaev expressed it, one must shoulder the burdens of culture and history, and deal with the world. One must do it because it is the nature of the human condition to develop itself through interacting with others. Aristotle was never wiser when he described man as a political animal, meaning one that interacts with his fellow humans.

~ ~ ~

Societies will be more livable when philosophers live in them, not as rulers, but as artists whose work affects the members of society. This was the case in ancient Greece and accounts for the continuing fascination that Greek culture exercises on the world. People live fruitfully only when the concepts that direct their lives undergo continuous evaluation and revision. This is not something to be delegated to politicians or religious leaders; it is a task every individual must perform for himself. Van Wyck Brooks, at the height of his powers before he sunk into depression, wrote, "no true social revolution will ever be possible in America till a race of artists, profound and sincere, has brought us face to face with our own experience and set working in that experience the leaven of the highest culture" (*Letters and Leadership*). One must learn to appreciate the creative work of the philosopher just as one learns to appreciate the visual or dramatic arts as part of the development of the interior self. This requires preparation of the mind; it is unrealistic to think that the apprehension of new ideas does not require experience with their reception and evaluation. Individuals need to receive ideas much as they need to receive food; the one is as important to mental health as the other is to physical health. Once people understand the importance of the life of the mind and of the necessity of grappling with the concepts underlying human activity, they will surely seek out means of developing their mental abilities. They can turn to philosophers, not as all-knowing wise men, but as those who have mastered the art of expressing significant ideas. The concept of philosophy as an art form needs to enter societal consciousness.

It bears repetition to say again that it was too bad that Plato, who still remains the most powerful force in western philosophy, should have desired to construct a new society rather than to be an artist within it. Satan seems to have tempted him rather easily. Later, Jesus was a more difficult problem for the Tempter; it required a different type of kingdom to attract his interest. Kingdom temptation is a perennial distraction for philosophers.

~ ~ ~

Farmers and philosophers have more in common than is generally realized. Xenophon had Socrates spend a great deal of time discussing agriculture and animal husbandry, and many of the noble Roman aficionados of philosophy yearned to return to the land. Nikolai Gogol, a founder of the Russian novel in the nineteenth century, saw return to the land as the solution to the problems of Russia (*Dead Souls*). But Russia in the twentieth century went in a different direction to its sorrow. The basis of material life is food production just as the basis of mental life is idea production. One may conclude that the society that does not value its farmers and philosophers is one that is defective in consciousness of reality. The neglect of the individual farmer on the land by technological societies is further evidence of the unreal vision by which they live.

People know who the farmers are in a society, but often confuse philosophers with psychologists, journalists, scholars, scientists, or theologians. It is necessary to be absolutely clear that independent philosophers (not the academic variety) are those who live the life of the mind as creative artists. They reflect on the nature of their experiences and express their reflections in a manner, as F.C.S. Schiller put it, that "gentlemen can read with pleasure." They nourish the minds of those who assimilate their writings. Perhaps farmers and philosophers should band together for their mutual benefit.

ASSERTION OF SOME REALITIES

The tragedy of subjectivity is that the most exalted feelings may fade, the deepest insights may turn to doubt, and high passion may be transformed into boredom. Humans are attracted to the siren song of a fixed object world as a means to avoid this vexing changeability of feelings. The meaninglessness of objects and of fixed relationships is often overlooked in exchange for the security of their stable position in one's life. Humans are not able to survive solely on the strength of their feelings but are also dependent on stability; a degree of constancy of the affective *milieu intérieur* seems to be as important for the wellbeing of the human organism as is constancy of the physiological milieu. Those individuals who cultivate feelings too intensely and exclusively may pay a high price for the purity of their experiences.

Yet all philosophers of the least distinction have realized that the facades of the *institution of marriage* can pose the greatest danger to the development of self. In past ages, and still to some extent today, marriage was a device to perpetuate family dynasties; hardly a value for individual development. Absolute conventional marriage pushes one into a tight corner, immobilizing the self and often becoming its cemetery. It is a considerable accomplishment to be able to enhance one's interior self within the institution. The fact that marriage is an ancient *more* in most societies is no justification for automatically accepting all its features; slavery was a constant feature in the world for thousands of years prior to the nineteenth century. One of the most dangerous aspects of marriage is the sense of proprietorship it can foster over the spouse. Proprietorship over another human being is the death of all aspects of a relationship that give it real meaning; symbols of proprietorship such as imposition of the name of the spouse or wearing of rings should be banned as have the more frank forms of human ownership. The erotic quality of a relationship vanishes at the instant when proprietorship is experienced. Chaucer put it perfectly in the Franklin's Tale:

> "When mastery cometh, the God of Love anon
> Beteth his wynges, and farewell, he is gon!"

It is vulgar and basically immoral to live in a condition of sexual intimacy with a person with whom one does not have an empathetic relationship. Such a situation is damaging to the self and to the self of the partner. One has no right to participate in the psychological damage of another even if one is willing to immolate his or herself for the sake of marital vows or of children. Separation from physical and psychological intimacy can be viewed as a moral requirement for those who have lost empathy with a marital partner.

Making a virtue of apparent necessity is treason to the self. To fossilize oneself in the cooled lava of a fixed marital relationship for the sake of family stability is a form of self-immolation like the suttee practiced by Hindu wives who still throw themselves on their husband's funeral pyre to maintain the relationship beyond death. It is an example of the weakness and lack of self-respect that can exist in individuals. Jesus never countenanced such attitudes; he preached departure from conventional situations for the sake of higher realities.

One of the most hypocritical attitudes of western religions is their sanctification of the family while ignoring the needs of the individual. The example of the domestic dog rather than the developing individual is utilized as the model for family values. This attitude is quite self-serving since the wellbeing of religious institutions is largely dependent upon stable families. But there is nothing spiritual about the institution of the family; it is completely based on societal and economic values and on the desire of many for a safe haven in an uncertain world. The presence of children magnifies all these factors but does not change their basic nature. It is really disgraceful for institutions purporting to value the spiritual aspect of life to undermine it for purely societal values.

~ ~ ~

William Blake wrote that he who does not form his own beliefs inevitably takes on those of others. In nothing is this truer than in the beliefs surrounding marital and family life. The values of a society in this area should not be accepted as overriding the values of the individual. Moreover, society is an illusory phenomenon; the fact is that every society is only a group of individuals clustered together for particular purposes. The individual who does not assert his own needs over those of society is an enslaved person who has lost touch with the realities of his personal existence. One often witnesses the living death of an individual for the sake of family obligations; this may be regarded as a form of suttee imposed upon oneself by acceptance of societal values. But individuals are required to develop themselves throughout their lives, not just at the beginning of them; they need to bring into consciousness the realization that the highest thing they can accomplish on this earth—far higher than child rearing which any beast can perform—is to make themselves into a human being worthy of his endowment. There is an old rabbinical myth that when an individual dies and appears before his God, he will not be asked what he has done for others, but what he has made of himself. The meaning of the myth is evident. If this process takes a lifetime of single-minded effort, it is in the best of causes. It is the proper show of gratitude for the gift of life.

    In western societies, child rearing often becomes a form of self-indentured labor for parents—a bondage that is far longer than the traditional seven years of biblical times or of the colonial era of the United States. It is usually impossible to engage in self-development while under the obligation to provide the kind of permanently secure, well-stocked, over-equipped household that is prescribed by societal custom in America. When it comes to education of offspring, the servitude becomes fixed for many years beyond the traditional seven. It is not at all clear that this type of servitude is beneficial for children; one can hardly claim that American society has discovered the secret for production of superior individuals.

    Bourgeois societies have accepted the ancient idea that one's children represent a continuation of self. There is no reality to this idea; children are completely different people with their own individuality and in no way should be regarded as a projection of the parental self. This egotistical thought is masked under cloaks of sacrifice and sentimentality. Dedication to one's children is put forth as the noblest manifestation of human feelings. Cultures that are based on child worship do not produce outstanding individuals; they produce people who are bound to their societies and limited in their mental development. The United States, for all its deification of the family and devotion to child rearing has not produced superior individuals on any level; the prevalence of the drug culture, endemic obesity and alcoholism, and the resurgence of cultism are not signs of a superior American society. Abdication of responsibility for self under the guise of parental responsibility is no different than similar abdications under the name of religion or patriotism; it results in developmental arrest of the parent and is probably detrimental to children.

One cannot predict what will lead to personal growth in another human being—least of all in one's own offspring. In my own humble opinion, the most important thing one can do for a child is to provide it with a model of what it means to respect and nurture one's own self. After that, one is in uncharted seas when it comes to 'raising' a child. Securely providing the essentials of life and the opportunity for learning is about the most one can count on to be of worthwhile. Everything else is of dubious value and sometimes harmful. Finally, a young person reaching the age of maturity needs to be left on his own to establish his independence without parental interference.

~ ~ ~

A principal task for independent philosophers is to stand against harmful influences of his day. Every age has its conventions that menace the individual. The greatness of Socrates lay in his willingness to oppose the bourgeois limitations of Periclean Athens. Voltaire stood up against the absurdities of Christianity. Nietzsche did the same, but he also resisted the Bismarckian nationalism that he thought was undermining genuine German culture. In the United States, it is not nationalism, however, that poses the greatest threat to individuals; it is the glorification of 'family values' because the family is so intimately involved with daily life. Forces outside the family such as business, political, and religious institutions shamelessly manipulate family values for their own ends. No society can flourish in the true sense when the family is held up as the principal value of human life. The increasingly frequent breakup of families does not obviate the problem; it exacerbates it by loading individuals with the burdens of guilt and anger. The concept of family values must be brought down to more modest proportions.

It is not happiness but human sacrifice that is usually to be found in the center of the American dream of family prosperity. The happiness in this dream is all too often the silence of the grave—if not a literal grave, then the grave of an individual's aspirations to make something worthwhile of his own self. The skyrocketing divorce rate in the United States is evidence of the disillusionment with the American dream. But the guilt over abandonment or rage in being abandoned often plagues the most blasé of divorced persons.

The real meaning of a marital relationship goes beyond the institution of marriage and the apotheosis of family. It is the erotic joining of two individuals. The need for this joining is not eliminated by the façade of marriage and the illusory American dream. The person who comes to feel as if there is nothing to be accomplished in his personal development is one who has been shell shocked by bourgeois life; he has succumbed to the combat fatigue engendered by societal assaults on his psyche. This is a special hazard of living in family-oriented, consumer-based, high technology societies. The person damaged by society with respect to his higher aspirations feels as if the outer world has nothing to offer him; nothing is then meaningful to him. The personality of such a person goes underground but may exert its revenge in subtle ways. American society is constantly being undermined by the distorted feelings of those whose lives have been stunted, in one way or another, by the American dream.

~ ~ ~

There is a close relationship between the prevalence of obsessive sexuality and violence in society and the absence of 'reality' in the lives of its members. All people yearn to experience *personal* reality in their lives; if it is not provided to them through their own experiences, they will seek it out through preoccupation with sex and violence. Those who feel they have little to lose in their own lives may engage in violent deeds, the extreme example of which is the fanatical suicide bomber. The more affluent bourgeois guarding their own possessions displace their feelings into conspicuous consumption, passive voyeurism, or the legal violence of litigation.

The distorted experiences of sex or violence are real compared to the unreality of life lived amidst a soulless technology. There is no use deploring the prevalence of these activities; they only represent the absence of more meaningful experiences in those who engage in them. When an individual's mental abilities are not developed sufficiently to permit him to develop himself within his society, he is condemned to obsessions with the sexual or the violent. These may be acted upon directly or, more commonly, displaced into control of others, meaningless travel, acquisition of fetishes masquerading as technology or art objects, or any of the numberless consumer activities invented by bourgeois purveyors. However, as Freud recognized, underneath all these 'civilized' trappings lie obsessions with sexual or aggressive impulses.

A violent and sexual mentality, whether expressed directly or indirectly, represents the failure of the individual to free himself from the stranglehold of societal control over his personality. There are psychological therapies offered for strangulated personalities. These are usually provided by those committed to bourgeois values and incapable of dealing with its problems, or those who do not grasp metaphysical need. It makes no difference whether one is strangulated by a spouse or by a family; whether one is strangulated by religion or by guilt over abandonment of religion; whether one is strangulated by an excess of possessions or by the feeling of failure of not having possessions. Oppressive institutions victimize people either way; there is no dealing with ingrained unhealthy values short of extirpating them, root and branch, from the depths of one's psyche. One must know how to be ruthless; it is necessary to break down in order to build up and to tear out weeds in order to grow flowers. This Freud and his followers would not do, but the searcher for reality must do it for himself before it is too late.

~ ~ ~

It is an unintelligent idea to think that violence in a society can be dealt with by making bourgeois out of the disadvantaged classes. At best, this will only convert active behavior disorders into passive voyeuristic ones. This transformation may make streets safer but it does not improve the quality of life for violent individuals. It does not confront the origin of the problem. The educational purpose of societies is to connect its members with self-enhancing experiences, not those destructive to self or to others. This is a task worthy of the high skills of real educators. An education oriented toward reality is what is needed, not one that is dominated by the unreality of technical devices. Given the present condition of American society, a good symbolic step would be to ban computers and cell phones from school grounds.

Another prevalent response to the unfulfilled yearning for reality is to dissolve it with alcohol or drugs, or, in the case of psychedelic substances, to substitute drug experiences for experiences with the world. In time, however, a heavy price is paid for either solution in the form of dissolution of brain functions through repeated exposures to toxic compounds. These are poor solutions to the unreality of societal living.

~ ~ ~

A striking example of the existence of repressed aggressive impulses in American society is the current debate over the right of pregnant women to undergo abortion. There is no society in the history of civilization that has forcibly required women to bear children. The right to terminate pregnancy was always respected; even during the worst excesses of the church, women were not persecuted for terminating their pregnancies. Infanticide was generally tolerated since it was the method of abortion for the poor and most societies had the decency to avert their eyes from the unhappy practice.

But now we witness a revival of puritanical tyranny in America under the banner of 'right to life', denying pregnant women the right to obtain abortions and threatening criminal action against those who might help them carry out their wish. One can only regard such a 'moral' crusade as barbarism and in the worst tradition of violence toward unbelievers that Christian societies have displayed in the past. The right of human beings to do what they want with their own bodies has been a principle laboriously acquired by western civilization. Slavery has been outlawed in the world since the nineteenth century. It seems inconceivable today that a government might tell a woman she is required to endure the stresses of pregnancy and childbirth and assume the responsibilities of motherhood once she has been impregnated—no matter what the circumstances. It is necessary to go back to the Salem witchcraft trials to find an equally tyrannical situation in American society.

The argument that a fertilized ovum or fetus has a right to life represents a biological naiveté of such astonishing proportions that one suspects that vengeful feelings are the true source of this attitude. If a fetus has a right to life, one may ask what about the ova or spermatozoa, since they are precursor forms of a human being just as is the fetus, only less along the embryonic developmental path. Will the next step be to prosecute boys who masturbate and spill their seed, thereby flouting the biblical injunction not to spill seed but be fruitful and multiply? The poor spermatozoa must die with no opportunity to fulfill their purpose of initiating life in an ovum. Or what about women who routinely waste their limited ova every month without giving nature the opportunity to do its divinely appointed work. Shall the government, in its wisdom, announce some day that premenstrual women not engaging in copulation are denying life to their living seed? Routine marriage at puberty, as has been the case in primitive societies, will avoid these infringements on morality. Why single out the fetus for special treatment? After all, the fetus is only at an embryonic stage in the road to independent life that does not always come to fruition.

But there are other aspects of the right to life that require consideration. There is the pathetic situation of the starving people of the world, largely due to overpopulation, that are so vividly portrayed by the media marvels of our day. Do not starving children elsewhere have a right to life also and are not the overfed legislators and churchmen who threaten pregnant women with dire consequences from induced abortions guilty themselves of not diverting their own abundance to needy populations? "Let him is who is without sin throw the first stone." How can anyone in America talk of the right to life of fetuses when it is the principal per capita consumer of the world's resources, the lack of which is the source of famine, suffering, and death in many parts of the globe. The truth is that the 'right to life' is an abomination in the mouths of those who have no respect for the quality of life of individuals and is motivated by their own psychological needs or societal ambitions. If there is a hell, its lowest level must be reserved for those who build careers upon the threat of force directed against those who help pregnant women who do not wish to continue their pregnancy.

The success of inhuman ideas is a sign of the ill health of a society. Adolph Hitler came to power in Germany because of the dysfunctional nature of German society—due in no small part to a vengeful world. The right to life movement is a straw in the wind; the problem is not that of dogmatic religions but of the undeveloped souls in a society that accepts such ideas. The apparent success of the right to life movement reveals that people are yearning for values of any sort; if they do not obtain them through their own life experiences, they will fasten on to any causes or cults that are available to them.

~ ~ ~

Every sentient human being is required to find an Archimedean place for his inner being—something to value absolutely in order to survive the vicissitudes of life on this planet. Without such a fixed place to stand upon, nothing of real significance can be accomplished in life. A person without a fixed value is a tragic figure since society will inevitably enslave him. Values are like possessions; a single value is worth more than a plurality of ones, which tend to obscure each other. Purity of heart, as Kierkegaard said, is to will one thing.

But some Archimedean places are more valuable than others. Those that are valueless for individuals are the ones inherited from the society in which the individual was born, rather than ones he has elucidated for himself. The former express an abstract society, not an individual himself. Religion used to be the principal hereditary value; now this dubious distinction falls to technology. If one must produce a categorical imperative (perhaps Kant was a good psychologist in his instinct for such a principle), it could be—*affirm personal reality.*

In fact, individuals tend to have a drive toward affirming reality; what they often do not have is the capacity to resist the demands and expectations of the society in which they live. Duty—Loyalty—Gratitude—Love—Faith—Compassion— Practicality—Humility—even perverted Reality itself—all these are used in a deceitful manner to trick individuals into the betrayal of self that has always been the usual fate of individuals. An honest person with a good character has two tasks in life: absorbing the world into himself through experience and giving to the world through expression. By accomplishing these tasks, he takes his rightful pace in a cosmic time-space continuum. To fail at these tasks is to remain in the limbo of nonbeing.

Q. But what of suffering humanity?

A. How do you know who is suffering? Or what you should do about it? Or if you do something, how do you know it is a good thing?

Przybyszewski – *Homo Sapiens*

Stanislaw Przybyszewski (spelling is correct!) was a Polish writer who participated in the Berlin *Schwarze Ferkel* (Black Pig tavern) group at the turn of the nineteenth century, including Strindberg, Dehmel, Munch, and other avant-garde intellectuals. His novel *Homo Sapiens* ends with the total collapse of the personal life of Falk, the main character. Finally Falk exclaims with a bitter sardonic laugh *"Vivez l'Humanité,"* as he decides to respond to defeat in his own life by joining the revolution.

The only real gifts that one has to give humanity are the products of one's creative expression. To the extent that creative art expresses the artist, to that extent they are gifts of genuine value. The artist takes pain to obtain clarity and harmony with art that expresses himself since he desires his inner self to be accurately perceived by others. It is 'art' grounded on the desire for lucre or power that is a worthless gift.

An authentic work of art is worth ten thousand charitable gifts. How often it has been proven that compassion and charity are harmful to the recipient. The expression of one's feelings through art is never harmful to anyone.

~ ~ ~

If the beginning of philosophy lies in understanding the illusoriness of phenomena, then its end is in comprehending the reality of the interior self. It is in the domain of the subjective that the meaning of life is to be found; only serfs dedicate themselves to service of the objective world, just as serfs served the nobility in the days of feudalism. Fulfillment, however, never can be found in the object world because that world can never belong to the individual; it is always outside and removed from him, a distant presence that may infatuate but never fulfills. The awareness of the reality of the interior self leads one out of the innumerable forms of indentured bondage that characterize the relationships of the individual with the object world.

Nietzsche's *amor fati*—to love one's fate—is the one legitimate attitude with respect to one's attitude toward the crumbling object world. It is the proper remedy for the resentment, envy, greed, and all the other petty feelings that can devour the interior self. The severest material setbacks are gifts for the mature individual to assist him in achieving his heart's desire—the deepening of his interior self, i.e., his soul. Beyond that, one can do no more as the limits of a human being are fixed by time and space. In the end, the shining image of the artistic Apollo overshadows that of the transported Dionysus.

SECOND PART

THE ART OF PHILOSOPHY

C URRENT PREFACE

This new version of the concept that philosophy is really an art form has been prepared some thirty-odd years after it was first set forth. Naturally, I cannot regain the youthful exuberance of those years when I had first accepted my vocation as an independent philosopher. I say youthful although I was not a youth chronologically, but youthful in terms of my commitment to philosophy. Some might replace the term 'exuberance' with 'hubris' but I will not pursue this issue. I prefer the positive term to a pejorative one. Below I have reprinted my first description of this part (with minor changes) in the first version of Philosophical Artwork published in 1983. I doubt that I can do better today in setting forth my fundamental view of philosophy, which has not substantially changed since that time:

> Philosophy is the expression of feelings of an individual generated in response to experiences. It differs from other art forms in that this expression is through concepts instead of through visual or auditory modes of representation. The scholarly values adopted by the academic professions have been the coffin of philosophy as an art form.
>
> The inestimable benefit to contemporary individuals in studying the philosophy of classical Greece arises

113

from the latter's devotion to a value that is only tentatively beginning to reemerge in modern culture: the concept of the individual, instead of society, as the centerpiece of human existence (latterly known as 'existentialism').

The whole purpose of culture is to crystallize an active consciousness of the realities of one's existence. It is the one thing needful for fulfillment of the human condition. Without an active consciousness, individuals are inevitably the victims of environments inhospitable to human development. Every free human being intuits the purpose of his life to be the deepening of his consciousness.

The distinctive trait of a philosopher is not merely the capacity to elaborate new concepts or the talent to put them into literary or verbal expression; rather it is the determination to vacate old values from the mind in order that he be free to create new ones.

The absence of philosophy in one's life leaves the interior self defenseless against the onslaught of exterior forces. The art of philosophy is the process by which concepts are developed and expressed in response to strife at all levels of existence; it is the only means one has to protect himself against the bourgeois and religious forces hostile to the individual. It is impossible to develop the self in all its dimensions of consciousness and expressiveness without engaging in philosophical activity.

The chapter entitled 'The Fate of the Soul' provides new thoughts on this subject.

ORIGINAL PREFACE

Since I regard philosophical writings as a category of artistic expression, none of the apparatus of the scholar is to be found in this work. The individual who wishes to write philosophy is naïve if he does not realize that his personality is molded by the society into which he was fated to be born. The clarification of this influence is one of the principal tasks of the philosopher. It is certainly futile to delegate it to the armies of scholarly specialists who abound everywhere in the factually minded, entertainment-oriented commercial activities that pass for culture in twentieth century western society.

This work deals with western philosophical culture, especially the ancient Greek heritage upon which western culture still precariously stands. I present my experience of this culture and my perception of its relationship to the one reality always needful of attention, the interior state of mind of individuals.

All translations are my responsibility unless stated otherwise.

THE ART OF PHILOSOPHY

There is a special problem connected with philosophy that does not exist in other artistic or literary forms of expression. It relates to the fact that unclear distinctions exist between philosophy as a mode of personal expression (which is its true identity), the history of philosophy as a branch of history, and philosophy as an analytic science dealing with language and cognition. No other genre of human expression has to contend with such confusion; for example, it is unthinkable that a literate person could confuse a poem with a tract on analysis of poetical metrics or that there could be any difficulty in distinguishing a novel from a critique of the novel. It is even more patently absurd to imagine that music could be confused with musical exercises for beginners or that the newspaper column of an art critic might be mistaken for the painting he has subjected to his critical evaluation.

Yet this is the predicament of philosophy; little distinction is made between its historians or critics and the form of expression itself. It is noteworthy that the latter is looked upon with suspicion when it exists independently of the products of the icons of philosophy enshrined for scholarly worship. For centuries in the Christian world, philosophy was only to be found within the confines of religious dogmatics according to prescribed limitations. Latterly, it has been viewed as a scientifically minded analysis of knowledge. The failure of European societies to recognize philosophy as an independent art form is responsible for its virtual demise in western culture. For these reasons, I wish to be explicit about the conception of philosophy that has given rise to this writing. I regard philosophy to be the expression of feelings of the individual generated in response to the experiences of existence. It differs from other art forms in that the expression is through concepts instead of through visual, plastic, musical, or poetic representations. Philosophical concepts express the interior state of the individual who experiences existence in a manner unique to himself, yet also in a manner shared by others. Personal expression is, of course, the essence of artwork but is often overlooked with respect to philosophical writings. The only matters of importance in philosophy so defined are the human feelings transmuted into concepts through a mystical process vaguely designated as art.

~ ~ ~

The identification of philosophy as a feeling-based art form is amply justified in its history, but is also evident in its etymology. It is said that Pythagoras first used the term φιλοσοφος, 'lover of wisdom', to refer to himself as one who was possessed by the passion for wisdom. The earliest use of the Greek word in literature that has survived the ages was by Heraclitus, the greatest of the expressive thinkers in Ionian Greek society. Later, Plato was clear both in the Socratic dialogues and in his own metaphorical style of expression that philosophy was an art, a means of expression of feelings in a rational manner. The Socratic questions having to do with feelings of virtue, justice, happiness, and love that develop in the minds of individuals are the very stuff of art; without these feelings, the rationality is meaningless and was illustrated in antique times by the image of the soulless sophist.

The evolution of Aristotelian natural philosophy or 'science' as it came to be known postdates the emergence of philosophy as an expressive art form and is distinct from it; in the past, all philosophers were viewed as followers of Plato or Aristotle. It would be more accurate to say all philosophers were either Heracliteans or Aristotelians since Plato may be regarded as being ambivalent toward philosophy as an art form, as will be discussed in 'A Downward Turn.' Natural philosophy, however, is today an archaic expression; it is much clearer to reserve the term 'science' for what used to be called natural philosophy and 'scientists' for those who devote themselves to the analysis of phenomena.

~ ~ ~

The self-image of the artist is a great boon to the philosopher, relieving him of the burden of the Aristotelian style of explication that is embodied in modern scholarship but that is the death of individual expression. The scholarly apparatus can only be the coffin of art. First and foremost, it is the task of the artist to express his own feelings; later he may consider how this expression can be made most coherent to his auditors. The artist does not have to instruct, amuse, or overawe his audience; it is only necessary that something of himself appear in his artwork. This is a more formidable task than that of the scholar, but it is one more in accord with the desires of human beings for self-expression.

When surveying the literary hodgepodge that currently goes under the name of philosophy, it is instructive to bring to mind the fearless judgment of the first Greek historiographer, Hecateus of Miletus, who began his pioneer work (unfortunately lost to history) with the following words: "What I write here is the account that seems true to me. For the stories of the Greeks, as they appear to me, are numerous and foolish." This thought may as well be applied to post classic western philosophy; this is not a manifestation of hubris, but a necessary response when dealing with the realities of a deteriorated form of human expression.

With artwork of any type, genuine personal expression should be the expectation of the viewer, as well as a requirement for the creator. In the processes of the give and take of personal expression, both must rely on the idealistic Heraclitean thought that has always motivated creation of culture; ξυνον εστι το φρονεειν, 'insight is common to all'. This is the concept that energized those remarkable individuals who created philosophy in the ancient Greek world; it is this concept that should be the task of a new philosophy to return to western culture.

ANCIENT GREEK CONSCIOUSNESS

Ever since the rediscovery of ancient Athenian drama, modern culture enthusiasts have been fascinated by the figure of Sophocles' Oedipus, the self-made fictional ruler of Thebes. King Oedipus, as Sophocles depicted him, had been blessed by everything that good fortune can provide to rulers—a stable government, a devoted family, and the affection of his subjects. Yet at the opening of the play, Oedipus' tranquility is threatened by inexplicable calamities and plagues that have suddenly descended upon his city. An oracle has rendered the judgment that the root of the troubles is the defilement of Thebes by its failure to punish the murder of Laius, Oedipus' predecessor as king. Oedipus is begged by the city elders to solve the crime. As his investigation proceeds, a fearful concatenation of circumstances emerges leading Oedipus to suspect that he himself might be the murderer of Laius. By a bizarre twist of fate, the latter seems also to have been the unknown natural father of Oedipus. Worst of all, since Oedipus has married Laius' widow Jocasta, he may have fathered children by his own mother.

His wife beseeches Oedipus not to proceed with the unearthing of the past for the sake of their children and their own happiness. But Oedipus will not desist from pursuit of the truth. When it is established beyond doubt that he has killed his own father and married his own mother, Jocasta hangs herself and King Oedipus, in a frenzy of self-hatred, uses her brooch to tear out his eyes. The elders of Thebes find him blinded, bleeding, and in a state of unrelenting self-condemnation.

It is ironic that the persona of Oedipus has come to be associated in western culture with incestuous feelings toward one's own mother, a symbol created by Freud to dramatize the onset of pre-pubertal eroticism. Sophocles undoubtedly would have been astounded and mortified by this trivialization of his dramatic work. The Oedipus story expressed a belief that had taken root among the Greeks—namely, that external success in life is ultimately threatened by certain demands of human character. Yet beyond the defects of his overbearing, imperious personality, the character of Oedipus required that he not shut his eyes to the truth and he sought it out at all costs—even when it threatened to be so damaging to his life. He never attempted to evade or conceal any aspect of the truth. Oedipus' desire to know reality was greater than his desire to preserve his own happiness or the happiness of his family.

The tragic events of Oedipus the King, the central feature of Sophocles' Oedipus trilogy, are balanced by the Promethean determination of Oedipus to face the realities of his life. The truth plunged him into suffering almost beyond human endurance, but ultimately Oedipus rose to the pinnacle of consciousness of human existence. In this way, Sophocles justified his suffering.

~ ~ ~

Contemporary western societies are presently in the predicaments of ancient Thebes; everywhere there are hints—and sometimes much more than hints—that there is some terrible defilement, which will destroy them. However, unlike Oedipus, the mentality of bourgeois leaders is not to want to learn the truth, but to lurch about trying to mitigate the volcanic rumblings through irrelevant economic measures or absurd militaristic posturing. Sophocles did not have Oedipus concern himself with crop failures, diseased livestock, febrile illnesses, and the like that beset Thebes, he went to the heart of the problem as he apprehended it; its citizens were under the influence of an evil influence that must be identified. When this influence turned out to be himself, he did not shrink from facing its reality.

There is no Sophoclean Oedipus to embody the defect of contemporary society. Of course, there never was even in ancient Greek societies; their tragedians spoke in mythic language their audiences understood. The Oedipus trilogy symbolizes the Delphic doctrine that every individual has to know and purify himself, whatever the cost. Purifying oneself is a task Greeks knew could not be delegated to outside agencies or be accomplished by altering outside circumstances.

~ ~ ~

Friedrich Nietzsche relates that the Romans referred to the intense preoccupation of Greeks (ancient) with their spiritual condition as nugari—trifles or nonsense. The Roman civilization had developed along entirely different lines than the Greek. The disciplined Roman was an individual oriented to exterior realities, principally concerning himself with his societal status, the well being of his familias, and the success of his patria. The mental gyrations of a Socrates or the psychological profundities of a Sophocles served as recreational activity, suitable as amusement after the day's labors were completed—although it was more likely he would prefer the relaxation of hot baths or the stimulating events in the Circuses. This attitude was not unknown in ancient Greece; Callicles in Plato's dialogue Gorgias mocked Socrates by referring to philosophy as an activity suitable for youths exercising their minds, but not for adults involved in the serious business of life. In antique Greece, however, the Calliclean viewpoint did not completely prevail, and Greek philosophic thought oriented toward interior development for its own sake. The so-called serious business of life was left to hoi polloi.

The concrete culture of ancient Rome is the prototype of western civilization. Inhabitants of Europe or English-speaking North America put back by some time machine into imperial Rome could easily adjust to language, habits, and local circumstances. However, if they were to move further back into a culturally vibrant Greek city of the fifth or fourth century B.C., their psychic bearings would be greatly disjointed. The mentality of the Greek of the classic period is foreign to the modern mind. Shakespeare wrote marvelous plays set in ancient Rome: his characters, it has been stated, were Englishmen with togas draped over their bodies. But his plays set in Greece carry no conviction and were relative failures. One senses that the flesh and blood Shakespeare did not intuit the Greek mentality.

~ ~ ~

The Greek attitude that was far removed from its Roman counterpart and is now light years in distance from the modern mind may be regarded as a commitment to the interior self, the soul, the psyche, or whatever expression one prefers in referring to the striving for individuality that characterized the Greeks at the height of their culture. Freedom was of the essence in accomplishing this goal, even if it led to conflicts among themselves. This commitment was the faith by which high-minded Greeks lived. Their society knew its bourgeois types and power brokers, but these were secondary figures; for a long time in the ancient Greek world, an orientation toward individual development and expression was the dominant feature of Greek society. It was what distinguished them in their own minds from barbarians and slaves. It came ahead of bourgeois comfort and security.

There was nothing godlike about the ancient Greeks—they possessed the full complement of human defects—but their example is vital for contemporary western culture. Their thinkers at their best had acquired what we lack—an absolute commitment to their own personal selfhood and to the consciousness of the reality around it; that consciousness stated in the epigraph of this work to be the most amazing fact of human life. The distinguished British neurologist F. M. R. Walshe once defined consciousness as "the condition of knowing," which is the heart of the matter whether one be a writer, philosopher, or neurologist. An unconscious person is not really alive in the human sense; he only possesses their biological attributes. Human beings who aspire toward self-development yearn for consciousness of reality to emerge from their own void. The remarkable intuition of Hamlin Garland cited in the epigraphs is evidence of the untapped depths that existed in the literature of the American frontier.

~ ~ ~

It is virtually impossible for denizens of the twentieth century to overvalue Greek culture when one realizes that culture is concerned with the emergence of consciousness of reality. This awareness does not grow out of antiquarian scholarship but out of the passion to know and express felt reality. However, access to much of Greek culture is difficult for general readers; the Greek literary sources are in a position analogous to that of the Bible prior to its translation into modern languages. In fact, Latin was far more widely known during the medieval period than are the classic languages now. Much of the remains of ancient Greek literature is buried in libraries only available to professional scholars. Of greater import, perhaps, is the fact that while the Bible is a sacred literary source, Greek literature is seen as having little more contemporary significance than crates of artifacts from an archeological dig.

~ ~ ~

Since the concept of art still has credit in society, it is worthwhile to consider a number of facts with respect to Greek culture. The ancient Greeks not only developed but also excelled in most of the art forms currently extant. These include the major forms of literary art—poetry, drama, and philosophy. They developed historia as a form of literature that, like philosophy, has also retrogressed artistically in the hands of their successors. The novel is the sole major literary genre that was not a Greek invention; the current efflorescence of novels makes one wonder if contemporary culture might be better off if writers confined themselves to art forms originated by the ancient Greeks.

A unique feature of antique Greek culture is that it was fertilized by philosophy at every level. The Greek dramatists, poets, and even sculptors were usually familiar with the writings of philosophers. Aeschylus, the founder of Attic drama, was deeply influenced by the ideas of Ionian philosophy, which often appear in his dramas. The relationship of Euripides to Socrates is well known to antiquarians. Sophocles was immersed in the intellectual life of Athens throughout his long literary career; he must have had contacts with Anaxagoras and Socrates, as well as with the numerous travelling philosophers who passed through Athens.

Only a small fraction of the products of the classical Greek dramatists have been preserved; yet these are universally regarded as the highest specimens of dramatic art. The power of their work derives from their reliance upon concepts evolved by Greek philosophers. These include awareness of the unseen depths of the human mind, recognition of the tensions underlying the surface stability of their characters, and the sense of evolution of wisdom out of strife. Similarly, the plastic artists of the Greek world obtained their inspirations from a concept of the propriety of a measured nature of all things. Out of this concept came the exceptional sense of form of the Greek architects and sculptors.

~ ~ ~

It is noteworthy that the artistic accomplishments of the Greeks were not made in large nations of the sort that maintain superiority in the modern world, but in the sparsely populated Greek polis of the eastern Mediterranean region. It has been estimated that, at the height of Athenian dominance, Athens and its surrounding territories contained a free adult population of less than 100,000 people. Subsequently, this number was diminished by plague and war; however, Athenian creativity in the arts continued unabated. Other Greek city-states were much smaller; the average polis generally contained a few thousand adult individuals. Yet within these towns that today would be considered mere villages, individuals often appeared who were destined to achieve artistic or literary stature. In spite of populations that were minute by contemporary standards, no other peoples have rivaled the ancient Greeks in terms of original accomplishments in the arts.

The inestimable benefit to individuals of the twentieth century studying the lives and thoughts of the ancient Greek philosophers arises from the latter's devotion to a value that hardly exists in modern culture—the concept of the individual human being as the centerpiece of existence. The antique historian Diogenes Laertius (hereafter referred to as D. L.), in spite of his own literary limitations (excessively stressed by modern scholars), is the most reliable guide to the mentality of the Greek philosophers. This is because he is closer to the antique philosophic mindsets than are contemporary academics caring more for the cult of scholarship than for the spirit of the individuals who give meaning to culture. If one wants to learn from Greek philosophy, he must immerse himself in its sources to the greatest extent possible, a task that has become easier because of the availability of translations (the scholar's greatest contribution to culture). If one goes beyond translations, he will find it an uplifting experience to develop familiarity with the ancient Greek language, which is unique in its expressiveness and depth of meanings.

~ ~ ~

It is incumbent upon we moderns who have a sense of responsibility for our own lives to become aware of the way of life that produced so many remarkable individuals among the ancient Greeks. There are many features of their lifestyle that can be clearly identified. They deserve wider recognition, not by academics engaged in scholarly grave digging, but by living human beings who desire direction in the creation of their lives.

Outdoor living—the Greeks spent most of their waking hours out of doors. Their homes were modest and suited for little more than sleeping, food preparation, and storage of possessions. It is of interest to remember the opinion of Henry David Thoreau who felt that houses were not desirable places for humans and that his own personality could only expand to its full dimensions surrounded by nature instead of walls.

Leisure—Leisure time was felt to be the birthright of every Hellene. The life of the interior self whose highest expression was Greek philosophy came to be the summum bonum of Greek society. They were scornful of a work ethic that they believed was only suited for barbarians (non-Hellenes). They achieved their leisure, however, through minimizing material requirements and lived in a remarkably simple manner, considering their intellectual accomplishments. The creative artist was the supreme figure in Greek society as witnessed by their phenomenal theater attendance; up to 17,000 Greeks were said to be spectators at Athenian dramatic festivals in which the mentally demanding plays of the great playwrights were performed.

Versatility—the Greeks did not believe in exclusive specialization, thinking such a way of life was the fate of slaves. (Although their slaves were usually better off than those in later Moslem or Christian societies, the Greeks did not attempt to rationalize their plight.) At the height of classic Greek civilization, most male Greeks engaged in civic functions, food production, legal activities, and military service. Unlike the Romans and except for dramatic festivals, they preferred participation or creative activity to spectatorship.

Autonomous culture—Greeks generally were only interested in their own culture and language. They did not learn foreign languages. During the classic period of Greek culture, they exhibited relatively little antiquarian curiosity prior to Homer, although they were aware of the existence of other cultures (Egypt, Phoenicia, Persia). During the heyday of their classic theater productions, audiences always listened to newly written plays. It was unheard of to repeat a play until well into the fourth century B.C. when the writing of drama had already gone into decline.

Verbal Expression—It is clear from the Greek literature that the Greeks were tireless speakers and listeners, often at the most complex level of discourse. The dinner conversations recorded by Plato and Xenophon are inconceivable in modern society. In time, written discourse came to be important but was always less significant than oral interchange among them. Aristotle's definition of man as a political animal does not have the usual meaning of its translation into English; rather it refers to the human intercourse occurring within the polis. Misanthropy was a very rare deviation.

Importance of Eros—The Greeks were open in their bisexual proclivity. Youth love held a higher status than heterosexual love for cultured adult males. The life of Socrates as depicted by Plato appears to have been an almost continuous exercise in cruising for beautiful youths who appealed to him intellectually as well (apparent abstention from physical contact in his later years does not alter the erotic backdrop of many Socratic dialogues). The Greek pattern of sexual behavior was highlighted by the handsome flamboyant Alcibiades of whom it was said as a youth he seduced husbands and as a man seduced wives.

Physical Fitness—The Greeks were oriented toward physical fitness out of a sense of the dependence of the mind upon a healthy body (they labeled the Indian yogis as 'gymnosophists'). Gymnastics was usually a daily activity for Greeks not disabled by disease. The longevity of many famous Greeks is remarkable; many lived well into their eighties or nineties without evidence of mental decline. One of the principal causes of their military superiority over the Persians was the poor physical condition of the Persian soldiery.

Absence of Priests—The Greeks had rid themselves of a priestly class before the flowering of their culture. They dealt with questions of metaphysics directly and assumed responsibility for any role of religious issues in their lives. Oracles and seers were available to a Greek according to his judgment of his need for them; many of these exhibited a high degree of philosophical wisdom. It was only required by Greek society that its members maintain a certain level of respect for traditional beliefs in the Olympian hierarchy of gods. The real reason for the execution of Socrates is unclear but was certainly not for impiety, as Plato clearly brought out in the account of his trial.

Little Interest in an Afterlife—By and large, the Greeks did not concern themselves with life after death, as did many of the societies that surrounded them. Their interest was focused on their natural life span, which seemed sufficient to them. They were concerned with the immortality of their memories, not their souls. The concept of Hades was a mythic one that had little impact on Greek consciousness; the famous Socratic discussion of an after life in the Phaedo is exceptional and probably not reflective of the historical Socrates. It is worth observing, however, that the absence of a belief in an after life did not deter Greek philosophers from the practice of voluntary termination of their lives when disease or aging had interfered significantly with its quality.

Democracy—The Greeks opposed dominant figures in government as much as they could. They felt it ignoble and barbarian for power to be concentrated in the hands of a tyrant or an oligarchy. Those who appeared to be accumulating too much power or influence could be expelled from the polis by the uniquely Greek device of ostracism in which an individual by popular vote had to leave the city for a specified, often prolonged, period of time. This became the fate of many of the most prominent Greek politicians and generals. Although at times he had no choice, the Greek believed himself to be demeaned if he did not share in some way in political power. The phenomenon of emperor rule was hated and the principal reason for the desperate opposition to Macedonian hegemony in the fourth century B.C.

Cuisine—There was little fish or meat in the ordinary diet, except on special occasions. Grains, vegetables, olives, and cheeses, along with olive oil and honey, formed the basis of their cuisine. They were vegetarians partially out of necessity but also out of a sense of the value of dietary restraint. A Sybarite entertained at Sparta is said to have exclaimed, "Now I understand why Spartans do not fear death!" But it was not greatly different in Athens or other Greek polis. They usually drank watered wine; reference to the drinking of undiluted wine indicated abandoned revelry. They knew nothing of hard liquor nor did they care for drugs that acted upon the psyche. Their own persona was sufficient for them.

~ ~ ~

The critical Greek accomplishment was to create a model of the unified self with which to confront the external world. They did not admire role players; their thoughts and lives reflected the unity of their personalities. There is an honesty and forthrightness in antique Greek expression that is disconcerting to the modern mind. Greek classic culture was an expression of Greek life in its totality; it was not a separate compartment of 'culture'. This is why Greek philosophers were sometimes brought to trial, exiled, or even put to death. Who can imagine contemporary western leaders having the slightest concern with the teaching of philosophers? However, it was different among the Greeks who did not believe in expending their energies on matters that did not directly involve their existence as human beings. The heart of the matter was discerned by the German classical scholar Bruno Snell who wrote, "A scientist or scholar acquires his knowledge through objective evaluation, whereas the discoveries of the Greeks, which is the topic under consideration, penetrate into the core of a human being and are revealed as formative experiences." In his book *Die Entdeckung des Geistes* (The Discovery of the Mind, 1948), Snell himself exemplifies his observation by engaging in the usual dispassionate scholarly analyses. However, his response to Greek culture is far superior to the bloodless format of most academicians, compared to whom Snell is a paragon of vital expression. This is the heritage of Nietzsche who has had his effect, albeit grudgingly, on German scholarship.

H IGHPOINT OF GREEK PHILOSOPHY

It is instructive to acquaint oneself with the development of Greek philosophy since much can be learned from it not only about philosophy itself but also about the tendency toward ossification of culture. The most important step is to discard the lumping of the 'pre-Socratic' philosophers into a group of somewhat primitive thinkers preceding Socrates, the watershed personality of philosophy, who supposedly revolutionized Greek thought. This concept is an invention of nineteenth century classical scholars who, like their Christian predecessors, were bemused by the literary skills of Plato. But this concept is a distortion of the history of philosophy. When one is freed from it, he will discover that not only the origins of but the highpoints of western philosophy are to be found in the Ionian and Italian Greek worlds of the 6th and 5th century B.C.

It is certain that most of the writings of the early Greek philosophers have been lost through the vicissitudes of history and the barbarous attitude of early Christian society toward 'pagan' literature. What the Christians overlooked in Ionian Greek society was often destroyed by fundamentalist Muslim successors. Yet the remnants that can be pieced together from the few surviving manuscripts, anthologies, and quotations reveal these philosophers to have been individuals of global scope and power. Appreciation of them has suffered through the preoccupation of classical scholars with the 'cosmologies' of the pre-Socratics, a topic of limited interest. It is in the image of individuals whose *consciousness of human existence* exceeded that of any subsequent writers of philosophy that their significance is to be found.

The boldness of spirit of the Ionians, upon which their philosophy depended, was phenomenal. The Ionian city-states on the west coast of Asia Minor and their colonies on the Mediterranean littoral were exposed to the influences of other civilizations in a way that the cities of Greece proper were not. Theodor Gomperz, an outstanding scholar of ancient Greek societies (a notable exception to criticisms of scholars leveled above), stated that Ionia was the cradle of the intellectual civilization of Greece (*Griechische Denker*). These pioneer thinkers, Gomperz wrote, addressed themselves to the eternal questions of mankind—the meaning of self, God, and the world. Their answers replaced and reshaped the former acceptance of religious beliefs. They relinquished all the roles and objects upon which modern humans depend to preserve their psychic equilibrium. Appearing out of the darkness of primitive thinking, they relied on just one thing to justify their activities—their faith in their own minds and souls. The early Greek thinkers on the periphery of *Magna Graecia* represent the human condition at its highest level of spiritual existence.

Lists of these philosophers can be found in any standard text of ancient Greek philosophy. Notable examples are Thales, Anaximander, Parmenides, Anaxagoras, Pythagoras, Xenophanes, and especially Heraclitus who is discussed at length below. By and large, only pathetic fragments of their works are available to modern readers. Heraclitus may be regarded as the dominant figure today of early Greek philosophy. Others, for example Parmenides, may have had disciples and greater influence during their lifetime, but in the opinion of this writer the judgment of posterity gives the palm to Heraclitus.

~ ~ ~

The clearing away of ossified mental habits is the necessary prerequisite for progress of consciousness; in this, Heraclitus of Ephesus was superior to all his Ionian peers. He proclaimed, "Homer deserves to be thrown out of the contests and thrashed and Archilochus as well." This is at a time when the Homeric sagas were the equivalent of the Bible for Greece. "Much learning does not teach judgment; otherwise it would have taught Hesiod and Pythagoras, and also Xenophanes and Hecataeus." These iconoclastic sentiments were deliberately exaggerated; they had the effect of reducing to human size figures that had been enshrined for public worship. Even the radical Cynics of a later age did not dare to speak so of the national idols. Heraclitus valued Homer, calling him the wisest of Hellenes in another context, but he realized that the concrete nature of Homeric thought stood in the way of deepening the mind, which for Heraclitus, was the supreme purpose of human individuality. "One should not behave as a child with parents" or "Men's opinions are toys for children" were statements of his long before Socrates was said to have cautiously intimated the same ideas. But Heraclitus understood the importance of boldly clearing space for new concepts and did not shrink from attacking the mentality of his day even though this might be a dangerous procedure.

~ ~ ~

This philosopher grasped the reality that energy in constant flux underlies the apparently stable phenomena of the cosmos and provides the unifying physical principle of existence. (Einstein believed in this principle but never could find the mathematical formula to express it.) Heraclitus expressed his insight with the famous metaphor of "an everlasting fire, flaming up in measure and quenched in measure." His metaphorical use of the symbol of fire resembles that of Jacob Boehme, without the latter's obscuring theological superstructure. The conceptions of modern physics are in accord with the Heraclitean worldview.

The greatest achievement of Heraclitus was his discovery of the depth and breadth of the human soul. "I searched after myself," he said in one of his masterpieces of compressed statement, and in finding himself, he learned that he "could not find the limits of his soul, so deep is its *Logos*." The inability to conceptualize the reality of the human soul is the fundamental limitation of the bourgeois mind. This discovery is never made by the analytical intellectualism of scientists or literati who brand as mysticism what they have been incapable of experiencing themselves.

By placing an elevated consciousness, which he called wisdom or "that which is wise" on the highest plane of existence, Heraclitus established the importance of personal autonomy of humans within the world order. He would have nothing to do with religious fictions. Unlike his Milesian predecessors, he did not dabble in engineering, astronomy, or agriculture. Perhaps he felt, as did Epicurus two centuries later, that the practical arts were already sufficiently well established. The luxurious life style of Ephesians needed no embellishment in his view. "The best choose one thing before all else," he said two and a half millennia before Kierkegaard. His ideal was wisdom; how to understand the plan by which all things are piloted through all." The Heraclitean image survives in the initials of the American College Honor Society, Phi Beta Kappa (ΦΒΚ), which stands for Φιλοσοφια Βιου Κυβερνητης; 'philosophy, pilot of life'. The term is a fossil relic; few members of the Phi Beta Kappa society, not to speak of others not so honored, know the meaning of the letters or even of Heraclitus. Use of the Greek expression is akin to display of American Indian paraphernalia in western towns for obtaining tourist dollars.

~ ~ ~

It was not possible for Heraclitus to have come to his conclusions without having had much experience of life. He was of royal descent from kings and priests of Ephesus. As a member of the aristocracy of the city, a place engaging in much trade with Persia, Lydia, Phoenicia, and Egypt, he must have experienced the opulent and sensual aspects of life in an Ionian city. He lived through the assertion of Persian supremacy over the Ionian city-states and the destruction of Miletus, which had been the cradle of Ionian philosophy. He probably survived to learn of the defeat of Persia by Athens and her allies. Heraclitus did not live in an ivory tower until he decided he had had enough of the society he lived in and retreated to an isolated cabin away from the luxurious life of Ephesus. He expressed his low opinion of his fellow citizens in his aphorisms. Thus he came to be regarded as a 'misanthrope', a hater of mankind.

The Greeks took for granted the experiential life. They could not take seriously a culture in which the individuals did not experience life fully. They accepted as inevitable the association of pain with experience; παθει μαθος, 'suffering yields knowledge' was a traditional Greek saying. To this doctrine, Heraclitus added the injunction that it was not enough to experience things; one must have a soul that can grasp the import of the experience. The 'barbarian soul', which to Heraclitus meant the soul with a limited consciousness, does not comprehend what it has experienced.

~ ~ ~

"What is wise is set apart from all things" was one conclusion of Heraclitus. This is the attitude of a sage, not of a café conversationalist or of the academic who lives in a network of supportive professional groups. Although there is little factual information about his life, anecdotes that have come down from antique sources indicate his strong sense of *autonomy* that did not require social approval. Unlike Socrates who often appears as a type of Uriah Heep with his false mocking obsequiousness toward important personages, Heraclitus did not stoop to banter with *hoi polloi*. He is said to have abdicated his rights of kingship of Ephesus and refused to participate in politics at all, claiming he preferred games with children, a most un-Hellenic attitude. But Heraclitus declined to play the game of fame with the notables of his day and even supposedly wrote a letter refusing an invitation to the Persian court, politely expressing his distaste of court luxuries. The authenticity of the letter is doubtful, but it reflects the image of Heraclitus in antiquity. D.L. reports that he experimented, Thoreau style, in living on grasses and herbs in the mountains—who can imagine Plato living an ascetic life in the wilderness? There are several unpleasant stories of his death that are probably fictional; antique literati do not differ from the modern versions in spreading nasty gossip.

~ ~ ~

The unusual personality of Heraclitus was as evident to the ancient world as it is to ours. D.L. states that he was exceptional from boyhood and "lofty-minded" beyond other men. There is no evidence that he was inclined toward forming a school or cult, a tendency that was strong in Greek philosophy. Heraclitus did not engage in florid poetics in the Homeric manner; he evoked the image of the legendary prophetic Sybil "uttering things unadorned, unperfumed and mirthless" in justification of his own condensed style. However, he was uncompromising in the statement of his opinions as when he suggests that "the Ephesians should hang themselves, all of them to the last man, and leave their city to their children because they drove out Hermodorus, the best among them." Nothing further is known about this incident but it is surprising that Heraclitus apparently lived out his life without being banished himself.

For this philosopher, one thing was needful, to be conscious of the reality of the divine *Logos* ruling the universe. One must admit his concept of the *Logos* is difficult to grasp but it was sufficiently known in antiquity to appear in the first lines of the prologue of the Gospel according to John (in the beginning was the Word [λογος, *Logos*], and the Word was with God, and the Word was God). Unlike philosophers of later times, Heraclitus did not compartmentalize his personality; since he felt Ephesian political life was childish ("toys for children"), he would not participate in it. He must have seemed to be a bizarre personality to his contemporaries, but the politicians of Ephesus have disappeared from history, while Heraclitus became a vital force in western culture.

~ ~ ~

According to the antique scholars, Heraclitus wrote one book, which he deposited in the famous temple of Artemis. It was probably more a journal than a book in the conventional sense but later commentators gave it a conventional book title *'On Nature'*. The book (or journal) was well known in antiquity; however, no copy of it has survived the vicissitudes of history. His influence in the intellectual Greco-Roman world was comparable to that of Plato; most of the significant literary figures of that era seem to have been aware of his writings. His influence was especially strong on the classic Athenian tragedians and in the Stoic school of philosophy. As mentioned above, an echo of his concept of the *Logos* can be heard in the prologue of the gospel of John.

Heraclitus was accorded a reputation for obscurity by those who were not responsive to his thoughts. Aristotle noted early in the history of Heraclitean commentary that he was not a follower of logical principles but expressed himself intuitively and metaphorically. Nevertheless, the intuitions that have given rise to his writings are usually quite clear to philosophically minded readers, even with only the fragmented remains of his original work.

~ ~ ~

The philosophers of Magna Graecia expressed their consciousness of the world by means of metaphorical cosmologies, but these were not meant to be taken in a concrete, scientific sense. The modern interest in controlling nature was of little interest to them. These philosophers especially differed from modern scientists in that they brought their values into the sweep of their ideas; they did not attempt to exclude subjective human beings from their cosmic perceptions. As sentient beings striving to *comprehend* existence, they developed a consciousness of nature at all its levels, not just a superficial catalogue of causes and effects utilized by the utilitarian sciences. Acquiring this consciousness was the purpose of human life as they conceived it. When Anaxagoras was asked the purpose for which he was born, he replied, "to view the sun and the moon and the heavens." He did not view them in order to obtain data for navigational purposes, but to heighten his consciousness of the cosmos. And the same was true for the other philosophers.

The earlier Ionians visualized a physical type of universe. Thales, the father figure of Ionian philosopher, spoke of water as the basic element. Later philosophers came to think of the cosmos as energy and some imagined that the human mind was the most concentrated form of that energy. Similarities can be seen with the Atman-Brahman concepts of the Hindu forest philosophers of the Upanishads. For Anaxagoras, νους or 'mind' was the central reality of being, whereas Heraclitus, who had reservations about the minds of his contemporaries, regarded 'fire' as representing the essential nature of cosmic energy. The details of these 'cosmologies' are not important today. Enlightened thinkers who have developed in an age of science may choose to elaborate different metaphors.

What is important is that the antique philosophers were Promethean thinkers urging the Greeks out of the morass of superstitions and material preoccupations that are the usual conditions of mankind. For them, human life was meant to comprehend the nature of reality, not to be dominated by it. The undermining of the promise of early philosophical culture by Christianity is the real tragedy of Greek civilization.

~ ~ ~

The value of ancient Greek society does not lie in the fact that philosophers appeared in their midst but that their society was *affected* by them and preserved their thoughts for posterity—albeit in a fragmentary manner. Societies can be judged by how they react to philosophers; our society historicizes them but is not affected by them. Heraclitus was recognized as an important spiritual force by ancient Greeks; today, he would have quickly faded into oblivion. His life, thoughts, and mode of expression would have no impact on contemporary society. It is likely he would have ended his days in psychotic withdrawal, as did Nietzsche. The glory of classical Greek culture was that it was influenced by such a personality as Heraclitus and brought him into its purview—even though he was disparaged by Plato and Aristotle. It is to the everlasting discredit of the Christianized Greco-Roman world that the one volume of Heraclitus' thoughts was not preserved. Perhaps it is not too much to hope that one day modern archeology will discover the full text of the work of a man who was "lofty-minded beyond other men." Meanwhile the remnants of his writings are sufficient to inform us that there was a time in western history when popular culture was not wholly dominated by the dismal arts of entertainment and scholarship.

~ ~ ~

The aspiration toward consciousness of reality by ancient Greek philosophers far outstripped those of our contemporary intellectuals. Nothing less would do for them than grasping the fundamental nature of existence and their relationship as thinkers to it. They were Faustian figures unburdened with the cultural legacies of Germany. Uniformly, they were disdainful of the bourgeois aspects of the society in which they lived (one wonders if they had any notion of what was to come in later centuries). By and large, Ionian society and its colonies tended to recognize the importance of their philosophers positively—not suspiciously as was the custom in Athens where several were brought to trial or compelled to leave. They did not have to train themselves to be stoical or ascetic; their consciousness of reality naturally provided them with a disdain for trivia and the ability to place the vicissitudes of life in a proper perspective.

More than in Athens or other Greek mainland cities, the Ionian world provided an environment in which individuals with a philosophic bent could grow to full mental stature. The philosophers of the Ionian world have disappeared, but their example remains, tempting those who are committed to interior development to try to learn the secret of their interior power. Certain liberating features of their lives can be discerned even at such a great interval of time; they did not harm their souls by role playing, they were not bound down by religious dogmas, they were not overwhelmed by cultural constraints. Above all, their lives were integrated rather than parceled out in a multiplicity of split personalities. One might also conjecture that they had a vision that there is more to human life than is revealed by bourgeois existence.

~ ~ ~

Western culture has taken the path of Aristotle who accused Heraclitus of not conforming to the categories of formal logic, a route he thought opened the door to the undisciplined superstitions of barbarian worlds. But the categories of Aristotle are also a superstition, one that is based on slavish conformity to analytically oriented thinking. The modern mind is chained to this heritage and to submission to the requirements of materialist thought. This way of thinking has become graven in stone, preserving society from the flowering of the individual. We moderns cannot live at the heights of the Ionian Greek philosophers because we are attuned, like it or not, to bourgeois utilitarian thinking instead of to the underlying metaphysical realities. Consequently, we are limited in the greatest of all gratifications, the development and expression of an individual consciousness.

DOWNWARD TURN

The thinkers of Magna Graecia made a ringing start in the development of a philosophical culture. However, it had hardly moved beyond its initial phases before it was overcome by the problems associated with great power politics in the Hellenic world. First, the Persian conquest of the Ionian heartland had a chilling effect on philosophy in what had been the epicenter of Greek philosophical creativity. Then, the endless internecine wars of the mainland Greek city-states were not conducive to the development of philosophy. Finally, the mythos of Greek military superiority that had been founded on Marathon and Salamis ended when militaristic Macedonia conquered all of mainland Greece in the fourth century B.C. Henceforth, the conquests of Alexander the Great became the symbol of Hellene achievement. Philosophy was pushed far into the background. It might have been better for western culture in the long run if Persia instead of Macedonia had maintained dominance over the Greek world; the Persians were better equipped by temperament to foster the spirit of Greek philosophy.

~ ~ ~

The western world today cannot be sure of the spirit of Socrates as a philosopher since he did not choose to write out his ideas. Because of this, Schopenhauer advised students of philosophy not to take the historical Socrates seriously as a philosopher—to no avail as it has turned out. His impact on western philosophy is entirely through his biographers and popularizers of which Plato is the chief representative. There is also the record of Socrates' conversations as reported by Xenophon, which are probably more historically accurate than the Platonic dialogues, but which may not capture his spirit. The fact must be faced that Socrates did not choose to express himself for posterity. He would have probably disappeared into oblivion had he not been given a martyr's death by an Athenian court and his memory immortalized by Plato. In any case, the surface personality of Socrates as handed down by his admirers does not reveal him to be a σoφoς, a wise man. He was, as he is said to have characterized himself, a gadfly or a midwife facilitating the questioning spirit of others. It is astonishing that such a person has been regarded as the cornerstone of ancient Greek philosophy.

~ ~ ~

The image of Socrates reveals the plight of the philosopher immersed in a bourgeois environment. The attitude of Socrates is usually mocking and invariably analytic, a style that often produces feelings of impatience in the reader. His frequent allusions to the "attractiveness" of the young Athenians who interest him bear the familiar hallmark of repressed sexuality. One cannot imagine Heraclitus or Anaxagoras preoccupied with young men (or women). It is not surprising that Socrates was a native Athenian, not an Ionian; his was a radically different type of personality.

Like Freud, Socrates did not appear to have an 'oceanic' sense and was not drawn to the larger questions of cosmic existence. In fact, he seemed totally insensitive to them as revealed by his famous complaint about the philosophy of Anaxagoras related by Plato in the *Phaedo.* Heraclitus was beyond him, he is said to have frankly admitted that only a 'Delian diver' could get to the bottom of the book by Heraclitus. Socrates was only concerned with individual psychological development within a society concerned with power politics. His preoccupation with personal psychological health is a trait well known to observers of the contemporary scene. He would have gotten on well with Freud and his followers. But he did not have the drive toward the deeper consciousness that is the identifying feature of the Ionian philosophers. Socrates was a common sense person, not a 'philosophic sense' one. His personality must have seemed strange, almost pathological, to philosophers who knew more profound forms of human feelings. Nietzsche's characterization of Socrates as a 'degenerate intellectual' may contain more than a germ of truth.

~ ~ ~

Socrates' appeal to the youth of Athens probably lay in his subtle defiance of the Athenian establishment. This was an understandable attitude but Socrates' failure to embrace cosmic questions limited his own philosophical development. The natural progression of Socratic thought led to the Cynic movement headed by Diogenes of Sinope, which was not interested in philosophy at all, except as a justification for discarding societal norms. Honest as Socrates was about his own worth, he may not have regarded himself as someone whose thoughts were worthy of literary expression. It was left to Plato and Xenophon to record the personality of Socrates and his ideas. However, the teachings of Zeno and other Stoics brought many of Socrates' thoughts to full flower beyond Cynic nihilism.

Socrates' decision to die rather than escape his jail was the sign of a person with a death wish—regardless of his sophistical arguments about duty to homeland. In fact, his yielding to the judgment of the Athenian court may be viewed as an undermining of philosophy. Xenophon stated that Socrates really welcomed death because of his age (70 years) and onset of infirmities; if so, Plato's account of his death is a misreading of the 'great man' unrivalled in the annals of literature. If Socrates had really wished to end his life, he could have done so openly—as did many other Greek philosophers who had felt the time had come to shed the mortal coil—rather than through a subterfuge that draped the mantle of a martyr over his memory. Perhaps his death should be regarded as the greatest piece of irony in the life of the great ironist of philosophy. But the Xenophonic age and infirmity explanation is not certain; possibly death became attractive to Socrates because of some discord within his nature that could no longer be kept in bounds. Now he enshrined in the Hall of Saints of the western academic world.

~ ~ ~

If it is true that the character of Greek philosophy changed after Socrates, it was a change toward security for self and away from cosmic consciousness. In the opinion of an original thinker like G. W. Patrick, the depth of philosophy declined (*Heraclitus of Ephesus*). The habit of the sophists in acquiring students for pay replaced acquiring committed disciples. Plato and Aristotle formed schools that institutionalized the style of sophistical teaching. Plato, who himself was a gifted litterateur, emphasized the importance of mathematics while Aristotle created the first research institute on modern models. Teaching was done didactically through lecturing just as it is today. The Academy and the Lyceum established the professionalization of philosophy. All this was very far from the aim of the first independent philosophers of Magna Graecia to discover the nature of the cosmos and find man's place in it.

Ultimately, philosophers of the schools tended to become skeptics and scholars. It was only amateurs of philosophy like Seneca and Marcus Aurelius who left writings that contain a semblance of philosophy as the individual's search for wisdom. Plato gives an involuntary intimation of this trend when, in the *Theatetus,* he has Socrates reminisce about Parmenides whom he had met in his early years with uncharacteristic respect, saying there was "a sort of depth within him that was altogether noble." This cosmic depth of the pre-Socratic philosophers disappeared in the antique world. The quality of mind developed by these remarkable individuals has not been seen again in western civilization. Their fragmented literary remains tower over modern culture just as the decaying monuments of Imperial Rome towered over the hovels of medieval peasants finding refuge within their ruins.

~ ~ ~

Nevertheless, if Socrates was a flawed personality, he deserves recognition for his defense of the ideals of philosophy against bourgeois influences. The same cannot be said of Plato who represents the triumph of literati in philosophy and who presents a duplicitous image of bourgeois values concealed behind a façade of philosophy. Plato, in fact, was the first Greek philosopher who strove to affect his public through literary style rather than philosophic wisdom. His contemporaries, according to D.L., virtually all disliked him. The available fragments of Diogenes of Sinope, who knew Plato in Athens, indicate that the perceptive Cynic regarded him as vain, verbose, and overly ambitious for fame.

The significant feature of Greek philosophers was its integration of thought and action. In Plato, however, the phenomenon of the literati appears, educated individuals who wrote one thing but lived differently. Consequently, one has virtually no sense of the personality of Plato in his writings. He published an enormous amount of prose, considering the primitive state of book manufacture in his day (unwieldy papyrus scrolls were still in use), yet he slyly asserted in one of his letters that his real teachings could only be obtained in his Academy— presumably for remuneration. Plato built his reputation by cleverly trading on the memory of Socrates and literary development of the Socratic persona. There is no question that Plato was a talented writer with a fertile mind capable of vividly expressing his ideas and portraying the personalities of those people whom he chose to give roles in his dialogues. He was the Mark Twain of antique Athens, except that the life at that city instead of on the Mississippi was his field of activity. Platonism represents the dominance of the philosophical literati in western culture and a movement away from the bold unity of self that had characterized earlier Greek philosophers.

~ ~ ~

One may suspect that Plato founded his Academy not only to further his philosophy, but also to prepare individuals for success in the life of the *polis*; such was its success that he was accused of running a school for tyrants. The Academy served as model for the rise of European universities and in it was evolved the elitist attitudes that have since characterized 'distinguished' university faculties. It is easy to imagine Plato as a distinguished professor at Harvard or Oxford (it is impossible to imagine Heraclitus or

Parmenides functioning in any manner whatever in academia). Plato's dream was in living out his concept of a philosopher-king; he journeyed three times to Sicily in fruitless attempts to accomplish that goal. There is nothing more revealing of Plato's personality than his repeated trips to a distant land for the sake of acquiring political influence. His basic weakness was that he could never get over his desire to become an important public figure within the state institutions of his times. Like Callicles, whom he portrayed with such insight in the dialogue *Gorgias*, the love of *demos* dwelled within his soul.

~ ~ ~

There is almost a pathetic note in Plato's negative attitude toward Heraclitus, especially at the end of the dialogue *Cratylus* in which he has Socrates (certainly not the historical Socrates) implore his listeners to explain what merit there could be in a philosophy in which all is in flux. The bourgeois mind is always frightened by instability and demands a stable environment. More significant, however, than Plato's difficulty with the Heraclitean cosmology, was that the bourgeois Plato who ran a school preparing students to be successful in public life, could not understand a person who was as disdainful of public opinion as was Heraclitus. Instinctively, Plato must have been aware of the contempt that his own personality would have elicited in Heraclitus. In a similar vein, Plato studiously avoided ever mentioning the philosopher Democritus whose fragments reveal a breadth of mind superior to that of Plato, but without his literary skills. One must wonder if, after all, Plato had been corrupted in some devious manner by Socrates.

~ ~ ~

If Plato might have been a Distinguished Professor in modern times, Aristotle, his onetime pupil, can be envisioned as the Director of a National Research Institute. Aristotle's critical views on Heraclitus have been previously mentioned. His scholar's mind was constitutionally at odds with the deeper insights of the Ionian philosophers. Aristotle was the quintessential one-dimensional scholar whose temperament was uniquely suited to the assembly and analysis of data. Contemporary philosophies adhering to offshoots of logical positivism or phenomenology are inheritors of the Aristotelian mentality. There was a distinctly absurd aspect in the efforts of Aristotle's less gifted successor Theophrastus to comprehend the cosmology of Heraclitus. Recent philosophy textbooks have usually followed Theophrastus' example with equally absurd results.

~ ~ ~

Philosophy is inherently a matter for individual consciousness. As sources of creative thought, the schools of philosophy at Athens never amounted to much beyond the original inspirations of their founders. A philosopher is only entitled to be an elitist as an independent individual; the moment he moves into the category of an institutional person, he becomes a figure that is blurred and ultimately ridiculous. 'Schools' quickly become institutionalized and thus act against the spirit of philosophy. It is astonishing to learn that the philosophical schoolmaster Epicurus required his students to memorize his writings. Inherent in all institutions is opposition to complete individual autonomy; at best, they are crutches to help an individual move toward intellectual autonomy, but they should be discarded as quickly as possible. However most institutions are not content to serve temporarily as crutches; the greatest spiritual institution of European culture, the Platonized Roman Catholic Church, has been the greatest enemy of individual autonomy throughout the history of European civilization.

NINETEENTH CENTURY REWAKENING

If culture in a society may be regarded as the drive toward a higher consciousness, then western culture has retrogressed since the days of the ancient Greek philosophers. It is not too much to say that in comparison with classical Greek culture, the two millennia of subsequent European history were a kind of Dark Ages that only began to clear in the nineteenth century. It is an erroneous notion to think that the Dark Ages in Europe were confined to the period between the collapse of the Western Roman Empire and the beginning of the Renaissance. This concept was based on considerations of social order and technological development, which should not be preeminent in human affairs. Nor does the emergence of scholarly studies mean the Dark Ages have become lighter. In terms of individual interior development, the Dark Ages for western society began with the replacement of Greek philosophy by Christian dogmas and proceeded, with only rare interruptions, to grow steadily darker during the dominance of institutional Christianity.

Western society has retrogressed during the Christian era because the prevailing religious mentality suppressed the development of self in its most important aspect, the consciousness of the relationship between the self and the cosmos. Every society has its share of 'spiritual' individuals but under the Christian tyrant over the spirit, such individuals were restricted in their metaphysical development. The springs of spiritual energy were closed off by the Christian dogma of Christ the necessary savior. Europeans were conditioned to believe that spirituality and Christian faith were identical in nature. The error of this concept is revealed in the huge difference that exists between the uninhibited consciousness of existence that was manifest in the Greek thinkers and the cramped 'spirituality' of Europeans in the Christian era.

~ ~ ~

Creative individuals who made their mark during the Dark Ages of Christianized Europe tended to be child-like individuals who had not reached full internal maturity. The Italian Renaissance was an age of youthful and talented artists who toyed with the dogmas of the Christian establishment much as children like to play with the weapons of their elders. It is evident however, for those with eyes to see, that the famed Renaissance art figures were restricted in their mental growth by the stultifying spiritual climate in which they lived. There is difficulty in bringing to mind genuinely autonomous personalities during the long period of Christian intellectual domination in Europe and the Americas. Creative personalities like Montaigne, Voltaire, and Goethe tended to retreat into sarcasm or skepticism. Christian Europe resembled the Islamic world of today—a society in which spiritual sterility is made inevitable by religious fanaticism.

~ ~ ~

It was not until the turn of the eighteenth century, after almost fifteen hundred years of Christian rule over the life of the mind, that the impact of religious domination began to dawn upon men of independent spirit. Thomas Paine, the painfully undervalued British-American writer, was the first to be explicit on this subject. His landmark work *Age of Reason* was written in a French prison during the Terror because the fanatical Jacobins did not trust his independent spirit. Because of his unyielding antireligious attitude, he has never been fully recognized by the literati who always make their accommodation with prevailing institutions. However, Paine is a landmark figure in the awakening of an intellectual conscience in the western world.

Philosophers who were quite open in their criticism of religious dogma were Arthur Schopenhauer and Ludwig Feuerbach, but both hesitated to fully confront the impact of Christianity upon European mental development. The most

Schopenhauer could bring himself to say was that religion was the metaphysics of the people. (Karl Marx went further in saying it was the opiate of the people, but Marx had abandoned the mantle of the philosopher in favor of the revolutionary.) The model for these philosophers was Immanuel Kant not Thomas Paine. Nevertheless, both Schopenhauer and Feuerbach brought new air into the intellectual climate of Europe.

~ ~ ~

In spite of their frequent quarrels with their countrymen, the ancient Greek philosophers never seriously questioned the worth of their Greek heritage and always regarded themselves as participants in Greek culture. Even the contentious Heraclitus talks of a 'barbarian psyche' (i.e., non-Greek) when he refers to those who can see and hear but do not comprehend. There is a feeling of belongingness and self worth that one feels has much to do with their accomplishments.

The panorama of the pioneer thinkers of the nineteenth century presents a very different spectacle. To a man, they seem to be desperate individuals trying to create intellectual autonomy in a society that was hostile to them. In their desire to avoid the disunity of self that characterized the European literati, they tended to separate themselves from intimate societal relationships. The later use of the term 'existential' merely refers to this sought after unity of self. Whereas friends and disciples mingled with the Greek philosophers, their nineteenth century counterparts were lonely recluses of the mind, tending to live in intellectual isolation. The nineteenth century independent philosopher outside of a university or a seminary evolved the radical concept of writing for posterity since he felt his contemporaries cared nothing for him or his work. Schopenhauer, Stirner, Feuerbach, Kierkegaard, Nietzsche—they all looked to the future and hoped for a posthumous life for their writings.

The psychological consequence of such a state of mind was unhealthy in the extreme; a human being cannot live an isolated mental life without harmful effects upon his personality. Schopenhauer kept a pistol under his pillow; Nietzsche exhibited increasingly evident psychotic traits; others manifested various forms of mental maladjustment. Their salvation, they felt, lay in their literary activity. Thus they tended, with a few exceptions, to pour forth great quantities of prose, so much so that it often detracts from their essential message. It would have been better if writers like Schopenhauer, Kierkegaard, and Nietzsche had not published so much; a smaller *oeuvre* would have facilitated entry of their ideas into culture and not made them vulnerable to their archenemies, the literati.

~ ~ ~

A significant feature that distinguishes the nineteenth century freethinkers from the Greek philosophers was their inability to attract the interest of the young during their lifetime, an interest that would have mitigated their isolation. The Greek philosophers were always in contact with intelligent and idealistic youth who sought to improve themselves by association with the most exalted type of individual, the philosopher. In the nineteenth century, however, European culture had created the system of scholarly-based education that destroyed the method of discipleship. Promising young men no longer sought the company of men with wisdom; instead they entered universities to obtain degrees and credentials. The attitude of nineteenth century society was that a young person would be foolish to give over his time and energy to the company of an eccentric philosopher. The value that ancient Greece had given to the tradition of discipleship disappeared.

~ ~ ~

The life of Mikhael Bakunin, the nineteenth century Russian anarchist philosopher, is a prime example of the difficulty an original thinker has in finding a place in western society. More than any other political figure, Bakunin had the Greek sensitivity to the degrading nature of societal tyranny. He recognized the importance of personal liberty in a way that his contemporaries did not. He was subjected to cruel and prolonged incarceration for his beliefs, managed to escape from his Siberian prison, but died prematurely after being isolated by the more Machiavellian communist revolutionaries.

Bakunin's posthumously published essay *God and the State* is an important milestone in recognition of the need for personal freedom in human life. But Bakunin's own example illustrates the fruitlessness of wasting one's energies in the politics of revolution. Like Karl Marx, a similarly gifted but more conspiratorial type of personality, Bakunin did not realize that what he valued most could not be obtained without a revolution at the deepest level of consciousness—the birth of metaphysical awareness. In ancient Greece, he would have been respected as a sage or perhaps exiled, but not cruelly damaged in prison. In our times, he has been condemned to that worst of all fates for an independent thinker— he has become the object of sociological study by scholars.

~ ~ ~

The writings of Friedrich Nietzsche are among the greatest events in western culture history since the creative accomplishments of the ancient Greek philosophers. One has only to begin reading the literary symphony entitled *The Birth of Tragedy* to realize he is in the presence of a philosophical mind of a fundamentally different nature than that usually classified as philosophic. Like much of Nietzsche's earlier writings, the style of composition was much affected by musical influences. (At one time, Nietzsche had thought of becoming a composer.) His musical experiences, especially with Wagnerian opera and the movement growing out of it, had a profound effect on Nietzsche's personality. This influence was not compartmentalized in his mind but permeated all of his thoughts and writings. For those who are accustomed to the dispassionate logical discourse of modern philosophy, the *Birth of Tragedy* can be better appreciated by having in mind the impact of Wagner's influence on its composition. The full title of the first edition was *The Birth of Tragedy Out of the Spirit of Music.* This ponderous title was nevertheless accurate; dropping the qualifying phrase as Nietzsche did in subsequent editions detracts from the understanding of this work.

~ ~ ~

At that time, Nietzsche conceived of human fulfillment to consist of the synthesis of the Dionysian and Apollonian impulses of life. Since images based on the figures of Greek gods may not be persuasive in an era in which science has replaced myth, we may properly substitute the term *experiential* for Dionysian and *creative* for Apollonian. With this altered terminology, the discussion becomes more familiar, albeit less endowed with imaginative spirit.

There are two principal ideas Nietzsche set forth in *The Birth of Tragedy*—the importance of the Dionysian impulse for health (an idea D. H. Lawrence later espoused) and his belief that 'Socratism' foreshadowed the decline of Greek philosophy because of its rejection of the Dionysian impulse. Furthermore, Nietzsche asserted, the triumph of the Socratic (i.e., analytic) influence in western culture in the form of the one-sided supremacy of the 'theoretical' man has led to his degeneration. Later, Nietzsche was to violently accuse Christianity of having finished the destruction of the spirit of Dionysus. In *The Birth of Tragedy*, however, he was content to refer circumspectly to "vicious dwarfs" who degraded German manhood without being more explicit.

These ideas were developed in the most flowing and evocative prose ever to emerge from a philosopher. A contemporary of his called it poetry, but not serious philosophy. The prose of Nietzsche is so alive with the spirit of its author that it is easy to become enchanted by it and ignore or forget the underlying ideas. But the profound thoughts of Nietzsche are of greater importance than is his extravagant prose style.

~ ~ ~

The Ionian Greek philosophers whom, as a professor of classical philology, Nietzsche had deeply imbibed, realized that philosophical consciousness bears the same relationship to experiential living as great rivers to mountain snowstorms; the former cannot exist without the latter. The idea that suffering begets knowledge was imbedded in Greek wisdom. Cosmic experience and personal creativity are joined together in the figure of Prometheus whom the playwright Aeschylus had endowed with

Heraclitean philosophy. Nietzsche grasped the antithetical and yet interdependent features of human life, expressing them in the prose poetry that is the hallmark of his writings. He knew that the lives of the ancient Greek philosophers had been enriched by significant experiences. If Aristotle observed that the type of 'insensitive man' who does not yearn for enriching experiences was a rarity in Greek society, Nietzsche noticed examples of such individuals everywhere in his day, especially in academia. He attributed the decline in the quality of western life to the depreciation of experiential living initiated by Socrates, continued by the later schools of Athens, transferred to Rome by itinerant Greek philosophers, and finally incorporated into Christian dogmas as the doctrine of 'sins of the flesh'. With his genius of elevated consciousness, Nietzsche perceived that the depreciation of the Dionysian impulse had led to a degeneration of personality in western societies.

~ ~ ~

Nietzsche's early life had been rich in experiential living. As a young student at the elitist school of Pforta, he had been immersed in classical Greek culture within an enriching environment that is no longer existent. Music, especially the new Wagnerian music, had a transforming impact on him—he wrote that he did not know how he could have survived without that experience. Although he wrote little about it, he was deeply affected by his participation in the Franco-Prussian war (1870-1); a war experience that touched every participant, especially a preternaturally sensitive individual such as Nietzsche. His decade of academic life at Basel was difficult for him but it was an experience he later claimed was necessary for the development of his ideas. Then there were his severe headaches and visual losses—likely due to a familial problem, since his father and brother had died of unexplained brain disorders—which Nietzsche said taught him to endure pain and invalidism. All of these factors in his life acted upon Nietzsche's fertile mind; his powerful creative drives assimilated them and produced a unique style of literary expression that represented the most important innovation in the art of philosophy since Plato's use of dialogue.

If Nietzsche's literary career had ended after the last of his *Untimely Reflections* appeared in the mid-1870s, he would have left to posterity a collection of writings, published and unpublished, that would have established his reputation as one of the most original thinkers of the nineteenth century. But much more was yet to come.

~ ~ ~

A few years after publication of the last of the *Untimely Reflections*, writings that elicited little public or academic interest, Nietzsche resigned his professorship at the University of Basel and went into self-imposed exile in Italy and France, a move duplicated some years later by James Joyce and Ezra Pound. Unlike most literary exiles, however, Nietzsche maintained virtually no close relationships, either in literary circles or with friends. He became a 'hyperborean', more and more isolated, until he was living as a complete recluse in Turin at the time of his nervous breakdown. The writings stemming from his years in exile have quite a different character from those of his early Basel period. His faith in the promise of German culture is gone; he is bitter, sarcastic, and pessimistic about every aspect of the German spirit. Although Nietzsche's love affair with German culture and especially with Schopenhauer was over, he could not rid himself of a the Hegelian orientation toward the 'spirit of a people.' The belief in the destiny of the German people turned out to be a passion he could not abandon without damaging his own spirit. Nietzsche became a hardened Diogenes; he regarded mankind as only fit for slavery and he felt there were no bona fide living members of a master race (other than perhaps himself). A passage in an unpublished preface in his notebooks reveals the mentality and the prophetic power of the gloomy Nietzsche. He says that those (obviously himself) who still hope for the appearance of culture must blot out the contemporary world.

~ ~ ~

As Nietzsche grew progressively negative about the human race, he perceived the full import of the impact of Christian domination upon European culture. His psychologically acute mind recognized the repression of mental growth produced by Christian faith. Even more importantly, he did not shrink, as Goethe and Schopenhauer had, from expressing his perception with all the power of his literary genius. Year after year, in the publications that he brought out annually (largely at his own expense), Nietzsche intensified his attack upon 'Christendom', an attack that was far more penetrating than the limited wars mounted by Feuerbach and Kierkegaard. His final long essay of 1888 *Der Antichrist* (The Antichristian), written shortly before his break, represents his most comprehensive statement against institutional Christianity. While one may wish that Nietzsche had been more in control of his prose and may become irritated by his literary posturing, the essential truth remains that Nietzsche was more in touch with the consequences of the Christian phenomenon than had been any of his predecessors or contemporaries—or followers for that matter.

There has been very little impact of Nietzsche's criticisms of Christianity upon western society at large. He has been regarded as a type of philosophical 'Peck's bad boy' by scholarly literati who admire his 'prose style' but ignore the substance of his writing. Many attribute his more radical statements to his purported syphilitic brain disease (a libel refuted in my *Legend of Nietzsche's Syphilis*). There is a clear embarrassment, even among his philosophic admirers, about the actual ideas he put forth, leading to the effect, if not the intention, of a conspiracy of silence. It appears that the post-Nietzschean western world cannot face the realities of two thousand years of metaphysically repressive Christianity. An example of the same type of phenomenon can be seen in the unwillingness of postwar Germany to face the horrors of the Nazi era. But Germany is now facing this reality and one day the entire Christian world will have to do the same.

~ ~ ~

Nietzsche has a claim to be the profoundest thinker in the history of European thought. He had gone through what was available to him in Greek and German culture and had drawn his conclusions. But he had his limitations; the erotic passions did not flower in him nor was he a child of nature; in this latter respect he was more

Socratic than Heraclitean in his preferences. One has only to compare Nietzsche to Thoreau to realize what an incapacity he had to experience nature in a meaningful manner. The paeans of praise of climate, sky, sea, winds, etc. are not persuasive in Nietzsche's writings.

It is interesting to compare Nietzsche's life with that of Goethe, the only German literary figure for whom the former had a high level of respect. Goethe's literary genius was accompanied by remarkable poetical gifts as contrasted to Nietzsche's musical sensibilities. However, Goethe had an intuitive sense of the importance of maintaining his connections with society throughout his life, even while conducting numerous illicit sexual liaisons. Such behavior was beyond Nietzsche's ability.

~ ~ ~

The titanic effort by Nietzsche to rejuvenate his spirit through the creation of *Zarathustra,* Nietzsche's literary *alter ego,* was a brilliant feat of creativity, but it did not serve to heal his psychic wound. Zarathustra did not substitute for his lack of meaningful experiences with others. His few clumsy efforts at erotic relationships were failures. Nietzsche did not really love eternity as he claimed; he loved German culture but it did not love him during his creative period and thereby lies the tragic element of his life. Heraclitus had seemed to Nietzsche to be the supreme example of a philosopher who was needed by the world but who did not need it. But no human being, philosopher or otherwise, can maintain spiritual equilibrium locked in a closet; the philosopher needs the world just as the world needs him. Nietzsche's *Übermensch* (superior man) could not survive without the vitalizing effects of significant personal experiences. Nietzsche himself finally bowed out of the world as he occasionally intimated he might—through recourse to insanity.

~ ~ ~

Nietzsche's writings as well as his life seemed to be fated for a tragic destiny. After his psychotic break, Nietzsche's sister, a woman unlike him in every conceivable way, took charge of his literary estate, withholding and altering his writings to serve her own purposes. (It must be admitted, however, that without her tireless publicizing of his writings, Nietzsche might not have achieved the posthumous fame that finally came his way.) During the Third Reich, the Nazi philosopher Alfred Bäumler became the official German interpreter of Nietzsche and linked his name with Nazi ideology, a movement that could only have evoked his deepest contempt. Nietzsche had openly expressed his distaste of Bismarck and the militarization of Germany—what might he have said about Adolf Hitler who represented everything Nietzsche detested in German civilization?

The fate of Nietzsche in English speaking countries was to have a Princeton professor, Walter Kaufmann, as his principal translator and commentator. Kaufmann was fluent in both German and English, and the excellence of his translations is unassailable. But Kaufmann brought a heavy-handed, dominating voice (Germanic?) to Nietzsche's writings via numerous prefaces, footnotes, commentaries, and explanations—all of which were far removed from the spirit of his subject. The paternalistic and condescending attitude expressed in print by Kaufmann remind one of an early comment of Nietzsche to the effect that certain people should not be permitted to even praise superior individuals. Nietzsche's message is damaged by the continuous intrusion of Kaufmann's opinions in the former's writings. The personality of a translator of important literature should be unobtrusive, lightly touching the writing with footnotes only when essential. Recognition is due to Kaufmann for his services as translator, especially for translating the difficult *Also Sprach Zarathustra* (Thus Spoke Zarathustra) but his many gratuitous remarks might be deleted from publications meant to present Nietzsche, not Kaufmann, to a reader. If there is anything that does not belong in the writings of Nietzsche, it is the ponderous apparatus of a scholar, especially one such as Kaufmann who takes advantage of his role as a translator to bring the attitude of a professorial critic into his work.

Kaufmann decided that Nietzsche's later works written during his period of isolation were his most valuable writings and he consistently depreciates the Basel *Untimely Meditations*. It is characteristic of Kaufmann's approach that he saw fit to translate only a part of the unpublished essay of Nietzsche entitled *Truth and Falseness in an Extramoral Sense* written in 1873. This abbreviation of an already short essay, which contains some of Nietzsche's most original thoughts, reveals a lack of respect for the former's writings. It may be compared to publishing only portions of a translation of Lincoln's Gettysburg address.

~ ~ ~

Although Nietzsche had an impact in European intellectual circles even before his physical death in 1900, this impact has been consistently resisted by both European and American literati and his ideas have not really been absorbed into western culture. Nietzsche seems to have disappeared as a significant philosophical milestone, especially, surprisingly, among the German-speaking intelligentsia. He is mainly attended to by academicians who enjoy dissecting the products of a mind they regard as talented, but diseased. It is true, however, that Nietzsche books seem to sell to the general public and most bookstores carry generous quantities of his books in the philosophy section. There are Nietzsche societies in North America and Europe that appear to be flourishing. The memory of Nietzsche seems to be maintained, not in the scholarly world, but by an educated public.

A similar fate has befallen the work of August Strindberg who was significantly influenced by Nietzsche and was one of the few modern dramatists with a philosophical consciousness. Like Nietzsche, Strindberg is valued for his literary abilities; like Nietzsche, his ideas are viewed as the products of a latent psychotic condition. Further considerations of the philosophical insights of twentieth century literati is a subject best approached from the vantage point of comedy, not philosophy.

~ ~ ~

Nietzsche during his Basel years created an image of 'The Last Philosopher'. The passage given below is a translation from notebooks that were not published in Nietzsche's lifetime. There can be little doubt it is Nietzsche's vision of his own descent into the hell of mental illness. The role of Oedipus is obscure;

translation into English of Nietzsche's word play is impossible, but the sense of the passage is chillingly clear:

Oedipus

Conversations of the Last Philosopher with Himself
A Fragment From the Annals of Posterity

The last philosopher I call myself since I am the last human being. No one speaks with me except myself and my voice sounds to me as one dying. With you, beloved voice, with you, my last breath of memory of all human joy, let me reminisce for but an hour, escaping solitude and deluding myself into love and friendship, since my heart resists believing that love is dead; it cannot bear the horror of unbroken solitude, it forces me to speak as if I were two.

Do I still hear you, my voice? You whisper while you curse? Shall not your curse burst the entrails of this world? But the world lives on; glowing coldly, its merciless stars stare at me; it lives on, blind and deaf as always, and only one thing dies, the human being.

And yet! I hear you yet, beloved voice! There dies yet another in this world beside myself, the last human being; there dies the last sorrower with me in protracted misery. Woe! Woe! Beside me mourns Oedipus, the last woebegone man.

~ ~ ~

Nietzsche's *Nachgelassene Fragmente* (unpublished notes; English partial translation, *Will to Power*) reveal his basic philosophical attitudes more clearly than his published works. In the fall of 1887, he wrote, "I don't worry about readers anymore, how could I write for readers...but I do make notes for myself." Further on he says,

"I read [present tense] Zarathustra, but how could I have thrown such pearls before Germans!"

But Nietzsche did write for readers and a great deal after he wrote these words. In 1888, he published (or prepared for publication) *The Case of Wagner, Twilight of the Idols, The Antichrist*, and *Ecce Homo*. He had recently revised the prefaces of most of his earlier books. Giorgio Colli, the erudite Italian editor of Nietzsche's *Nachlass*, thought Nietzsche wrote as a philosopher for himself and as a literary artist for the public. But I think it goes deeper than that. Nietzsche came to feel that the 'public', hitherto unresponsive to his books, would respond to more aggressive writings, *boshaft* writings, and stylized hyperbole; thus he gave the public what he thought would impress them. In the long run, he was right; these writings greatly contributed to his iconoclastic image, especially abroad; although also to the perception his brain was ravaged by syphilis. His serious thought subsequent to *Thus Spoke Zarathustra* (1884) and *Beyond Good and Evil* (1885) remained buried in the *Nachlass*. However, always publically expressing himself as a malicious, sarcastic, angry person may have undermined his personality and led to his mental breakdown.

L EAP OF CONSCIOUSNESS

The purpose of culture may be regarded as crystallizing the realities of one's existence into a higher consciousness. It is the one thing needful to fulfill the destiny of the human condition. Without a meaningful culture, human beings inevitably become victims of environments inhospitable to human development. The ancient Greeks took a higher consciousness so much for granted that they had no word for it; lack of a higher consciousness was often referred to as a state of sleep. Barbarians were human beings asleep throughout their lives. The Greeks distinguished little between physiological sleep and the lack of a higher consciousness, which they referred to as being 'asleep'.

Heraclitus perceived the underlying reality of the cosmos as a 'logos' that in human beings manifests itself through consciousness. The so-called progress that has occurred in the western world largely has to do with the development of technologies—ant-heap progress instead of progress concerned with elevating or deepening consciousness. The consciousness of reality of members of primitive groups may exceed the consciousness of western man; for example, American Indians were often superior as conscious human beings to the technologically superior Europeans who destroyed their civilization. The consciousness of the Ionian philosophers, and of the populations that engendered them, was superior to the Christian cultures that replaced them. It is probable that the Christian and Islamic societies that sit upon the ruins of ancient Greek culture represent a retrogression of human consciousness.

Simply being alive does not satisfy the energy within the human organism. Humans are creatures who desire to become aware of the ultimate reality. Although they cannot perceive the purpose of cosmic existence, they feel the purpose of their own life is to *establish and express* their consciousness of this reality. But a higher consciousness is not a matter of information acquisition. It arises as the outcome of the strife of living and the emergence of a 'mystical awareness' that transcends 'common sense'. It is here that the later Greek schools, the Buddhists, and the armies of contemporary psychotherapists who urge tranquility tend to devitalize individuals. Without love and hate, the specifically human forms of attraction and repulsion, human life withers; its passions are the yeast of consciousness without which it cannot arise out of the meaninglessness of reactive existence. It is only necessary that passions be attuned to a vital balance so as not to destroy consciousness itself.

~ ~ ~

The biological evolution of life forms is essentially the development of survival abilities and human evolution is no exception. The domestic cat is not intrinsically superior to the saber-toothed tiger nor is the elephant superior to the wooly mammoth; they are only more adaptive to their environment. Contemporary Europeans are not superior to the ancient Greeks but they have been more skilled in adapting to their environments. One must keep in mind that the human species tends to adapt to its environment by altering it rather than adapting to it, but the goal of species survival remains unchanged. Nevertheless, species survival per se does not satisfy human aspirations and human progress cannot be measured with longevity charts or death rates. Every sentient person intuits the purpose of his life to be the elevation of his consciousness of reality. Consciousness relates to human beings as a Chopin sonata does to a piano. The silent piano is an inert structure occupying space to no purpose. Sentient human beings who survive for a limited time period are part of the cosmic flux of existence, but those who survive without a higher consciousness are a dead weight diminishing the worth of humanity.

Consciousness cannot be divorced from life activities; it is impossible to be actively conscious and not *will to exist in accord with that consciousness.* A philosopher is a person not satisfied with object-oriented living; he desires to exist in relationship to an ultimate reality. His distinctive trait is the determination to vacate old values from his mind in order that he be free to create the new ones. Without this freedom, philosophy is reduced to monkey chatter. The goal of philosophy is the refurbishment of the values of the mind.

Jesus said that one does not pour new wine into old wineskins, a reflection of his remarkable ability to simplify the complexities of human life. This was also the distinctive feature of Heraclitus whose power stemmed from his ability to get beyond Homer, Hesiod, and the other traditional Greek icons, an accomplishment surpassing even that of Jesus who could never quite break away from his tribal Judaism. Nineteen hundred years later, Nietzsche was similarly handicapped by his bonds to German *Kultur*. Yet these individuals were heroes of the human race; when one is exposed to the pious platitudes of scholarly 'philosophers', one realizes their limitations do not lie in their capacity for thought but in their inability to relinquish their traditional values.

The values that have to be relinquished in order to make way for individual development have already been specified. They are the Judeo-Christian heritage, which has long outlived its value for western civilization, the one-dimensional technological preoccupations that have to be greatly downgraded in their relevance to the human condition, and the obsessive scholarship, which is often inhibitory to a genuine culture. When the mind of an individual is cleared of antiquarian notions and mental bonding to an obsolete religion, it becomes free to develop its own values that all lead to one goal—consciousness of an ultimate reality. This is the program of the individual; it supersedes that of society.

~ ~ ~

The concept of an irrational mental 'leap' required by Christian faith was enunciated by Gotthold Lessing, a leading figure of the enlightenment in the German cultural world. Unlike Kant, Lessing had a strong intellectual *conscience*, manifested by his publically admitted inability to base unlimited faith in an historical personage such as Jesus of Nazareth. Søren Kierkegaard utilized this unusual candor of the eighteenth century writer to reveal what he thought to be the 'one thing necessary' for a human being, a leap of faith transcending a universe seemingly regulated by natural law. The convoluted mentality of Kierkegaard settled on identifying this faith with becoming a Christian, meaning acknowledging the emergence of a metaphysical God into history as Jesus the Christ.

Kierkegaard himself was unwilling to define Christianity. The closest one can come to it is his statement in the *Concluding Unscientific Postscript* that "it is not a doctrine but an existential communication expressing an existential contradiction." Clearly, for Kierkegaard, Christian faith is a state inexpressible by literary means. The obsession with Christianity seems to have been implanted in Kierkegaard by an overbearing father who was morbidly preoccupied with his religion.

~ ~ ~

Kierkegaard's spiritual insights led him to recognize the role of faith in human existence; it was his perverse nature that made him identify it with a commitment to Christianity. There is only one leap of faith that an individual raised in the scientific western culture must make—the leap from faith in an exclusively empirical orientation to faith in the metaphysical interior self. There are no scientific data that can demonstrate an interior self since science functions within a different dimension of existence. Efforts at equating the interior self with the brain can only lead to intellectual monstrosities such as a scholarly tome I recently encountered entitled *The Self and Its Brain*. Faith in one's interior self (otherwise known as the soul) is consciousness of one's own metaphysical existence; this consciousness does not arise from the facts of the external world. The failure to admit the reality of the soul is the tragedy of modern life, which only believes in object existence and the empirical facts connected with it.

The faith-oriented Kierkegaard, who had great difficulty in defining his faith, came to describe sin as the absence of Christian faith. Modern western culture reeks with the greater sin of having no faith in the existence of a soul in human beings.

~ ~ ~

The ancient Greeks knew about the interior self, which they called the ψυχη (psyche). The development of this faith can be perceived in the emergence of Greek philosophy in which the ideal of the heroic but reactive man of action is gradually replaced by the inwardly directed sage, a soul dragging about a corpse as Epictetus once pithily observed. It is faith in his own soul that is necessary for the individual to be able to stand firm against the encroachments and impositions of object oriented societies. Kierkegaard was right to create the noble image of the knight of faith; but this image was marred by his obsessive Christianity. The knight of faith is one who believes in his own soul; this must be the proper meaning of Kierkegaard's heroic defense of his own soul's integrity.

In last analysis, scientific knowledge connected to the external phenomenal world is mainly of interest insofar as it pertains to survival of individual human beings. Philosophers who are oriented principally toward science, toward objective cognition in order to ascertain 'facts', and toward logical processes in order to arrange facts are of limited interest since philosophers have little to contribute to survival of individuals. These philosophers only live on in the academic world because they are subsidized as culture fetishes by universities. Lately, some have also become public personalities, which provide them with a broader basis of support.

~ ~ ~

The Ionian philosophers, solely on the basis of their own unaided observations and awareness of the nature of existence, made the crucial discovery that the object world is regulated by a natural law. It is not necessary to fill in the details; all the discoveries of technological astronomy have done little to heighten the consciousness of the cosmos that was acquired by Thales and his successors. When Anaxagoras asserted that his purpose in living was to perceive the universe, he expressed a consciousness of the human condition that eludes twentieth century technologists who know only mastery of the world. Consciousness of man and nature is not enhanced by the avalanche of scientific data that daily pours forth from over-endowed laboratories. The human senses provide fully adequate perceptions of the world; the limiting factor in consciousness is the mind behind the perceptions.

The tidal wave of physical data is not only largely useless; it serves to distract their observers from the goal of *metaphysical* consciousness and promotes technologies that victimize people instead of enlightening them. The mastery of nature is the goal of scientists, but in the end it is human beings who are mastered by science, as Samuel Butler foresaw in his uncanny vision of the dominance of machines related in his novel *Erewhon*. Butler did not fully grasp the meaning of his vision but it is impossible to read his book without glimpsing the unconscious prophetic powers of its author.

Objective empiricism leads in one direction, subjective consciousness in another. A certain amount of empirical knowledge is necessary to survive in the world. Every individual has to assess his own needs for survival and develop his capacities to the extent necessary. But what is sorely lacking in western societies is the higher consciousness that cannot be acquired by further technological development. A redirection of energy toward deeper levels of existence is required. Such redirection requires a genuine culture divorced from the materialist mentality.

~ ~ ~

An active metaphysical consciousness establishes the centrality of the interior self, cut loose from the dead weights of superstition and empiricism. With a higher consciousness comes recognition of the interrelationships of all things, the *logos* defined by Heraclitus; this is why analogy and metaphor are at the heart of philosophical expression. They form the language of consciousness while quantification is the hallmark of empiricism. The Ionian philosophers were pioneers in formulating these relationships, albeit they conceived of the ultimate reality in primitive terms.

Religiosity and empiricism impede the emergence of a higher consciousness because they place the center of existence away from the self—whether toward worship of an imaginary deity or toward an external object world. They represent immature levels of development retaining control over the interior self. One may physically survive as *homo adorans* or *homo faber*, or combinations of these two childish conditions of human existence, but under these circumstances, one cannot aspire toward the true goal of human beings—the goal of consciousness of reality, epitomized by the conception of man as *Homo sapiens.* Western society today is blanketed by the suffocating atmosphere of empiricism; it devoutly believes in the object world and has lost consciousness of the metaphysical interior self—the soul.

The proliferation of empirical information that has reached epidemic proportions serves only to depress interior consciousness. The final outcome of an exclusively empirical self is a robotic individual unaware of its interior self or manifesting it only by a surface sentimentality. "I searched out myself," said Heraclitus; he moved toward a consciousness of an ultimate reality and along with his fellow Ionian philosophers planted a light that still serves as a beacon to the embattled representatives of western culture.

~ ~ ~

The highest human achievement is creation of artwork—the objective phenomena that represent human consciousness in the form of feelings, emotions, and conceptions. Everyone instinctively recognizes the importance of art, whether pictorial, plastic, or literary. Philosophy falls under the literary category. The spirit of art, however, is poisoned by bourgeois institutions that attempt to capture it for the profit motive. Mind and talent are hired out for wealth accumulation. The true artist is one who strives for self-expression through an art form, which is the achievement most worthy of sentient human beings. In the end, working for bourgeois approval is working for survival in the societal world. But human fulfillment comes through self-expression, not survival in society.

This kind of fulfillment is difficult and often painful in a bourgeois dominated society because that society begins shaping the behavior of its members from the first years of life and never ceases until death. The behavior shaping is always in the direction of conforming to values that strengthen materialist society; all other proclaimed values are false or cosmetic. Behavior shaping in contemporary western societies is not carried out by overt indoctrination or brute force; it is done through conditioning procedures in which positive or negative reinforcement is continuously conducted by the society. The craving for signals of approval can be developed to such a degree that the most meaningless happenings are experienced as gratifying events.

~ ~ ~

An accomplishment of the Greek schools of philosophy was to help the individual resist behavior shaping by replacing fear of the gods with indifference to them. Socrates, Antisthenes, and Epicurus made their contribution to Greek culture by personally demonstrating the ability of the individual to rise above the vicissitudes and threats of society, which were more menacing in the ancient Greek world than in the cushioned societies of today. The image of the relaxed Socrates calmly discoursing with his friends on the eve of his execution was the model on which Greek cheerfulness and Roman stoicism was based. Similar examples were provided by other philosophers in other ways.

However, the antique world did not have to contend with the force of the conditioning imposed by modern western societies. In the ancient Greek world, bourgeois psychology was a tendency, not a dominant aspect of the culture. We in the western world are heirs to centuries of ever growing bourgeois behavior shaping; our bones and brains have been saturated through and through with the mentality of wealth and object acquisition. When we modern humans come in contact with non-bourgeois cultures (of which a few still survive), we are amused by attitudes that seem to be primitive and ignorant. Yet it is we who are primitive and ignorant for we are not conscious of the realities of existence, which were beginning to be known by our cultural forebears in ancient Greece. We may try strenuously to educate ourselves, but often we find ourselves in the position of Eugene O'Neill's Emperor Jones who, as the bongo drums continuously beat out their ominous message, abandons his civilized veneer for the paranoid fears of the Haitian black. The bourgeois lures of object possession are the bongo drums of modern man; he may strive to develop his soul but when the drums beat, his earliest training propels him back to the jungle of bourgeois mentality. This training has permanently altered our minds; the most intense and sustained effort of will is required to lift us above the primitive object-oriented world of bourgeois existence.

ARTISTS AND ARTWORK

Out of their essential vitality of spirit, the Greeks were able to dispense with the study of culture. They themselves represented culture. However, we moderns, fenced about as we are by decadent and petrified institutions, are not able to afford such a luxury. It is necessary for us to distinguish genuine artwork, the expression of the consciousness of existence of another human being, in order to maintain the human quality of our personalities. It is necessary to extract from the artwork of artists the essential nature of existence. The philosophical culture of the ancient Greeks is the art form best suited to provide this lesson since they, among all the civilizations known to us, reached the highest peak of artistic achievement.

It is easy for naïve individuals to mistake pseudo-culture or philistinism, using a term coined by Nietzsche, for the real thing. The key to the recognition of genuine art is that one's interior self is affected by it, whether it be visual or literary art. The bourgeois philistine is the Pharisee of culture; he likes to be associated with art objects but they do not touch his interior self. They serve decorative or social purposes. Genuine artwork has a force greater than any product of bourgeois endeavor, but it is impotent if it does not act on the interior self. The bourgeois personality is incapable of being affected by this force—when it is so affected it is no longer bourgeois.

It is important to understand the meaning of the term 'bourgeois' in contemporary usage. The bourgeois condition as used in this writing does not refer to economic or social class arrangements; it is entirely a matter of individual psychology. The bourgeois mind is oriented to the external object world and has no consciousness of an interior self apart from this world. It represents a habit of thought arising from an aggressive need to dominate the external world. Clearly we live in a bourgeois era in which bourgeois civilization is en route to covering the entire face of the earth. It is interesting to note how the Hegelian mentality of the communist world that assigned spiritual value to the 'proletariat' has largely given way to the acquisitive bourgeois mentality of the capitalist world. The latter has created a world of 'dead souls', to borrow a title from Gogol.

~ ~ ~

The deepest meaning of art is not to be found merely in appreciation of artwork but also in the artist's subjectivity of which artwork is the phenomenal representation. Everyone who experiences art knows that it exerts its power only for a finite moment in time—a painting, a novel, a philosophical work, a musical composition all exert their effect briefly and then the memory fades. However, what remains behind or what should remain behind, is the awareness that another individual, the artist, has perceived some aspect of existence in such a manner and communicated this perception through his artwork. The creative subjectivity of the artist becomes transferred, albeit to a lesser extent, to the one experiencing the artwork. Genuine art is a representation of the consciousness of the artist; if the viewer can absorb this consciousness, he has been transformed by his contact with the artwork.

How this occurs is a mystery since such transformations do not occur through the ordinary channels of communication. Labeling it mysticism explains nothing. Art is the highest form of human activity because it is the highest goal of human life to attain to consciousness—and perhaps to communicate this attainment to others.

The plight of the bourgeois mind is that it does not aspire to consciousness; to the bourgeois, art is a means of further embedding himself in his society, not of leading him out of it. He does not refer the meaning of art to his interior self because he does not truly believe in the existence of an interior self. Thus he fails to create his own soul through the varieties of experience, artistic or otherwise. The term 'soul' to the bourgeois mind is an archaic term referring to the medley of brain neuronal activity acquired during the course of adaptation to one's environment. What helps him adapt, he values; what does not is of no consequence to him. The bourgeois is all brain and no soul. He has lost touch with the essential element of human life.

~ ~ ~

The creative act, objectifying the mind's perceptions of the world of phenomena, establishes the mind's autonomy—if only during the moment of creativity. Human beings are the sole form of life that engage in art because they are the only ones with the desire for mental autonomy, for creating their own soul. One may define the soul as an autonomous mind, not a mind in bondage to the external world but a mind free, conscious of its own autonomy and productive of original concepts. Humans are meant to have a higher consciousness; experience has shown that without it, they become a devouring cancer within the bosom of the natural world.

Philosophers worthy of the name have known that philosophy is not a matter of scholarship but is an affair of the soul. Scholars are only the copyists and historians of these affairs. With this in mind, it is necessary to remind oneself that the significance of art, and of philosophy as an art form, has to do with the establishment of the spiritual autonomy of the artist. The bourgeois mind does not become a soul because it has not forged it in creative endeavors. In spite of the most elaborate deceptions, it is ignominiously chained to the object world as its slave.

~ ~ ~

Loose talk about a child's soul, or worse yet, about the soul of an unborn fetus, denigrates the development of the human spiritual condition. A child does not have a soul because it has not yet forged its autonomy in the strife of life. A child's mind deserves respect because it has the prospect of forming a soul, but its soul does not truly exist until the mind has become autonomous in relation to family and society. The Christian establishment has been allowed to prate too long about the sanctity of all souls without contradiction. The Christian concept of the soul's role is its seeking bondage to a controlling deity, not seeking its own autonomy. This concept completely distorts the human spiritual state. The idea of an autonomous soul responsible only to a universal *logos*; first conceived by the Ionian philosophers, ought to be returned to its original independent form. Its presence within Christian dogmas is like the presence of the Elgin marbles in the British Museum. It is a reminder of the acquisitive nature of European civilizations.

~ ~ ~

The emergence of consciousness in the human mind is a destiny, not a pleasure; herein lies the inadequacy of the concept of Epicurus that pleasure is the ultimate good. The significance of consciousness lies in its independence of the principle of sufficient reason. A sense of the mystical element of human life is necessary to grasp its meaning. It is an amazing phenomenon as was stated by Hamlin Garland in the epigraph chosen for this writing. Without consciousness, the human psyche is a speck of sand on an infinite beach—a feeling that has greatly contributed to the ubiquitous presence of theistic belief. But theology is unnecessary; it is only necessary to apprehend the soul as a movement out of time-bound objectivity into metaphysical timelessness. Dissolution of time-space constraints that block experience of other souls is the unique function of art; it is how individuals can span over two millennia of inferior cultures to experience Greek philosophers. Let us say that art is a sacred bridge by which one soul can communicate with another, but let us not forget that the foundation of this bridge rests on the strength of the interior self of both the artist and his viewer-reader.

Artistic consciousness forms the basis of philosophy as an art form, because only to the extent that the philosopher projects his interior self into his writing and teaching are they of consequence. It is this ability that makes Kierkegaard, Nietzsche, and Berdyaev philosophers of enduring interest. It is what can be clearly discerned in the writings of Heraclitus, Democritus, and other early Greek philosophers. It is this ability that literati do not possess as they are basically either entertainers or scholars, and more at home in the domain of the bourgeoisie. As for the scholar calling himself 'philosopher', he is 'the fool of all the centuries' occupying himself with searching out the meaningless details and trivia of philosophers and philosophy, which are the province of scholars. Genuine philosophers only reveal their secrets to the souls of seekers capable of receiving them.

~ ~ ~

The value of the artwork of an artist is integrally connected to the unity of his personality, since artwork that reflects a unified self is far more meaningful than that which stems from the bits and pieces of a divided self. Writers more than other artists are predisposed toward a divided self; perhaps because they are more focused on 'success' than are other artists. However, success in society is always in conflict with artistic success. Henry David Thoreau is the best example of an American writer who exhibited a unified autonomous personality—in contrast to his patron Emerson who never could fully emancipate himself from his Protestant origins. Thoreau's place is in the forefront of philosophers of the western world because his life and writings complement each other in a manner rarely seen since the era of the ancient Greeks. He has exerted a cultural influence far beyond that of more prolific but less significant literati.

The secret of Thoreau's autonomy was that he was that great rarity among writers and philosophers—someone who did not concern himself with fame. It was sufficient to him to present his writings to whoever might be interested. Thoreau's respect for himself was such that he did not require the approval of others. He had a healthy suspicion of his society and did not think it necessary to mix himself with it. The power of Thoreau as a philosopher has only begun to reveal itself more than a century after his death. There are some signs in America of the emergence of awareness of the philosophical depth of Thoreau's mind, and not merely of him as an advocate of nature.

~ ~ ~

Creation of artwork is the best preparation for developing a philosophical consciousness. Through engaging in artistic activity, one obtains the experience of self-expression and of apprehending the expressions of other artists. Art requires a radically different form of cognition than that of scholarship or science; it requires the development of the receptive-expressive self rather than the analytical self. It is fruitless to labor over the receptive-expressive self by means of analytical techniques; it is even more fruitless to bother with the irrelevant esotericism of modern science. One does not apprehend Rembrandt or Van Gogh by puzzling over which half of their brain exerted a dominant influence. Either half would be more than a match for the intelligentsia of neurology.

Art is emasculated in a world controlled by scientific modes of thought. The psychoanalyst, the scholar of culture, the neurologizer of creativity—all these types do a great disservice to individual artists by intruding into their affairs. Even more disconcerting is the involvement of computers, the ultimate negation of the meaning of art, into artistic processes. The unprecedented spread of computers into modern life reveals that the vision of Samuel Butler in *Erewhon* was more prescient than that of the politically preoccupied George Orwell in his novel *1984.*

An individual interested in art should approach it as he would a loved one—desirous of the experience of love. If he cannot obtain such an experience from a work of art, he ought to move on to other encounters. The notion, however, that the programmed study of the history of any type of art develops appreciation of that art form is as fallacious as the idea that analysis of the human brain develops appreciation of the soul of human individuals. The reverse is true, since the analysis of mind and brain hinders appreciation of the human soul as has been proven beyond doubt by the modern obsession with the scientific study of the brain. The decline of Greek art began with Aristotle; it could not survive the substitution of loving attention by analytical study.

~ ~ ~

The absence of philosophy in one's life leaves the soul defenseless against the onslaught of societal forces. The art of philosophy is the way by which concepts are developed out of life's experiences;

it is the only means the individual has to protect himself against bourgeois and religious forces that threaten his autonomy. It is impossible to develop the interior self in all its dimensions without engaging in philosophy.

The heritage of ancient Greek philosophy is a priceless treasure gathering dust in funereal libraries. It possesses great powers, however, for those who know how to unlock its treasures. There is more wisdom in Democritus than in Whitehead, more in Heraclitus than in Einstein. The philosophical culture of the antique Greeks provides models and lessons for subduing an out of control technology on the verge of overwhelming individuals. The direction toward life fulfillment is not through political, economic, or technological machinations; if that were so, western first world societies would have long since become utopias. Development of the interior self, the soul—the heart's desire of every human being no matter how bonded he is to society—lies in the emergence of a higher consciousness and in the expression of that consciousness through artwork. Authentic wisdom is the recognition of the road toward interior development; its rewards have been as they ever have been—a sense of deliverance and a brightening of the spirit that far exceed in value the childish pleasures that technology can confer upon the individual.

~ ~ ~

The pathological tendency in every complex society is the splitting of personality that undermines the unified interior self; regardless of appearances it is better to be an integrated misfit than a split personality success story. August Strindberg was one of the most penetrating writers of the modern era whose prose writings deserve wider translation into English. He wrote at the end of his novel *Black Banners* that dilettantism is the cardinal sin to be avoided. He did not mean only artistic dilettantism but also dilettantism in living. For him, human life was not a toy to be played with but was to be treated reverently as befits the dignity of a sentient being with consciousness of the worth of his existence. Strindberg struggled furiously in his own life to escape bourgeois dilettantism—as a consequence often appearing to be mentally ill to those around him. But as the perspective from history emerges, it becomes evident that he was a great artist striving to integrate his personality and whose insights into human life far exceeded those of virtually all of his contemporaries.

~ ~ ~

The issue of unity of personality is a crucial one in culture. Without it, philosophy tends to become, as Nietzsche put it, "a harmless chatter among senile academics or immature children." It is true that individuals with undeveloped minds are likely to have relatively unified personalities since there is not the specialization of mental structures that predisposes toward a split personality. However, as the mind develops, there inevitably appears the tendency toward compartmentalization of it. This phenomenon is seen in all advanced societies. Extreme forms are the habitual criminal who is a loving parent, the successful businessman who embezzles from his firm, the genial entertainer who brutalizes his family. The behavior of the Reverend Davidson in Somerset Maugham's short story *Rain* is a classic example of the split personality produced by the conflict of Christian doctrine with erotic passion.

The more complex the society, the more complex is the phenomenon of personality splitting. The example of Sigmund Freud is a particularly bizarre case of personality split. Freud probed more deeply than any other into the sicknesses of bourgeois society, yet he himself exhibited a degrading subservience toward its customs. Like Hegel, Freud was a person who completely divorced his own existence as a human being from the products of his mental activity. All the accusations leveled by Kierkegaard against Hegel are equally applicable to Freud; both ignored the reality that the worth of mental concepts is in direct proportion to their connection to the life of those who produce them. The life of the mind is degraded by individuals such as Freud; the psychoanalytic movements he spawned and for which he serves as inspiration have done as much to set back the cause of a genuine Euro-American culture as have all the political disasters of the twentieth century.

~ ~ ~

Philosophy stands for wisdom; violation of the integrity of the interior self is always unwise no matter how expedient at any moment in time. Philosophy is moribund as a vital force today because of the split personalities of the sophistical pseudo-philosophers who serve as its models. What would the ancient Greeks have thought of the example of Immanuel Kant, the father figure of modern western philosophy, with his fawning, bowing, and scraping before the authorities of his day. He was the prototype of the 'university philosopher' that now dominates the philosophical scene. Some Greek philosophers were brought to trial, banished, and even executed because of their unwillingness to split their personalities. Their bravery exceeded that of the early Christian martyrs because they did not depend upon an afterlife with Jesus to reward them for their pains. Theirs was a consuming passion for reality rather than a passion for God. It is difficult today to appreciate the force and vitality of the Greek philosophers as a consequence of their unified personalities. Because of their mental powers, they promoted the quality of life in their society and their memories are the greatest monuments bequeathed to modernity by ancient Greece.

~ ~ ~

Nietzsche once wrote that important thoughts are the greatest events of history; he might have enlarged upon his epigram by stating that the artistic expression of important perceptions are the great events of history. New accounts are needed that will vividly describe the literary and representational artwork that are the great events of our planet instead of the boring recitations of one dimensional historical episodes generally filling history books, even the history of culture. Great individuals are those who express new perceptions, not the demagogic mediocrities who achieve political prominence. The French, Russian, and Nazi revolutions were conducted by split personalities in which one aspect was hypertrophied beyond all reason. The fact that they affected the social history of Europe qualifies them as great events only in the sense that the eruption of Mount Vesuvius or the Lisbon earthquake were great events. The same can be said of most wars and revolutions; they are volcanic events that alter the surface of human affairs but rarely bring genuinely new developments into human existence.

Modern historians are generally inferior to their antique predecessors because of their disinterest or incapacity to represent the personalities of individuals who form the true history of human development. Historians are usually unconscious Hegelians who are preoccupied with the history of nations. It is remarkable to discover how much more interesting are the works of Thucydides, Xenophon, or Plutarch than are contemporary historians. The Roman historians Tacitus, Livy, Sallust, and Suetonius are preeminent in this regard, having been influenced by Greek historiography. The founders of western *historia* understood the importance of individuals for history. They were inquirers into human activities, not academicians preoccupied with scholarship or entertainers transforming history into soap opera.

~ ~ ~

Recognition of the great events in history is not difficult if one is attuned to the expressions of the human spirit in art forms. One can recognize a concentration of great events in western civilization within two particular times in history: the efflorescence of Greek culture, especially philosophy, in the sixth and fifth centuries B.C. and the existential-expressionist reawakening in Europe during the nineteenth and early twentieth century. The influence of European rebirth of higher consciousness extended into pockets along the northeastern seaboard of the United States, but the rest of the continent largely remained in the Dark Ages of Christendom.

However, the nineteenth century rebirth does not appear to have survived the twentieth century explosion of technology. At the present time, a serious observer can find little evidence of great cultural events in contemporary society. If they have occurred, they are not recognized as such by the shakers and movers of society. Genuine culture—which always has to do with expression of consciousness of existence—has been replaced by such a descent into triviality that one feels human life must either undergo a radical transformation or some cataclysmic event must occur to relieve the unbearable tension of spiritual suppression. A third possibility is that the evolutionary forces of biological adaptation will result in the loss of spirituality in the human race.

~ ~ ~

An artist is a person who commits his energies to the expression of his feelings and thoughts to his artwork. He works at the higher elevations of human affairs, since it is involvement with art that elevates the human spirit above other animal species. Technological development is at the same level of activity as the anthill or beehive. For this reason, the individual who is conscious of his human status feels compelled at some time in his life to involve himself with the processes of art. Mature individuals who expend all their energies in non-artistic activities are not worth taking seriously and are invariably tiresome personalities.

As sure as anything is known about the human condition, fame destroys the higher qualities of an artist. Leisure and solitude are essential for the interior self to maintain its integrity; the person who has been caught up by fame cannot fend off the world sufficiently to attain them. Goethe, who was one of the most naturally gifted artists of all time, said that the public destroys in writers the very qualities that they admired in them. Goethe himself did not age well in spite of all his desire to protect himself from his idolatrous public. One need only compare Faust, Part I, the product of his early manhood, with Faust, Part II composed during his later years. A cynical nihilism under the guise of practicality became the dominant trait of the elder Goethe.

An artist is fortunate if he can avoid fame and still escape poverty, since there is much more gratification to be found in the company of an occasional like-minded individual than in the childlike adulation that is the lot of a famous person. There are ways of maintaining oneself materially and psychologically without becoming famous. The talented artist ought to hope that fame, should it ever come upon him, will be safely deferred until his life is out of harm's way.

~ ~ ~

The relationship of an artist to his audience involves deep philosophical issues. An artist cannot dispense with the concept that his work may touch other individuals although he can project this occurrence into his posterity. Most really original artists of all types think their true audience will not appear until after their death; generally, they have been correct in their assessment.

However, one must also envision the artist who never gains an audience, either contemporaneously or posthumously, not even a single individual who responds to his work. It is certain that there are many such examples; virtually all artists must face the fear of their work disappearing into oblivion. What is the meaning of genuine art—artwork that expresses the unique perceptions of the artist—that attracts no audience at all. The question of whether talent and creativity really existed in such an artist is not the issue; if only one talented, creative artist has ever existed whose work has not been noticed by society, the meaning of such a circumstance must be considered. Actually, it is quite likely that most significant artwork has disappeared into oblivion because of failure of critics to judge them meritorious. "A thousand unsung Miltons" must have disappeared from societal sight. When considering his failure to obtain readers, Nietzsche dryly remarked there were no fish in the lake he fished in. The meaning of the fisherman artist who catches no fish is deserving of close attention.

~ ~ ~

The most important consequence, perhaps the only real consequence, of the creative act in art is to establish the artist's personality as an autonomous individual. One might say that a new Cartesian doctrine relevant for today is "I create art, therefore I am an autonomous human being," acknowledging the uniqueness of humans as artistically creative beings. If it is the perception of *meaning* in the world that distinguishes sentient humans from all other living creatures, it is the expression of this meaning in artwork that gives it a stability that does not exist in the flesh and blood of its creator. The artist depletes, yet mystically *immortalizes* his spirit, irrespective of any audience, by following the mandate given mankind by a symbolic Lord in the Prologue of Goethe's Faust, Part I:

New creation, eternally occurring,
Ye shall contain with love's kind attention,
And what freely floats, dimly swaying,
Surely shall ye fix, with lasting conception!

~ ~ ~

Time changes everything, including artists. They may improve or deteriorate, but they never remain the same. Once created, artwork is no longer part of the artist's interior state. Like a child grown to maturity, it assumes a life of its own and may soon appear as a foreign object to its creator. When the artist's artwork has grown unfamiliar to him, it has the significance of any other artwork; it is the objective representation of the interior self of another sentient being, in this case, the artist himself at an earlier stage in his life. Since the purpose of art as object is to affect others, the artist should be receptive to his own work from a different period in his life and allow it to exert its influence upon him. The artist who is unaffected by his own work is like the artist who will spend no money on his vocation. Neither can expect others to find value where he finds none.

The consequence of an artist's valuation of his own art is that he has, as an assured audience, his own self. He may elevate himself to a higher level of being by means of art produced at a stronger period of life. The importance of this phenomenon should not be underestimated. There is nothing more important, more worthy of valuation, than the spiritual state of an individual. No one knows the significance or consequences of the soul's condition. Philosophers, in particular, have recognized the importance of their own work to themselves. Kierkegaard, Schopenhauer, and Nietzsche constantly referred to their own writings, not out of a desire for self-glorification, but out of a genuine awareness of the meaning to them of their own creative activity.

~ ~ ~

The proper attitude of presenting artwork to the public is that of bestowing a gift, not of selling a commodity. The question posed by Ezra Pound as to what will become of cultures that turn artwork into commodities has been answered in the twentieth century—they become pseudo-cultures, diminishing the human condition. Justice requires that every individual present meaningful gifts to the society out of which he has emerged, for, whatever its faults, it has provided him with the opportunity of forming his life, without which no perceptions, no desires, no art, nothing is possible. The artist who expects society to reward him for his artwork is like a child who expects his parents to pay him for graduating from school—something that is not unheard of in our society. The model for the artist is not provided by the high-priced lawyer or physician but by Aeschylus' Prometheus who nobly endured a thousand years of torment as a result of his gift to the human race.

~ ~ ~

Those who are creative for commercial purposes, for indulgence of personal vanity, for the excitement of fame will find no satisfaction in the thoughts expressed in these pages because their needs will not be met by them. They gain no gratification from engaging in artistic activity that does not bring them monetary or psychological rewards from the world. Such individuals are not artists in the deeper meaning of the term; the creative process is a tool to them, not an end in itself. They are part of the culture of entertainment and instruction, which has its own defined purposes. Contemporary western society is entirely oriented toward rewarding those who entertain or instruct them. But genuine artists motivated by their own spiritual desires need a philosophy of art that will protect them from the corroding influence of bourgeois pseudo-culture.

FATE OF THE SOUL

In order to take seriously the question of fate of the human soul after death, it is first necessary to accept its existence as a reality. If one thinks that what the term 'soul' refers to is basically certain qualities of the brain, then there is no point in considering its persistence. When the brain dies, its 'qualities' disappear with it. However, if one is emancipated from the dogma of materialist monism and recognizes his inner self as a 'metaphysical' reality, then he must accept this reality for what it is, and consider the possibility of its persistence after death of his body.

The phenomena of life and death are fundamentally 'mystical' circumstances in spite of the usual Talmudic obsessions of modern science for accumulating information about these phenomena. Enumerating *ad infinitum* all the properties of living organisms does not explain the reason behind the vital impetus of life and its increasing complexity in time (see Henri Bergson's *Élan vital*). Biology describes in minute detail how life at all levels behaves, but the fundamental difference between animate and inanimate existence remains a mystery to the scientific as well as the philosophic mind.

~ ~ ~

The intuitive explanation of the vital principal of life throughout human history is that there is some type of metaphysical reality determining the material aspects of life; it has been called spirit, soul, 'breath', ruling principal (the Stoics), ghost, god (pantheism). In Eastern religions, this metaphysical reality is regarded as the only reality and the material world is looked upon as illusory. It is

184

only in recent times as scientific thinking has become dominant throughout the world that the metaphysical reality is looked upon as illusory, and material being is viewed as the sole reality. However, this view is based upon scientific dogma, not human intuition.

Advances in physics in the last century have called into question many of the previously established beliefs of science and philosophy. The old idea of a four dimensional universe now seems to be simplistic; it appears that there are several additional dimensions beyond the scope of human representation. An 'uncertainty' principle (Heisenberg) appears to affect efforts at precise measurement of the quanta of energy. The principle of sufficient reason to explain everything has been called into question. Einstein's general relativity theorem has revealed that measurement of movement and passage of time in the universe is relative to the observer. The special relativity theorem establishes that matter can be transformed into energy. These concepts are difficult for individuals who are unaccustomed to the arcane world of mathematical physics to visualize. In view of the shakings of the foundations of the traditional dogmas, one might consider metaphysics, not as a domain of understanding separate from physics, but as an extension of it, an *epiphysics.*

~ ~ ~

All this undercutting of conventional 'common sense' beliefs make it quite plausible to question the monistic dogma and to think that there is a metaphysical dimension of existence that exists beyond the physical one. The old scientific criteria of truth based on measurement, quantification, and verification have no meaning within the metaphysical dimension. Human intuition rather than scientific measurement is the means to metaphysical understanding. It is intuitions that need to be compared, not measurements. The *logos* of the universe is not only based on scientific knowledge but on metaphysical understanding as well. The history of thought shows that intuition of the interior self or soul by human beings is the principal subject of metaphysics, even though, as Ludwig Feuerbach showed, many have comingled ideas of God with the qualities of the soul of man.

~ ~ ~

Once one accepts the existence of the soul, many other insights come into view. Who can doubt that the soul consisting of emotions, desires, insights, will, understanding, 'wisdom'—all forms of consciousness—are the most important part of one's status as an individual member of the species *Homo sapiens*. It follows that his physical self can be regarded as a means for developing the soul. The entire sensory-motor system of a human being is admirably suited for relating the external world to the soul. The soul cannot develop without contact with the world outside of itself. When a human being emerges from the womb into the outer world, its energies consist of undeveloped desire—nothing else. 'Desire' is the metaphysical wellspring of the soul. Some like the devout Père Gratry have said it is the voice of God. Whatever its nature, it is the experiences of the world that allow the soul to fill with consciousness and expand its mental and spiritual horizons. Learning to walk, talk, read, contemplate, and write allows the soul to take wing. The brain is the executive organizer of these processes.

The apparently insuperable objection to the thesis expounded above is how events in the physical sphere can affect metaphysical realities. Aristotle counseled against arguments requiring movement from one category of reality to another. How can neuronal discharges in the frontal cortex be related to feelings of fear, love, creativity, or conscience? Descartes proposed that this process takes place in the pineal gland, a small structure centrally located in the brain. His idea has been greatly ridiculed, but even if it were correct, the problem of relating one dimension of reality to another one would remain. One is reduced to accepting on faith and the weight of circumstantial evidence that such relationships must exist.

But perhaps such a concept is not so objectionable. Neuronal electrical activity is a form of energetics that may not be so far removed from the metaphysical dimension of the soul. In view of the necessity to surpass the limitations on imagination of human beings, it may be that 'quanta' of energy can actually be *transfigured* (a better expression than transmutation) into spiritual realities. Perhaps Democritus and Epicurus were not far off the mark in conceiving souls to be merely composed of finer types of atoms than those of material substances. These speculations may be looked upon with suspicion but speculations ultimately lead to understanding. What is necessary today for the human condition are not more physiological data and more artificially colored photographs of the brain but more creative thought that can lead to a better understanding of *Homo sapiens.*

~ ~ ~

Once one accepts the compelling intuition that the soul *exists* within a different dimension of reality than the physical self, one can at least imagine the possible disconnection of the two. Here one must resort to *teleology,* a concept that has been described as "the unacknowledged mistress" of scientific research into life. In the case of the higher life forms, all physiological studies utilize teleology—the investigation of the purposes of metabolic and organ functions. The heart pumps blood *for a purpose*, the gastrointestinal tract digests food *for a purpose*, the liver detoxifies noxious substances *for a purpose*, kidneys secrete urine *for a purpose*. And ultimately the brain receives and sends electrical impulses *for a purpose*. These examples do not exhaust all the purposeful activity of the mammalian body but the point has been made. In Aristotelian terms, the final cause is more important than the efficient cause. The latter is at the service of the former.

Aristotle who was master of all the knowledge of his day, metaphysical and scientific, said that man is characterized by the *desire to know.* He might have been talking about himself but it is clear that he was referring to mankind as a whole. Aristotle and his *Lyceum* had little interest in the possible utilitarian consequences of knowledge. More than anything else, this placed the Greek mentality above the contemporary one. Today, all scientific advances are related to the benefits that they can confer on society. But Aristotle and his followers were out for knowledge because they intuitively knew that knowledge expands the interior self. Beginning with his first efforts at independent motility and prehensile activity, the developing human being wants to learn about the world outside of itself. This desire never leaves him although it may be expressed in more and more complex forms culminating in arcane scientific studies and esoteric philosophical speculation. The desire to know in its broadest sense characterizes the human individual.

~ ~ ~

From whence comes this desire to know, which can be readily distinguished from the lower desires of survival and procreation? One can once again resort to a teleological question and say, "Why this never ending motivation to develop the interior self through knowledge?" For the coarser type of individual, knowledge may represent power as is everywhere trumpeted today; but for higher-minded personalities, this is merely one more perversion of thought to which human beings are prone. The best human beings are intuitively aware that knowledge develops the self, not the powerful self, but the spiritual self. The Judeo-Christian scriptures say somewhere, "Be ye as Gods" and that perhaps is the motive force for acquisition of knowledge as understanding and not mere information acquisition.

But to push teleological thinking further, what would be the point of being little gods during life if, upon death, the soul evanesces into thin air, just as the body is reduced to dust? Why all this effort into building one's interior self for the briefest of moments in time, if it comes to nothingness upon death? Then life is truly Shakespeare's "tale told by an idiot, signifying nothing." This is in fact the attitude of many contemporary intellectuals. But if one does not desert the unacknowledged mistress, there is a reason for all of life's activities, including development of a human higher consciousness. However, the reason can only be conceived through persistence of the soul after death.

Death, even more than life, is a mysterious event. The compelling feeling of those who have thought clearly about this event is that there is a withdrawal of an animating force that previously stimulated the conscious activities of which human life consists. If one is not a dogmatic materialist, one may say that in the case of human beings, this animating force is what is referred to by the concept of *soul*. Withdrawal from the body does not imply death of the soul; it implies separation. By a flight of speculation, one can imagine that on separation, the body returns to the dust from whence it came and the soul to the ultimate metaphysical reality from whence it came. As Heraclitus said, the details of the process resist human knowledge or imagination. But now the soul returns in a more developed form and adds something to the ultimate metaphysical reality. Man's soul may need God, but God may need the soul of man as well. In this way, the purpose of spiritual development in individual human beings can be envisioned. However, pursuing this line of thought any further would be approaching the excesses of Gnostic speculation.

~ ~ ~

The ancient Greeks speculated more about the nature of the universe, the nature of God, and their own nature than is currently the case. There was a reaction against these speculations in the form of a philosophical movement known as *skepticism.* The philosopher Pyrrho was the first to organize this movement in a coherent form and Greek skepticism is sometimes called Pyrrhonism. Pyrrho recognized that there is no absolute knowledge and what is called knowledge is usually opinion. One must reserve judgment about most assertions of others; he used the term 'suspension of judgment' (*epoché*) about virtually all forms of presumed knowledge. Edmond Husserl, the founder of modern phenomenology, made use of this expression, although for very different purposes.

Critics of Pyrrhonism raised the objection that in life one cannot reserve judgment about everything; one must act in order to live. Later adherents to the skeptical viewpoint met this objection by developing theories of *probability.* One could act on the basis that a certain assumption is probably true even though there may not be enough reason to believe the assumption is unassailable. Most of our daily activities are based on assumptions of probability rather than absolute truth.

This writer approaches belief in the persistence of the soul after death in the same spirit as the antique skeptics. Even if one wonders whether the soul loses its reality upon death (according to the antique Eleatics, an absurd idea), there are good reasons to think and act as if it persists in its existence after death of the physical body. Some of these reasons are summarized in Plato's dialogue *Phaedo* in which Socrates argues for an after life of the soul. Persistence of one's soul after death has a profound significance for an individual, far greater than leaving behind children, money, memories, good works, etc. One is entitled to believe it has the possibility of serving a divine purpose. It may be the whole purpose of terrestrial life is to fit the soul for serving this purpose. Teleology may well be a tool of divinity. One will think and act very differently with this in mind than if he follows the maxim related by Boccaccio: 'eat, drink, and make merry for tomorrow we die.' There is no need to require absolute truth regarding the fate of the soul.

I have avoided the expression 'immortality of the soul' because immortality has a temporal connotation that has no place in metaphysical thought. Furthermore, the concept of immortality of the soul is associated with myths of hell, punishment, resurrection, and the like that have virtually no degree of probability. It is enough to assign it a purpose after death without invoking eternity.

~ ~ ~

Every thoughtful individual if he examines carefully his sense of self will realize that he intuitively feels a sense of permanence about himself. He cannot imagine his non-existence. Unlike the inevitable aging of one's body, the soul can grow in substance throughout all of one's life. The idea that his soul will disappear some day is an intellectual, not an intuitive feeling. It is impossible to feel reverence for one's own soul if one thinks it will become non-existent upon death. The main function of philosophy should be to help an individual discard 'materialist common sense' in favor of 'metaphysical common sense'. The discarded metaphysical common sense that was present through much of the history of thought must be regained if there is to be real progress in cultural development. Accepting the persistence of the soul after death is the central element of metaphysical common sense.

SUMMING UP

One might venture an opinion that the core problem of contemporary society is lack of regard for the interior self, traditionally known as the *soul*. The technological culture in which individuals live has engendered an attitude of respect only for the tangible and concrete. Thus there is the inane spectacle so often seen of gigantic technological efforts made to keep soulless moribund bodies alive, while no attention is paid to the desperate circumstances of many sentient humans.

The concept of 'subjectivity' refers to the manner by which the interior self manifests itself. This self is not 'objective' and will never be displayed on lifeless instrument panels or be perceived by electron microscopes. But the phenomena of subjectivity are the most real thing in the life of a sentient human being; everything else is a pale imitation of that reality. By ignoring the energy of the interior self, a human being is deprived of the essential nature of his life.

It is of interest that modern 'sub-particle' physics has come to the realization that even the most inert forms of matter are non-particulate in nature. It is an abject failure of consciousness to be unaware that the same is true of the soul.

~ ~ ~

The spiritual correlate of a technological culture is the allegiance to an Almighty God who demands absolute obedience of its worshippers. Most of western culture since the Greco-Roman era has been spoiled by monotheistic ideologies and the delusions that they foster. The unity of self that was exhibited by Greek philosophers has not been maintained because of the compulsion to project the spiritual nature of the self onto a fictitious supreme Deity. The landmark book of Ludwig Feuerbach entitled *Essence of Christianity* (1854) more than a century ago fully documented this situation. Unfortunately, those who come to reject this deity often then reject all spiritual realities. These facts should be realized by those whose minds have been formed within a trusting relationship to Euro-American theistic culture. They have been damaged by this trust whether or not they express surface allegiance to any monotheistic religion. The attitudes of a society are extremely contagious. Within contemporary western societies that do not value the interior self, it is necessary to live as if in a leper colony, taking great care to avoid contagion.

In the case of philosophy, there have been very few spiritually independent thinkers since the devout Roman Emperor Justinian closed the schools of Athens in 521 and exiled the last Greek philosophers to Persia. One has only to experience the writings of the antique Greco-Roman philosophers to become aware of the penalty paid by philosophers coming to maturity in a Christian world.

~ ~ ~

The depth of consciousness characterizing ancient Greek writers is like the sound of the pterodactyl in the twentieth century; there is no experiential basis to envision it. Modern western society does not accept or comprehend an integrated individual since role-playing is the essential element of modern life. Furthermore, the deceitfulness embedded in the ethos of marketing, law, and public relations is so pervasive that language—the principal means of expression of the individual—has been debased into something very different than it was in ancient Greek society. The antique sophists are like idealistic adolescents compared to modern politicians or advertisers. The debasement of language in the decaying Austro-Hungarian Empire was perceived by disillusioned intellectuals like Karl Kraus at the turn of the nineteenth century, but this debasement is far greater today in Europe, the Americas, and elsewhere. Honest expressions of the interior self have become virtually extinct.

~ ~ ~

One could say that communication of a higher consciousness is not an approved cognitive style in modern societies. Our cognitive styles are developed in response to bourgeois values and requirements. From the very beginning of childhood, individuals are oriented toward the analytical evaluation of the space and time-based *hic et nunc*, the 'here and now' that is always the standard of technologically based cultures. A subjective and unified style of thought is discouraged from the beginning of the socialization process, and exaggerated by mass production schooling. The kind of mental activity that a technological culture cherishes is far better performed by computers than by unpredictable humans. Consequently, there is a continuous replacement of human subjective thinking by objective mathematically-based processes.

A society is characterized by the values that are communicated to its members. One has only to be exposed to the contemporary communication world to see that its energies are put into popularization of goods and technologies, which the public has become habituated to desire and believe are essential for civilized living. The ancient Roman public believed that gladiatorial 'games' and free bread were essential to the good life. A classic example of induced dependence in the modern world is provided by the passenger automobile. We are now seeing computers and cell phones following a similar route. An individual who desires a different kind of life becomes a recluse, or even worse, a divided self who cripples his psyche through the splitting process. Misanthropy is the great temptation to someone who values his soul in a bourgeois society.

~ ~ ~

An autonomous individual values leisure far above acquisitive bourgeois activity. However, the person who has come to maturity within western societies, especially that stronghold of bourgeois culture, The United States, needs rehabilitation rather than leisure. Just as a wild animal raised in captivity cannot survive abrupt release into nature, so humans, raised in bourgeois barbarism, cannot be abruptly deprived of their supports and be expected to thrive. The average person under these circumstances will turn to alcohol, drugs, gambling, dogmatic religions, cults, electronic screens, or any of the other soul-destroying vices flourishing in western societies to compensate for lack of interior development. Compulsive golf and supervised travel certainly fall under this heading. The work ethic is often another device utilized to occupy energies of those who have no capacity to utilize leisure for personal growth. At best, there is the harmless pottering about with hobbies or home improvements so popular today. Bourgeois do not have the ancient Greek concept, ψυχης ταμιευομαι, 'storehouse of the soul', to turn to for interior development.

Consciousness of the interior self is an attribute acquired slowly, maintained with difficulty, and dissipated easily. The communities of the aged that have sprung up all over the United States in which are found the usual pathetic obsessions with health, financial security, and family supports are reminders that bourgeois life does not lead to flourishing of the soul. Elderly individuals should study the Greek philosophers and tragedians who flourished in old age. Nothing less will overcome the effects of a lifetime spent in ingesting the poisons of bourgeois existence.

~ ~ ~

Just as the adolescent youth requires freedom from his family to develop his individuality, so the mature individual requires freedom from his society. Modern society, however, is so encompassing and subtly controlling, that it has become virtually beyond human abilities to wrench free from it. Only a powerful and determined movement toward philosophical consciousness can provide an individual with the resources necessary to accomplish his task. The value of philosophy is that it teaches one such a feat is possible even amidst the lures and entanglements of a materialist civilization. The Greeks were not subject to technology as we know it, but they were exposed to the pressures of ambitious politicians, unrestrained hedonism, and ensconced religious traditions. It was the Greek philosophers who helped them overcome these pressures. The role of philosophy is highlighted in Xenophon's dialogue *Symposium* where Antisthenes tells his listeners that philosophy has taught him how to develop and draw upon the storehouse of his soul. In this way, he established himself as an independent entity within his society.

There is no direction in an authentic philosophy that does not lead toward independence from one's society. In the current era, it is only philosophies that teach the meaning and importance of the interior self that are relevant to sentient human beings. The deceptive scholarly learnedness that purports to be philosophy is just monkey chatter to which no attention need be paid.

~ ~ ~

One has difficulty in escaping from the ominous feeling that the contemporary era is a time of increasing spiritual darkness. The literati are largely concerned with amusing their readers so as to retain their popularity. The only so-called spiritual forces currently extant are conventional churches and mindless cults. The former derive their authority from superannuated traditions, the latter from unscrupulous, often mentally ill leaders. It is as if the long period of Christian tyranny over the spirit has rendered the populace incapable of independent spiritual consciousness and left it fit to function only in the domain of mechanistic technology.

However, dark ages seem to precede periods of cultural development. The ancient Greek philosophers appeared at a time of darkness in Greek civilization. The world that they knew must have seemed frightening to them. It was unclear whether the Ionian cities and mainland Greece afterwards would be overwhelmed by political conflicts, by religious obscurantism, or by the Persian Empire. Fear and superstition were rampant. Yet, through an unparalleled effort of mind, philosophers brought to their society conceptions of universality, natural law, and the autonomy of the individual. Their messages must have been heeded by many; otherwise, we would know nothing of them now. The great leap forward of Greek culture arose out of these conceptions.

The specific problems faced by classical Greek society were very different from the problems society faces today. Yet the basic challenge is the same, the need to develop new attitudes and concepts that promote human spiritual development. We westerners need to expel the vestiges of religious idol worship of every type, bring under control a soulless technology, and replace bourgeois values with the values of the interior self. Underdeveloped societies need to be disabused of the belief that scientific knowledge brings beneficial power. This is an idea that is destroying the cultures of the third world as much as smallpox and measles once decimated their populations. The way toward a new culture will not be pioneered by clever technicians or split-personality literati, but by those individuals who have the capacity to unify their souls on the basis of consciousness of the human condition. It is they who will provide the models that are nonexistent at the present time.

~ ~ ~

The ancient Greek philosophers did not represent a biologically superior breed of individuals. Rather the conditions under which they lived permitted the development of the interior self to a greater extent than is possible today. The Japanese people were stunted in their physical growth for centuries because of inadequacies of their diet. During the latter half of the twentieth century, following the example of the healthier western dietary habits, the Japanese have grown to almost western bodily stature. There is every reason to believe a similar phenomenon is involved with the development of the interior self. It is astonishing to realize that entertainment of *hoi polloi* in Greece centered on daylong performances of classic Greek drama. Who knows what other forms of profounder entertainment may have been lost to history? One can be confident that freed of the effects of technologically-dependent, oversensualized, religionized western culture, the interior self would expand to greater depths and heights. But this freedom is not yet in sight.

The ancient Greeks lacked a developmental sense because personal development came so naturally to them. We moderns, however, cannot ignore the nurturing of the interior self since the environment is so inhibitory to its development. An educational system that functions as it should, would above all, teach a child how to utilize leisure for heightening consciousness and developing skills for creative expression. Among other things, this means learning Greek and Latin before computer technology.

~ ~ ~

Elevated consciousness and self expression are the right and left wings of the human spirit aloft; one cannot beat long without the other participating. At all cost, one must express oneself. This is the only means of maintaining individuality in society. Even if the sense that no one listens is overwhelming, that the 'icy solitude' is infinite, one must pay attention to the ferment within and express it to the best of one's ability. There is reason to expect change. There is a profound dissatisfaction with present bourgeois existence that can be found everywhere. There is an insoluble contradiction between the excessive bourgeois consumption upon which the current western system of prosperity rests and the deterioration of the interior self that is the inevitable consequence of these excesses. Other economic ideologies have been no solution, as evidenced by the absurd spectacle of 'communist' societies whose members wanted nothing more than to participate in western bourgeois consumerism. The contradiction in capitalist culture is not between the need for expanded markets and the impoverishment of the working class as Marx thought; it is the incompatibility of consumerism with the growth of the interior self. But the latter is the destiny of the human condition and no economic system that stands in its way can survive indefinitely.

~ ~ ~

Learning through suffering was a profound pedagogical principal discovered by the ancient Greeks. The Greeks suffered and they learned. It may be, however, that contemporary societies have not suffered enough to have learned as a population—or that they contain populations incapable of suffering and therefore incapable of learning. Heraclitus believed that the fate of an individual lay in his own character and therefore in his capacity to learn, which is the basis of character. This is the same as saying one can't rely on society; one has to rely on his own self. One might as well berate cattle for failing to run from the stockyards as to condemn humans of limited character for failing to defend and value their individuality. Perhaps the phenomenon of Greek philosophy may be the result of some cosmic cycle that will repeat itself, perhaps in an even more illuminating manner. Human development does not follow the straight line of historical time, but is cyclical as befits its status as part of the cosmos. Those who are preoccupied with the moment of existence tend to lose sight of cosmic happenings.

A gap of twenty-five hundred years is no bar to a return of the Ionian Greek spirit of philosophy; it is actually an inconsequential pause in the context of the hundreds of thousands of years human beings have existed on the planet before the appearance of historical cultures. When the self-destructive delusion of a dominating deity begins to fade, as it is has already, and the obsession with bourgeois consumerism becomes nauseating to the human soul as it inevitably must, then will exist the possibility for resuming the creation of an *authentic* culture founded upon the interior self and its primacy in human existence. Its American patron saints would be Ralph Waldo Emerson and Henry David Thoreau.

~ ~ ~

The most significant step that could be taken for public education as a means of interior development instead of interior suppression would be the reinstatement of classical languages in the curriculum—Latin as well as Greek, since enlightened Romans carried on the Greek traditions of philosophy. Most important thinkers in the history of modern existential thought created their own work on the platform of ancient Greek philosophy. Goethe, Kierkegaard, Emerson, Thoreau, Nietzsche, Unamuno, Pessoa, Heidegger—all possessed grounding in the Greek language and Greek literature. One might suggest that it was their assimilation of Greek consciousness that prepared them for their contributions to western culture. The abandonment of classical languages is the intellectually emasculating inheritance of bourgeois utilitarian attitudes. Thoughtful individuals need to realize that they cannot regard themselves as 'cultured' persons if they are not familiar with the ancient Greek spirit, only available in our times through their surviving literature.

The Roman ruling class, destitute as they were of a culture of their own, recognized the value of Greek culture and strove to acquire it by learning Greek and sending their children to the philosophical schools at Athens. Ancient Greek culture no longer resides in Athens but its literature, sculpture, and architecture survive, albeit in a tragically decimated form. Every literate person should have an acquaintance with the ancient Greek language and literature because they are a stimulant to interior development and a way out of the Dark Ages of Christian metaphysical obscurantism. Technological, bourgeois, theistic cultures everywhere desire to abolish the interior self. The mentality of the ancient Greek philosophers serves as a powerful antidote to protect the thoughtful individual against suppression of his interior self.

~ ~ ~

If one studies the ancient Greek philosophers, the insights of Emerson and Thoreau, the commentaries of Nietzsche, and the highly original revelations of Nicholas Berdyaev, one has fairly well mined the significant veins of western existential philosophy. Plato is more littérateur than philosopher; he can be left to the literati or perhaps delved into as an antiquarian hobby. All the rest are studies of the various human deviations and divagations, including the Christian variants, and can be safely left to gather scholarly dust in university libraries. Thus conceived, the study of philosophy is a quite straightforward task.

~ ~ ~

The principal pitfall in Christian cultures that prevents the formation of a unified personality is the glorification of Christian 'love', αγαπη, *caritas*, whose meaning is better translated into English by the term *compassion.* Two millennia of a dominant Christian ethos have established compassion for others as the ultimate spiritual value (albeit many groups throughout history hardly have experienced it). In its extreme form, it means the willingness to sacrifice everything, including one's own life, for the object of compassion. When the apostle John preached that God is Love, he drew upon the abstractions of Greek culture to embed this feeling in the Christian mind. This concept of compassion has expanded into the vacuum left by absence of any other aspects of the interior self. The Christian soul feels

200   Philosophical Artwork II

compassion toward biological human life but strangely seems to have no compassion for the life of the human interior self, for what another apostle called "the higher powers." In fact, western culture has lost all consciousness of the presence of higher powers in the human spirit. They have all been given over to worship of an almighty deity or his surrogate manifestation—or more lately, to an omnipresent scientific technology.

Uncontrolled feelings of compassion tend to keep an individual within the bourgeois network of society and its values. Turning away from these values invariably causes pain to those others who are affected; this is why independent individuals in Christian societies are often quite isolated. Yet it is better to have relationships and restrain compassion than to turn to misanthropy. By giving up relationships, one gives up an essential component of human life.

~ ~ ~

The misery threatening the human soul is not that it will be condemned to purgatory or suffer in hell, but that it will remain in the limbo of non-being, a limbo that is all too common in the inhabitants of materialist societies who have lost all feelings for the soul. *Dead Souls*, the title of the major novel of Nikolai Gogol, could apply to much of the population of today, as well as to defunct serfs of Czarist Russia. No assistance in regaining a soul is to be expected from obsolete churches or object-possessed bourgeoisie. The consciousness of one's own soul will emerge through a gradual movement back to its origins from whence appeared the concept of the human soul. It is likely that the appearance of this feeling will be associated with a new appreciation of Greek philosophy. Concern with personal creativity and the arts will replace bourgeois preoccupations with material acquisitions or social development. Stirrings in this direction can be perceived in the vibrant energies of oral poetry circles evident throughout the United States. The daemon of our time will soon tell us to practice ancient Greek—in thought more than in language—in order to recover its lost heritage and set about forging our souls.

~ ~ ~

What individuals should require of future societies is that they allow them the leisure to fulfill and express their interior selves. How to do this as an independent individual is the conundrum that any future society must resolve to justify its existence. T. S. Eliot advised budding poets to obtain employment in the post office so as to free their minds for their versifying. Other solutions may be possible. But it is degrading to be content with an existence that prepares one to be a cog in a bourgeois social system. There are always slaves in societies founded on the bourgeois mentality as earlier defined; this is so whether they are pressed into such a condition by physical force, or second hand, through wage slavery, family slavery, military slavery, commercial slavery, or any of the other techniques devised that suppress the human spirit. However, a society in which the values of interior development predominate does not foster slavery since consumerism and acquisitiveness are reduced to a subordinate role. One can recognize the glimmerings of such attitudes in individuals within the Greek polis distinct from the destructive political chaos that characterized the Hellenic world. Overcoming of materialist values came about then—as it can now—through consciousness of the depths of the human condition, a consciousness that is the mission of philosophical thought to further develop. All other approaches to the flourishing of the interior self have been failures.

THIRD PART

THE MEANING OF THE EROTIC IMPULSE

CURRENT PREFACE

C I think it essential for the growth of the mind to experience a powerful erotic infatuation. Person-centered erotic infatuations should occur at least once during a person's lifetime—and preferably more often. Infatuations are usually principally erotic in nature, but also may directly involve the mind. Philosophical infatuations have a beneficial effect upon one's mind because then one becomes strikingly aware of the force that concepts can exert upon an individual. Actually, there is something strangely erotic about philosophical infatuations. Some of the most memorable periods in my life are connected with philosophical infatuations. Naturally, like person-centered erotic infatuations, such passions fade in time, and one acquires a more measured if less uplifting attitude toward writings that once seemed so powerful.

The Meaning of The Erotic Impulse was first written almost forty years ago while I was under the spell of the Russian philosopher Nicolai Berdyaev and his book *The Meaning of Creativity*. The ideas of Berdyaev, written in his unique Gatling-gun style, no longer have the visceral impact upon me that they once did, although I still have the highest regard for his books. Later, I utilized a different style in significantly altering the writing, although I can still detect the odor of a scholar clinging to parts of it. There are more footnotes in it than in the other two parts of this book. Nevertheless, the essential substance of this work reflects my own experiences and thoughts about that strangest of phenomena in the human condition, the feeling known as the erotic impulse. I believe that it is the philosopher, not scientific psychologists or endocrinologists, who must work out the meaning of erotic impulses. Since I first wrote this part, I have become more convinced that the way in which they are handled by individuals plays a key role in development of their personality, their philosophy, and ultimately their souls.

ORIGINAL PREFACE

It is remarkable how little value has been placed upon erotic experiences in human life. This essay deals with the metaphysical meaning of the erotic impulse. It does not reflect the Dionysian element, which has been more than adequately described by others like Henry Miller and to a lesser extent D. H. Lawrence. The writing is set forth in a philosophic spirit and assumes philosophic attitudes on the part of the reader. It is not a scholarly treatise, still less is it a vehicle for sexual stimulation. The ideas to be discussed may be summarized by stating that erotic feelings are primarily metaphysical in nature, meaning that they arise in the interior self; that the erotic element in life heals one's sexual dividedness and is essential for personality development; and, finally, as in all other aspects of human life, they must be free in order to be authentic.

I have been strongly influenced by the writings of Nikolai Berdyaev whom I regard as the greatest metaphysical philosopher of all time, not excepting Plato, Kant, or any of the other giants in the history of philosophy. The relative neglect of his work can only mean the western world has not been ready for the depth of his insight. Although I quote him liberally throughout, the quotations do not really convey the full impact his writings have had upon my thought.

With Berdyaev, I believe philosophy is not dreaming but action. My life has been an active one; I have been vigorously involved in medical science, in family life, and in intense, at times highly unconventional, personal relationships. Books, which to me represent the available living spirit of their authors, have always been an essential element in my life. I cannot imagine my own life, evolving as it has, without my experiences of the universe of the written word. All these are the experiences upon which I have formulated my conceptions of the erotic impulse. I deeply believe in the privacy of intimate relationships so that I do not intend to advertise the details of mine. However, those who have shared my life will recognize familiar thoughts in these pages. I am grateful to those individuals with whom it has been my good fortune to share intimacy.

It should be understood that the term 'man' as used in this essay usually refers to persons of either sex. English translations of extended quotations that have not been acknowledged are my sole responsibility.

METAPHYSICAL MAN

> Man is a metaphysical animal.
> —Schopenhauer, *The World as Will and Idea*

> Man's essential idea is spirit.
> —Kierkegaard, *Either/Or*

> For there is only one great adventure and that is inward toward the self, and for that, time nor space nor even deeds matter.
> —Henry Miller, *Tropic of Capricorn*

> It is the Spirit that quickeneth: the flesh profiteth nothing: the words I speak to you, they are spirit and they are life.
> —*Gospel According to John* 6:63

It is a revealing feature of modern society that the concept of the *metaphysical* is regarded with distrust. For many, it has a vaguely ridiculous sound, implying superstition, irrationality, or hypocrisy. The materialist worldview so dominates our culture that non-scientific modes of expression hardly receive any attention. There is a general belief that if an idea does not stand up to 'scientific' scrutiny, it is not worthy of serious notice. The role of philosophy is akin to the position occupied by 'culture' in the American frontier where the pressing concerns of survival were all important. In those societies, culture was the domain of Sunday clubs or newspaper writers. Other than men of the cloth, women were the usual bearers of culture, often as a substitute for the spinster state. In contemporary society, concern for culture is perhaps more

206

widely diffused, but the majority of individuals still occupy themselves primarily with the material elements of life, not thinking that in so doing, they consign themselves to a limited, almost infrahuman, aspect of the human condition. They have no awareness of the metaphysical nature of human life.

The metaphysical aspects of existence have always been regarded with suspicion by men of the world. Twenty-five hundred years ago, Plato related his version of the response of one of these men to Socrates' vision of a fulfilling life:

> Callicles: Of course, Socrates, philosophy does have a certain charm if one engages in it during one's youth and in moderation; but if one dallies overlong, it's the ruin of a fellow. If a man, however well endowed, goes on philosophizing throughout his life, he will never come to have the experiences which one must have if he is going to be a man and have the world look up to him...
> Plato, *Gorgias* (trans. by W. C. Helmbold)

This view of the position of philosophy in the minds of practical men has little changed throughout the centuries. Yet now, with the enormous success of science in overcoming nature, men are even more confident in their belief that material 'reality' is at the core of human life. Today, academic philosophers usually also adopt this attitude.

In actuality, the 'reality' is that the scientific worldview is the result of man's long struggle to protect himself from the forces of nature and to gain dominance over them. This is the underlying motive of science and the explanation for its vast elaboration. Since the dawn of civilization, man has struggled to secure his existence against the perils of a hostile world. The technology of science has been his most effective weapon in this struggle. The protection from harsh elements, the dominance over other animal species, the conquest of disease, the securing of food supplies, the harnessing of the energies of nature to enhance the power of men—these have all been the fruit of scientific achievements. It is hardly surprising, therefore, that men tend to worship science and regard it as deserving of their total allegiance. Science has revolutionized their life.

Yet, in spite of its accomplishments, science must be considered as merely a utilitarian aspect of human life. It provides tools for dealing with the material world within which humanity exists. Science requires objective observations, analysis, and verification. The laws of science have to do with the causality relationships of the object world without reference to human values. Science teaches man nothing about the meaning of his life. From the point of view of science, the individual is a meaningless thing, a trivial speck in a space-time universe, hardly different from inanimate matter. Science deals deterministically with the external attributes of man, but has no contact with his interior being, recognizing only a brain that transforms, albeit in a complex manner, sensory inputs into motor responses. The human desire for freedom, his belief in values, his notion of himself as a creative being are, scientifically speaking, totally unreal imaginings, out of touch with the 'realities' of man's place in the universe.

Sooner or later, however, all individuals become dissatisfied with the scientific worldview. They must find reasons for living; they must have a guide to choose between different directions in their lives. This is the domain of *metaphysics* where men create the values in which they believe and by which they should live. The quotations heading this chapter are meant to illustrate that serious thinkers of every type have regarded the human spirit as man's central feature to which all other aspects of his life are secondary, and without which, life is ultimately not worth living.

The spirit of a human being possesses a claim to reality that is every bit as compelling as his perceptions of the external world. In fact, one may consider his interior state to be his truest reality as it has become clear that men's representation of the exterior world is a highly simplified one. Modern physics has revealed the material universe to be a very different place than human sensory perceptions imagine it to be. (It was Kant with his German thoroughness that first clearly separated the world of science from that of spirit.) Even in the simple domain of biology, a human being's sensory apparatus cannot perceive the instinctual drives that propel animals to perform their functions when alive. The 'reality' is that man as observer has a quite superficial view of the world around him; the fact that he can predict and influence certain natural events tends to conceal his limited understanding of them. The only things that science truly teaches men are the means for acquiring additional powers to dominate nature and protect themselves from it.

But the assurance of his physical survival for a limited time period does not satisfy man's yearning to find significance in his life. He desires to have a fuller conception of the meaning of his existence and is inclined naturally toward a metaphysical view of the world. These are truer realities for him than the scientific technologies that give him power over nature. This is the reason for regarding man as a metaphysical (i.e., spiritual) being. "Metaphysical" refers to man's consciousness of his personal reality and his mental connections with the external world as distinct from his biological functions. These apprehensions are at a subjective level of existence. It is pointless to attempt to deal with them with the methods of science. The proper role of science is the study of the world of objects. In so far as man is a part of this world, he is subject to scientific analysis. Insofar as he is a spiritual being he exists in a world beyond science. The unfettered spirit of an individual always responds to metaphysical awareness, surprising those who are enchained by organized, scientific systems.

The need for spiritual self-development in life is man's central task. But men often hesitate to face this task as if they doubted their capacity to respond to such a weighty problem. The massive structures of accumulated sciences and traditional religions act to dwarf the individual's independent thought processes. They often prefer to delegate the spiritual questions of life to agencies outside of themselves. The burdens of civilization lie heavily upon man, the ubiquitous pressures of technology and communication tend to overpower him, and he is tempted to passively take his place as a cog in the machinery of society. He doubts his ability to influence the world and retreats from the ultimate questions of his existence. By adopting a naïve, concrete realism as his world outlook, he submits to society, perhaps only rebelling in minor or inconsequential ways.

Through following such a path, however, man abdicates his position as a spiritual being. Basically, he *is* a spiritual being whose distinctive feature has been his strivings for spiritual development. At his best, this has been his passion and preoccupation. These values are not to be found in the materially based concepts of scientists; they are found in the metaphysically based concepts arising out of consciousness of self and its relationship to the outer world. It is these values, formed out of the tensions arising from living, which influence an individual to establish his own directions in his life. Otherwise, he is aimlessly driven by a myriad of environmental, societal, and physiological influences that affect his being. As long as he relies on values provided by others, man lives as a child, or even worse, as a robot. Independent value formation is the key to the spiritual maturity of individuals.

The linkage of metaphysically based values to institutional religion has been disastrous for spiritual development. Organized religions are social institutions molded by social needs of society. They establish dogmas, demand intellectual conformity, and deal with individuals in their roles as members of society. As does the family, religions nurture and even inspire men. Yet all organized religions are by their nature antithetical to freedom of the spirit. It was the particular genius of Kierkegaard to fully grasp this aspect of Christianity (cf. his *Attack Upon 'Christendom'*).

Since metaphysical matters have not been regarded as a serious topic in the world of science and have been relegated to the domain of religion, it is not surprising that metaphysical meaning has not been found in the subject of *Eros*. For there are no institutions that have been more hostile to the erotic impulse than the organized religions of western society. Between the materialistic scientific world on the one hand and the hostile religious world on the other, the metaphysical erotic impulse struggles to survive in the human spirit. It has been exclusively confined to physical instincts (i.e., sexuality). Freud in his highly influential writings asserted that asocial sexual drives are always at the basis of erotic feelings. They require strict societal control. However, humans have not realized that the withered metaphysical impulse can turn poisonous and produce far-reaching derangements of their personalities.

HISTORICAL

> Man's concept and feeling for the world depends on sex. Sex is the source of being; the polarity of sex is the foundation of creation. The sense of being, its intensity and coloring, has its roots in sex.
>
> –Berdyaev, *The Meaning of the Creative Act*
> (transl. by Donald Lowrie)

> To love all ages owe submission.
>
> –Pushkin, *Eugene Onegin*

The nature of erotic love has largely eluded the intellect of man. It is in poetry and myth that the forces of erotic desire have been best represented. Plato said that love makes every man a poet (legend has it that the aging Plato destroyed the poetry of his youth). One must turn to the medieval troubadours or poets such as Shakespeare, Donne, or Pushkin to gain some idea of the nature of erotic love. Greek mythology regarded *Chaos*, *Gaia,* and *Eros* as the three primal mythical figures in the beginning of the world. The ancient Greeks assigned a most important role to *Eros*.

There is a remarkable lack of serious consideration of erotic love in contemporary philosophical and psychological circles. Schopenhauer, in his sardonic manner whenever speaking of sex, viewed erotic and romantic fantasies as tricks played upon unsuspecting men or women by an omniscient Nature, determined to have her way in the propagation of the species (*Metaphysics of the Love of Sexes*). The commonly held intellectual view on the nature of erotic feelings regards them as an offshoot of the reproductive instinct. As is the case with all animal species, man is instinctively driven to multiply himself. Thus, behavioral

211

psychologists assert, man relentlessly seeks out an appropriate member of the opposite sex to fulfill the mandate of biology. (The question of homosexuality is usually ignored or regarded as a psychological deviancy.)

Sigmund Freud based his theories of personality development upon sexual drives (*Eros* or love instinct) and aggressive drives (Thanatos or death instinct). He conceived of the mind of man as a battleground over which two implacable enemies warred for supremacy—*Eros*, man's inborn biological urge for sex in all its manifestations, and Civilization, the societal world deeply hostile to *Eros,* except for the purpose of maintaining family life. Freud's deep awareness of the nature of the human personality revealed to him distortions imposed by sexual repressions. In his famed essay *Civilization and its Discontents* (1930), Freud catalogued the stressful effects of sexual repression. He expressed doubt that contemporary society could long survive the tensions imposed by these repressions.

Today, in this era of behavioral freedoms, it is curious to see that Freud did not seem to conceive of opposition to the mandates of his society. He regarded rebelliousness against society as outside of the realm of human development. In his pessimistic and socially submissive manner, Freud saw man as a passive object in the grip of societal forces oblivious to his personal desires. This may seem an archaic attitude, but his attitudes toward sex dominate present day concepts of erotic love.

There is an interesting letter written by Freud in response to a French publisher asking him for a contribution to a book planned on the essence of love beyond the realm of sex (quoted in *The Search Within,* T. Reik, 1956).

> My Dear Sir,
>   It is quite impossible for me to fulfill your request. Really you ask too much. Up to the present, I have not yet found the courage to make any broad statements on the essence of love, and I think that our knowledge is not sufficient.
>   Very truly yours,
>   Freud

This response from a man in his fifties who had spent a lifetime probing the innermost recesses of the human mind. Freud's refusal to face the metaphysical element of human sexuality was an obsession with him although his later writings reveal his interest in metaphysical matters. In his discussion of Plato's myth of the origin of sexual dividedness, Freud takes an exclusively physiological approach toward Plato's metaphysics (*Beyond the Pleasure Principle*, 1926), just as he does toward all signs of spiritual life in man.

Many have charitably attributed Freud's attitudes to philosophical naiveté (D. N. Morgan, *Love: Plato, the Bible & Freud*, 1964). However, whatever Freud was, he was not naïve, in philosophy or in any other matters. He was broadly educated, in the classics and in world literature. Freud's deep negativity toward man's creative spirit, especially in the domain of erotic life, brings to mind the words of Mephistopheles in Goethe's *Faust* (Freud greatly admired Goethe and quoted him often):

> *Ich bin der Geist, der stets verneint*
> *Und das mit Recht; den alles was entsteht*
> *ist wert, dass er zugrunde geht…*

> (I am the spirit that always denies,
> and that is right; since all that comes to be,
> deserves to come to nothingness…)

Mephisto tends always to take a dim view of the higher aspirations of mankind and is pleased when humans reveal themselves to be essentially animals, subject to their animal drives. One wonders if the nihilistic spirit of Mephisto entered into Freud's soul. Another letter of Freud's (1918) reveals his attitude toward his fellow man:

> I don't cudgel my brains much about good and evil, but I have not found much "good" in the average human being. Most of them in my experience are riff-raff, whether they loudly proclaim this or that ethical doctrine, or none at all.
> (E. Jones, *The Life and Work of Sigmund Freud*, Vol. II, 1957)

While Freud was a profound thinker, contemporary views indicate a marked trivialization of attitudes toward erotic love. One encounters interpretations of erotic experiences as fun, play, pleasure, joy, etc. Sometimes erotic expression seems to be a form of acrobatics analogous to gymnastics in which the essential element is positional. It is not surprising that in a society dominated by scientific thought, *Eros* becomes an exercise in the technology of copulation.

Freud's views were founded on the Judeo-Christian ethic, which has long regarded erotic love mainly as a means for initiating family life. The significance of erotic feelings is subordinated to the purposes of the family—the key element in social and religious life. St. Paul, the founder of the Christian religion and a highly metaphysical personality, did not extend his metaphysics to include *Eros*. He thought sexual contacts should be completely avoided, but if that severe recommendation was beyond the capacities of an individual, marriage was advised to damp down sexual lusts. It may be that Paul was reacting against the phallic cults of his day. Yet his attitude has greatly influenced contemporary Christianity. There are occasional gestures of valuation of erotic love in liberal religious circles but these are token in nature. The fanatical obsession of the Roman Catholic Church with suppressing artificial birth control reveals the true face of Christianity toward erotic expression. The latter can only be justified in marriage for the purpose of propagation of more Christians.

It is difficult to find philosophers since Plato who have undertaken a serious examination of the meaning of *Eros*. He must be regarded as a landmark figure in this area, albeit as litterateur as well as philosopher. In the course of 2500 years, no other thinker has approached the originality and intensity of his thought on this subject. Plato dealt creatively with this topic because he combined a genius for both poetical and philosophical expression. The harsh sentences of Heraclitus were not for him. In his two great metaphysical dialogues, Phaedrus and Symposium, Plato examined the nature of erotic love. His ideas are expressed through myths related by Socrates and his companions. These dialogues reveal Plato as less of a didactic formalist he is in the *Republic* or his later works. Here he offers thoughts that reach the heights of metaphysical expression never to be surpassed in the history of philosophy.

One of Plato's most seminal ideas (no pun intended) is the conception of the sexually divided nature of men. In a myth recounted in the *Symposium*, Plato attributed this dividedness to man's having been cut in two by the Gods as punishment for his daring effort to scale the heavens and supplant the Gods. Thereafter, all men have been sexually divided creatures, differing from the gods who are whole. Because of their dividedness, men are forever searching for the missing half that will complete them. (In view of the prevalence of homosexuality in ancient Greece, it is not surprising that Plato does not specify a gender for the missing half and does not relate *Eros* to procreation.) The force of erotic desire stems from the overwhelming urge of man to find his missing half. When such a one crosses his path, all his faculties awaken and he experiences erotic love, ερως. He feels an intense desire for union with his missing half.[*]

Plato ultimately goes on to develop his doctrine of *Forms* in which man's human objects of desire become supplanted by the disembodied forms of supreme Beauty and Good. It is his doctrine of *Forms* that came to be known as Platonism and gave rise to the concept of Platonic love.

In western culture, there has been little further development of thought about the metaphysical nature of erotic love. Vladimir Soloviev, often regarded as the founder of Russian philosophy, expounded one of the few substantial contributions to the topic since Plato (*Meaning of Love*, 1895). Soloviev conceived of three levels of 'sex love': animal-physical bonding, social-moral family structures, and spiritual love. True erotic love lies in the integration of all these elements into a harmonious blend, leading the individual out of evil egotism. He recognized the great difficulties

---

[*] The notion of the divided sexual nature of man as the motive force of erotic love is found in religious myths of the beginnings of man. In *Genesis*, sexuality is a result of the 'Fall', a punishment inflicted upon humans by God because of their disobedience. Previously, Adam and Eve had lived in a state of asexual repose. Hindu mythology tells of the androgynous nature of man before the creation (P. Rawson, *Erotic Art of the East*, 1968).

in preserving love in an imperfect society. Soloviev developed a moral view of love as an achievement of faith, transcending the biological and societal elements in life:

> ...for this keen emotion of love comes and passes away, but the faith of love abides... In our materialistic society, it is impossible to preserve genuine love, unless we understand and accept it as a moral achievement.

Nikolai Berdyaev, a younger contemporary of Soloviev, had a powerful sense of the significance of sexuality in the human condition. He vividly described the depth and energies of erotic feelings as illustrated in the epigraph at the head of this chapter. Berdyaev developed a Brahmanic-like notion of conservation of sexual energy for the purpose of creativity. Essentially, Berdyaev believed that the mixture of the physical and the spiritual in erotic expression should gradually give way to the purely spiritual. Both Soloviev and Berdyaev exemplify the type of passionate Russian thinker whose views on sexuality are strongly affected by a fusing of Platonism and Christianity.

Herbert Marcuse expressed the view that sexual repression by society is "surplus repression" and that humanity should move toward eroticization of all aspects of activity (*Eros and Civilization* 1955). Marcuse was much more interested in Civilization, especially in means of controlling it, than in *Eros*. His interests are political and sociological, and in the 1966 preface to his book, he states, "Today the fight for life, the fight for *Eros*, is the political fight." There is actually little to be found about the phenomenon of *Eros* in Marcuse's writings other than a review of psychoanalytic (Freudian) theory.

A more relevant approach to erotic activity was taken by the psychologist Erich Fromm (*The Art of Loving*, 1956). Fromm endorsed the Platonic concept of overcoming sexual polarization as the basis for spiritual love. He proposed that erotic love necessitates an act of will and is not simply the consequence of biological instinct.* Fromm believed that Freud's attitude toward sexuality was too narrowly physiological, suggesting that this narrowness was due to Freud's "extreme patriarchalism." But in his voluminous writings, Fromm subordinates erotic life to the broader issue of human love in all its forms. He asserted, "The most fundamental kind of love, which underlies all types of love, is *brotherly* love." In Fromm's view, *Eros* becomes *Philia.* Fromm's conception of love approaches the Christian tradition in which love of one's fellow man (*Agape*) through love of God is held to be the pinnacle of human affective life. It is interesting that in Fromm's last book *To Have or to Be* (1976), he evinces little interest in erotic love in his vision of "The New Man and the New Society." Like Marcuse, Fromm turned to social engineering as the path to human fulfillment. Yet Fromm thought deeply about the human condition, and his books are rich mines of insight into the subject.

Norman Brown was a twentieth century mystic who enthroned erotic love as the central feature of the human condition (*Love's Body*, 1966). Brown wrote in a Joycean style of stream of consciousness and did not elaborate a coherent concept in his writing. He believed that sexual energies are a means for fusion of mankind into a state of cosmic oneness, reminiscent of Soloviev's idea of *syzeugy.* Brown seems to fall within the tradition of Eastern mystics who see the destiny of man fulfilled in the achievement of a state of silent Nirvana.

Procreation, family life, brotherly love, social justice, and mystical states all have their own justifications. Even casual sexual intercourse has its place alongside athletics, dance, games, etc. However, these forms of activity do not meet the human need for erotic love. Experience reveals it to be a unique *feeling* in the soul of an individual unrelated to social relationships. Preoccupation with false issues or submission to societal controls ultimately leaves the individual unfulfilled and depressed. Erotic expression has a far deeper meaning in the life of man than could be surmised by exposure to current attitudes toward it. In its essence, it must be

---

* A penetrating discussion of the superficial attitudes toward erotic life is found in Rollo May's *Love and Will*, (1969). "Man's task is to unite love and will" was May's central theme.

apprehended as a *metaphysical desire* that arises from the metaphysical nature of man.

The natural inclination of an individual for erotic expression is always rejected by society. An individual must value his erotic feelings in order for them to survive in the world. Therefore, he must have a conception of the meaning of erotic love. As a metaphysical being, man requires a concept of the meaning of things for them to play a significant role in his life.

It has been a loss to modern culture that the Platonic tradition of philosophical consideration of erotic life has been abandoned.[*] His ideas deserve reconsideration in the light of the history of thought and the complexities of contemporary life. It is not enough to describe erotic feelings—there is no shortage of such descriptions in literary history—there must also be understanding of the meaning of the erotic impulse for the development of personality. In one of the great creative metaphors of poetic imagination, the Russian poet Pushkin intimated his understanding of the role of *Eros* in personality development, and also revealed his own awareness of its tragic potential for human beings:

> To love all ages owe submission,
> To youthful hearts its tempests bring
> the very boon they would petition
> as fields are blessed by storms of spring:
> the rain of passion is not cruel,
> but bears refreshment and renewal –
> There is a quickening at the root
> that bodes full flowers and honeyed fruit.
> But at the late and sterile season,
> at the sad turning of the years,
> the tread of passion augurs tears:
> Thus autumn gusts deal death and treason

[*] C. J. Jung in his discussions of *eros, ego, logos, self, anima, animus, etc.* elaborated an imaginative terminology for the metaphysical self. But like many psychiatrists, Jung does not abandon the posture of the analytic psychotherapist pontificating from on high. He is more interested in psychoanalysis than philosophy (*Aion: Phenomenology of the Self*).

and turn the meadow into a marsh
and leave the forests gaunt and harsh.
                    Alexander Pushkin, *Eugene Onegin*
                         (trans. by Babette Deutsch)

ORIGIN AND NATURE

Leporello – "Only leave the women alone."

Don Giovanni – "Leave the women alone! Idiot! Leave the women alone! Don't you know they are more necessary to me than the bread that I eat, than the air that I breathe!

–Mozart's *Don Giovanni*

Every person yearns to be fulfilled in erotic love and openly or secretly dreams of its possibility. It is sad to see how either restless or depressed human beings can become over lack of erotic fulfillment. There is great difficulty in achieving a sense of self if one has not loved and been loved in the spirit of *Eros*. This need for erotic love is the Achilles heel of mankind.

Kierkegaard believed that *Don Giovanni* by Mozart was the greatest of all operas because of its successful evocation of the erotic impulse. However, for individuals, it is not enough to sing of love. One also needs to understand it and the actions that stem from it. The lack of comprehension of the meaning of erotic love makes it vulnerable to hostile pressures at many different levels of society.

Fundamentally, the erotic impulse stems from man's *sexual dividedness*. An individual is either male or female; he cannot be both. (Hermaphroditism is an anatomical anomaly having nothing to do with gender identity.) Yet in his depths, he longs for his missing sex and therein lies the secret of the erotic impulse. It is in the nature of human beings that they strive to enlarge and complete themselves. As an individual organism, man is little different from other animals; he is tiny, insignificant, a grain of sand in the immensity of the universe. However, within him lies the seed of a desire to be more. Each individual recreates his own history of the race by the means he chooses to develop himself.

The essential feature of erotic expression is a desire for fusion with the loved one. Sexual intercourse is an integral aspect of this desire as individuals attribute special significance to the sexual relationship. Yet other forms of mingling may have equal meaning. "Letters mingle soules," wrote John Donne bearing witness to the powerful impact of the written word. The one indispensable requirement for erotic expression is a personal relationship that humans, with their complex mental apparatus, can achieve in many ways.

The significance of authentic erotic expression lies in its spiritual nature within an increasingly spiritless society. In no other human activity does man's body and soul act in such harmony. When an individual is joined to his lover, he leaves mundane daily life and receives an intimation of escape from time and space. Lost in the depths of erotic feeling, he undergoes an experience like none other in society's vale of tears. Restlessness and striving fly away through the miracle of erotic fulfillment. For once, a lover is at peace with himself. It goes without saying that mere spiritless copulation does not produce this experience.

The attribution of erotic feelings to the procreative instinct is most charitably described as simplistic materialist thinking. Any experience with erotic feelings confirms that, consciously or unconsciously, they have nothing to do with reproduction. On the contrary, great lengths may be resorted to in order to prevent insemination. Nor is erotic love connected in any way with family formation. The erotic lover has no thought of creation of new life or of family.

Those who believe that the goal of sexual orgasm is at the heart of erotic activity are preoccupied with the price nature demands from erotic activity. But the orgasmic experience is different from the erotic one; it is demanding, violent, and irresistible. Through orgasm, man's biological nature preempts his personality, revealing a human being to still be an animal. However, the force of orgasm should not dominate an individual any more than his other material needs.

An act of imagination and a leap of faith are necessary for man to love erotically. The risks that are taken for erotic expression require that the lover see only the essential sexuality and the unspoiled personality of the loved one. All of the deficiencies and faulty human traits must be passed over as trivial. Someone inspecting a portrait by Rembrandt does not minutely inspect the details of the execution. This would destroy the spiritual experience conveyed by Rembrandt's artistic genius. This is not 'unrealistic'; rather it is supremely realistic. It is a refusal to become entrapped in the layers of materialist minutiae that often consume individuals. The Schopenhauers and Freuds of this world teach 'reality', but behind their words, one can smell the whiff of fear of the dangers of erotic commitment. Even Kierkegaard, who had a keen appreciation of erotic experience, ultimately denied it a place in his own life, and thereafter, wrestled with its significance in his own writings. Those who fear the loss of control in their lives that erotic expression entails, always deny the spiritual element of such expression.

The tragic nature of erotic love lies in the fact that man can never overcome his sexual dividedness with the limits imposed upon him by it. Erotic experience will give him moments of peace, but he will always return to his natural state. Even more, the conditions of erotic life will expose him to grave risks and adversities that may overwhelm him. There are no material or social advantages associated with authentic erotic experience. Energies devoted to it will not be available for other activities that may be necessary for personal survival. The legend of Don Giovanni reveals the fate that lies in wait for whoever gives oneself over totally to erotic life.

Therefore, it is essential for the individual to understand the value of erotic experiences in his personal development. He knows that his destiny is to make more of himself than he is at the moment of his birth. He may choose to acquire learning, wealth, power, family, creativity. He wishes to enlarge himself in all areas; one might say he wishes almost to become godlike. In some sense, the Faust motif applies to all men even though they are limited by their energies, age, and the constraints of their circumstances. Yet every man knows his human destiny and strives to accomplish it to the extent possible for him.

For some reason, men have not really grasped the fact that their greatest limitation is their sexual dividedness. Half the world is denied to them; they are not woman or not man. Most men fatalistically accept their condition just as previously men accepted poverty, malnutrition, or disease as acts of nature over which they had no control. History reveals, however, that man is not fatalistic by nature. He acts to surmount fate wherever and whenever he can. The fact that he is born male or female does not mean he cannot strive to overcome this limitation. Erotic expression is his challenge thrown out to his anatomical fate. Denial of *Eros* leads to stunted personalities. This unique form of self-development is only to be found in advanced societies. Erotic life is not seen in primitive cultures.

Men often strive to develop themselves through proximity to ones possessing the desired attributes. Men may wish to associate with the rich, the powerful, the learned in order to acquire their virtues, and become like them. Development does not occur merely by proximity, yet others influence us and it has been long known that a person often grows to resemble his friends. The analogy cannot be extended too far as the sexual self exists at a different level than affluence, celebrity, etc. Androgyny as a permanent state is a delusion since it is at odds with the basic makeup of human beings.

Modern interest in the concept of androgyny focused on freeing men and women from extreme forms of sexual polarization, particularly for women who have been restricted by male domination. Androgyny was a central theme of the London Bloomsbury movement, especially as exhibited in the life and writings of Virginia Woolf.[*] There is little doubt that gender assignments have often been harmful; again especially for women. Sex gender is not an assignment of personality style, still less should it be a justification of power for a dominant sex. Nor is prowess in intercourse the main sign of the sexual nature of men. This is clearly illustrated by the intense erotic experiences of many men not involved with physical sex. Even celibacy is not

---

[*] An interesting discussion of androgyny and the Bloomsbury movement can be found in the book *Toward a Recognition of Androgyny* by Carolyn Heilbrun.

sexlessness—Jesus has appeared to many as an erotic personality as evidenced by his effect upon women and his own affinity toward them.

But misconception of the nature of human sexuality should not obscure its essential meaning in human life. The absence of sexual identity results in a deviant personality who has great difficulty fulfilling himself as a human being. Every aspect of animal existence reveals sexual polarization; microscopic studies show that every cell in the human body has a sexual signature in the form of chromosomal patterns specific for males or females. Other differences also probably exist. Human beings cannot become androgynous without doing violence to their human status. The instinctive revulsion against androgyny is well founded; it is a serious deformity of a human being. Those who reject their sexual identity become dehumanized and are objects of scorn or pity, whatever their accomplishments in other areas. True sexual androgyny is a more extreme deviation than homosexuality since it claims total sexual self-sufficiency, which is only possible at the expense of one's human qualities.

Thus erotic expression may be metaphorically viewed as a gesture of defiance of the human spirit against the mandate of biology. It is an expression of rebelliousness against sexual limitations. Immersed in the erotic experience, man is complete for a moment, healed, escaped from the state of sexual dividedness. But, tragically, it is not forever as the erotic experience quickly fades and erotic love is the most fragile of flowers.

The concept of 'healing' is important to the understanding of the erotic phenomenon. Sexual dividedness may be regarded as a deep biological wound of the human condition. From this wound grows many of the evils of human life. Erotic love briefly heals this wound; it reestablishes the metaphysical harmony in man that is disrupted by his sexual wound. Erotic love requires metaphysical consciousness; one loves the qualities of womanhood or manhood in another. When someone experiences erotic love, he is cultivating awareness of his metaphysical nature. This is a highly beneficial act for his personality. Absence of erotic expression leads to desiccation of one's personality, premature aging, and perhaps even senility.

Plato was interested in erotic love because its metaphysical aspect related to his doctrine of forms. 'Platonic love' is not asexual; it is the setting aside of physical sexuality in order to give room to metaphysical sexuality. Plato did not accept the intimate association of both forms of sexuality. However, Plato lived at the dawn of western thought, he did not appreciate personal freedom and he was diverted by preoccupation with homosexuality. A mythical interpretation of man's sexual wound and its significance can be found in Genesis 2:21-24.

Although an individual can never permanently escape sexual dividedness, his drive toward erotic expression and experience can transform his personality. It has been learned that personality is formed through the efforts of self-expression and the suffering entailed by it. Those who love and have been loved erotically differ from those without such experiences. A 'woman who has been loved' is a transformed person but the same is true of a man. A life devoted to bourgeois trivialities becomes quickly boring to those who have experienced erotic fulfillment.

The effect of erotic experience is not as a passive personality change, but is an unveiling of new dimensions of the spirit and a stimulus toward creation of new values. Individuals are strongly affected by deep experiences and they should choose them with the greatest of care. Intelligent individuals greatly value the experience of erotic love. A cursory survey of evil men of history reveals they knew little of erotic love (e. g. Napoleon, Hitler, Stalin). It is difficult to avoid the conclusion that failure to experience *Eros* leads to diversion of energies into destructive activities. At the source of human desire, both erotic and aggressive expressions stem from a basic energy inborn in the individual.

It is desirable for men and women to cultivate their awareness of their sexual 'wound' and realize their dependence upon each other for healing. It is only from erotic feelings that men develop consciousness of themselves as limited sexual beings. Erotic experiences reveal that sexual dividedness has an existential significance, that through it they relate to and are dependent upon others in the external world.

The bourgeois individual thinks to escape this dependency by possession of objects (including human ones) and through organization of life into fixed patterns. In the depths of bourgeois acquisitiveness lies an unconscious fantasy of permanent healing of the sexual wound though acquisitions. This is an absurd delusion. It is not the destiny of human beings to ever achieve such a state without loss of their humanness.

Women are similar to men in that they experience *Eros* as a healing phenomenon. Through the intensity of a man's desire to merge with her, a woman becomes aware of both his and her sexual dividedness. The philosopher Miguel de Unamuno, in a typically Spanish thought, emphasizes women's compassion for men's sexual need (*The Tragic Sense of Life*). Women can also be sadistic and torture men out of resentment and envy. Such women are drawn to the violence of orgasm, while disinterested in erotic expression.

A woman differs from a man in that she has motherhood as another way of dealing with the sexual wound. The newborn infant creates a new harmony for the mother. The mother-infant dyad is a metaphysically healed state. Yet the fate of the mother is to become again sexually divided. Infants grow and leave their mothers. Again, the sexual wound reappears in a woman and her erotic desires reappear. The maternal experience added to the erotic one produces more instability in a woman's life compared to a man.

A man's contribution to the mother-infant dyad is through impregnation. Unconsciously, he carries a healing seed for a woman within him. Man does not love in order to impregnate; he does so involuntarily as a consequence of erotic fulfillment. It was diabolically clever of nature to connect impregnation with *Eros* and most fortunate for the survival of the race. Animal species have died out because of loss of the procreative instinct.

Sexual desire draws man into this world; spiritual desire draws him to another world, the metaphysical world. Both of these forces play upon him during his lifetime. They form the fundamental dichotomy of the human condition. The formation of his personality is based upon the way he harmonizes these forces.

It can be concluded that the purpose of erotic activity is to heal the sexual wound of human beings. The concept of sexual dividedness and its implications ought to be brought into conscious awareness of the individual. Through this concept, he can better deal with his erotic drives that seek wholeness, albeit only temporarily. However dimly it may shine, the light of metaphysical awareness justifies, strengthens, and supports the erotic desires of individuals.

D EVELOPMENT

When I was a child, I spoke as a child, I understood as a child, I thought as a child; but when I became a man, I put away childish things.

−St. Paul, I Corinthians 13:11

A sense of the importance of development in human life is essential for understanding it. Man does not magically spring to the fullness of life all at once as in a fairy tale or myth. He begins as a helpless newborn possessing energy and instincts but nothing indicating the human potential within him. The miracle of creation is recreated every time a newborn infant develops into a spiritual human being. There is nothing in the natural world that can account for the appearance of the human soul. It is the only miracle men have ever witnessed yet its commonplace nature leads them to ignore its significance. The study of human development does not explain this miracle but it does allow one to have a closer look at its enactment.

Man's desire to experience erotic feelings appears soon after birth when he moves from the protection of the womb into a cold external world. At that time, he is in the most vulnerable period of his life. One of the contributions of Freud to the understanding of human behavior was the recognition of infant sexuality. The infant's pre-erotic expression lies in participation in cuddling and in responding to the nurturing overtures of its mother or surrogate mother. When infants cannot cuddle, because of brain damage or other reasons, they often go on to exhibit serious defects in all forms of social development. Infants who exhibit childhood autism, a condition of profound disturbances of personal relationships, do not participate in cuddling during infancy. It is a plausible hypothesis that the absence of early pre-erotic experience may be responsible for subsequent personality disorders.

Sometime during the third year of life, children become aware of their sex identity. From that time on, erotic expression and sexual awareness become increasingly fused. Freud drew attention to the early erotic interest of a child in its opposite sex parent through his description of the *Oedipus* complex (a better label might have been found!). This is later followed, its tempo depending on the emerging temperament of the child, by interest in other members of the opposite sex. Children are curious at an early age about the opposite sex. They sense the barrier that divides the sexes even though there is a tendency by adults to minimize this distinction in children.

Early sexuality is exploratory and playful, reflecting the curiosity and playfulness of children. On the other hand, children have a strong sense of modesty unless they are severely emotionally disturbed or maltreated. The need for privacy of their sex organs is one of the earliest manifestations of human sexual awareness. In a certain sense, the sex organs *are* shameful as they indicate the primal deficiency of man, his sexual dividedness. Exposure of the sex organs reveals this deficiency to the world at large. It is quite significant that the biblical account of the origin of consciousness in the first humans referred to the covering of their sex organs. Mental development of children tends to recapitulate the mental development of mankind.

The sexual development of individuals becomes more apparent in puberty with the hormonally induced appearance of secondary sex characteristics—breasts, genitalia, body hair, etc. The maturing individual becomes aware of the ability to engage in sexual intercourse—in the broadest sense of the term. As this awareness grows, the desire to do so grows accordingly. This knowledge of one's sexual potential and desire to fulfill oneself sexually is more important than the instinctive drive to copulation. The interest in sexual intercourse is largely a psychologically determined state. As in all forms of human activity, the mental conception is dominant. It can be observed that those who have no contact with the opposite sex and no opportunity for heterosexual experience have little sense of need for it. Sexual intercourse may also be expressed through same sex activities or other deviant sexual habits. The most common form of deflected sexuality is self-stimulation through masturbation. There is a street saying that no one with an agile hand need be sexually frustrated.

Early adult modes of sexual expression are quite varied depending on the personality of the individual. Joining with an object of erotic desire takes different forms in men and women, involving personality traits like forcefulness, seductiveness, or submissiveness. Stages in erotic development produce many challenges to the ingenuity of an individual, much as do games of skill or strength. However, the underlying motif of all developing eroticism is overcoming the consequences of existence as a sexually polarized human being.

The awareness of the capacity to reach full physical orgasm is an important psychological need of adult humans. The dominant thought after orgasm is a sense of accomplishment rather than recollection of pleasure, which is instructive as to the meaning of the act. There is an ancient association of orgasm with death, because of the weakening of life force immediately afterwards. (Death can occur after orgasm, regarded by some as the supreme exit from life.) In certain societies, sexual intercourse has been regarded as an obligation rather than as a gratification. This is a key tenet in polygamous societies that still persists in the world. Those who are unable to reach orgasm during the sex act may become obsessively concerned with their inability to do so. (Fear and guilt are the main barriers to orgasmic experience.) This can be an insuperable obstacle to erotic development.

Physical sexuality can be elaborated to involve a great variety of sensual experiences. Currently, there is much interest in foreplay and mutual pleasuring, reminiscent of the hedonistic activities that flourished in ancient Greco-Roman society. The Christian attitude toward sex suppressed the open display of sexual hedonism, although it always survived through prostitution and other various concealed ways. Sensuality is an important aspect of human sexuality but ought not to be identified with erotic love, to which it is related as a precursor.* There is little of the spiritual in

---

* In Hindu culture, sexuality was joined to religion as revealed in Hindu temple 'erotic' sculpture. This has been viewed by some as spiritualization of sexuality; however, spiritual erotic expression is

carnal hedonism; the latter principally provides physical sensation and relief. Organized commercial hedonism (prostitution) is mainly directed toward the orgasmic aspect of sex. Societal attitudes that criticize prostitution while allowing pervasive sexual stimulation in the form of advertising are totally hypocritical.

It is usually necessary for individuals to involve themselves with pre-erotic experiences before erotic life can appear in spiritual form. There is great variation in tempos of erotic development according to circumstance and personality. The earlier forms do not disappear completely but are superimposed upon as in embryological development of organ systems. One may often find vestiges of early pre-erotic sex in the erotic life of men and women.

As the soul of a human individual develops and spiritual values emerge, his relatedness to the other sex assumes spiritual forms. With experience, man learns of the correspondence of mind and imagination that obviates need for force or seductiveness. Physical sexual qualities become subordinate to a dominant spirituality. Music becomes a significant avenue of erotic expression (as with Don Giovanni). Popular love songs often exhibit a far greater understanding of erotic love than do societal attitudes or textbooks of psychology.

Through poetry, one can concentrate the core of his erotic feelings. The love poetry of Shakespeare and Donne are illustrations of the intensity of feeling communicated through poetic expression. It is their metaphysical awareness that lends passion and depth to their work. The gift of a love poem is one way for an individual to communicate erotic feelings.

These spiritual modes of expression are not sublimations of animal instincts as Freud claimed, but rather represent a higher development of the soul. It may be that sexual intercourse itself is a potent stimulus to erotic relationships. It is lovers in each other's arms, having given all they possess to each other, who are in a true state of spiritual communion. The momentary exhaustion of physical energies is the prelude to the state of erotic fulfillment. Only reluctantly do lovers return to the world and to their state of

---

difficult to find in the impersonal phallic worship found in parts of India.

sexual dividedness. The fusion of man and woman through erotic expression is the ultimate ecstatic experience in life. Its meaning for personality development is yet to be fully comprehended.

L OVE OBJECTS

> ...some women fascinate by their beauty, or by anything you like, all in a minute; while you may ruminate over another for six months before you understand what is within her; and that to see through and love such a woman it is not enough just to look at her, it is not enough to be simply ready for anything, one must have a special gift besides.
>
> –Dostoevsky, *A Raw Youth*
> (trans. by Constance Garnett)

The key to understanding man's erotic activity lies in grasping its metaphysical nature and the distinction between sensual and erotic expression. The sensual is the physical aspect of *Eros*, but does not capture its essence. What mature humans seek with erotic desire is only found through awareness of its metaphysical aspect. The essential quality possessed by the recipient of erotic love is one's missing sexuality. This may be discerned at a glance by a lover. Shakespeare wrote that he who did not love at first sight never loved at all. Yet erotic love may also grow gradually. Dostoevsky was more profound than Shakespeare when he wrote the passage prefacing this chapter. In this passage, Dostoevsky reveals his understanding of the metaphysical nature of erotic love.

Erotic attraction is a truly mysterious phenomenon reflecting the metaphysical depths of erotic love. Not much has been written on the subject. Plato believed that like sought like in accord with the homosexual proclivities of his society. Plato's failure to grasp the metaphysical significance of heterosexual love is a serious flaw in the otherwise cosmic scope of his thought. Schopenhauer expressed his awareness of the metaphysical nature of *Eros* by concluding that men loved intelligence in women and women character in men. (But Schopenhauer's own choice of street women as love objects suggests hypocrisy on his part.) In today's era of scientism, the topic is not regarded as a subject for serious discussion by philosophers. If the subject is discussed, it is usually from the perspective of eugenics.

The face and the form are the two physical elements that initiate erotic attraction. In facial and bodily configuration, man recognizes his missing sexuality. For those with a discerning eye, the spirit of the love object emerges through facial expression and bodily movements. Human eroticism requires the integration of the physical and spiritual aspects of sexuality. Mature individuals search for this integration in their quest for erotic fulfillment. One without the other is of little value. Attraction by facial expression alone leads to sexless relationships, attraction to form alone leads to hedonism. Neither by itself can result in erotic fulfillment.

Besides the erotic impulse, other forces act to attract humans to each other. Often these are interwoven with erotic attraction reflecting the complexities of human relationships. People are attracted to polar opposites in areas other than their sexual nature. Beauty, youth, character, wisdom, and maturity are traits that are valued in different degrees. Wealth and power notably attract those who yearn for these attributes. Friendship, loyalty, and compassion are important feelings that arise in the course of relationships, especially family relationships and sometimes work relationships. Vows of fidelity may bind individuals together for a lifetime. Yet erotic attraction remains the most fundamental and pervasive of all forces drawing individuals together. Sooner or later, its power makes itself felt in the lives of everyone.

The characteristics of the object of erotic interest correspond to the stage of development of an individual. Man's unconscious sense of the nature of his sexual dividedness determines his choice of love object. This changes throughout his life. Efforts to rigidify his attraction and rendering immune to change are doomed to failure—except at the cost of devitalizing the erotic impulse. Such pressures are applied by men or women who have been de-eroticized themselves and wish to establish stability in an area of life where no stability can exist. Erotic love cannot be forced—only embraced or abandoned.

'Deviations' can occur in the course of the development of the capacity for erotic love. The most common is homosexuality. This ancient sexual habit of mankind has been usually condemned by society (Greco-Roman society was an exception) although the reasons for so viewing it have been clouded by religiosity and bigotry. The defense of the practice by Plato is persuasive but in the end untenable. Essentially, Plato saw homosexuality as the affinity of like for like, thus justifying the habits of his society. He regarded heterosexual intercourse as a form of animal behavior whose only value lay in production of new citizens for the state. The approach to heterosexual love found in *The Republic* is that of a cattle breeder. Yet, shot through the characterization of Socrates in the dialogues is evidence of Plato's discomfort with the practice. It was through his doctrine of forms that Plato succeeded in separating the *Ideal of Beauty* from the body of the boy lover. His prejudice in favor of homosexuality prevented Plato from recognizing the significance of sexual polarity in human beings, which his profoundly metaphysical mind would have otherwise certainly perceived.

In contemporary times, homosexuality is again, as in ancient Greco-Roman society, viewed as a normal alternative to heterosexuality. Homosexuals are human beings and are justified in resenting persecution or ridicule. Yet the meaning of this sexual practice is that individuals do not move beyond the condition of sexual polarization, regardless of surface behavior. It is a problem, not of a physical preference but of a metaphysical one. Homosexuals are not physically or psychiatrically deviant, but they are metaphysically constricted. They are same sex limited. Without metaphysical awareness, one cannot understand the basis of homosexuality or its effect on personality development (cf. Berdyaev, *Destiny of Man* and Fromm, *Art of Loving*).

Excessive preoccupation with physical aspects of erotic love is common in today's metaphysically empty societies. Obsessions with sexual experiences expose individuals to sordidness and distortions in their lives. In more subtle ways than prostitution, women are often sex objects to men without spiritual interchange. Commercialism usually exists in these 'mistress' relationships but not in the manner of organized prostitution. '*Hetaera*' relationships with highly cultured courtesans that existed in ancient Greece are rare in English-speaking countries. They may be more common in France. Even in family life, the woman may be in a type of legalized prostitution where she serves only the physical and social needs of the husband.

Concentration on adornment of face and body are signs of primitive sexuality; cosmetic preoccupations often coincide with an absence of the spiritual aspect of eroticism. Other, more florid deviations and perversions can be found described in psychiatric texts. However, the most common and yet least recognized distortion of erotic expression is in marriage. Married individuals accept, to a greater or lesser extent, loss of freedom of their erotic life. The nature of this suppression will be considered in 'Fetters on Erotic Love.'

In its most meaningful and healing form, erotic expression relates to both the body and spirit of the loved person. 'Beauty' refers to the integrated sexuality of the person as in a 'beautiful person'. Reference to a 'beautiful face' or a 'beautiful body' suggests absence of integrated sexuality. These must be thought of as relative judgments as no human being possesses a perfect erotic harmony of body and spirit. Dostoevsky has one of his characters state that "beauty will save the world!" revealing his intuition, albeit exaggerated, of the relationship of person beauty to the human need for erotic fulfillment.

Shyness refers to inhibition of erotic expression. It is based upon unconscious shame of one's own state of sexual dividedness, which is uncovered by the feeling of *Eros*. It is a sign of metaphysical awareness to be shy; the absence of shyness is associated with absence of spirituality. Shyness can be dissolved by alcohol; it is no accident that taverns are the common refuge of those seeking erotic fulfillment. The embarrassment of nudity stems from the same origin as shyness. Those who have no sense of shame upon exposure of their sex organs have no metaphysical awareness of sexual polarization. There is meaning to the biblical account of the origin of shame of nakedness in Adam and Eve corresponding to the origin of human thought. Habitual nudity probably diminishes the awareness of the metaphysical meaning of sex identity. One has empathetic shame at the sight of the sexual organs of a member of one's own sex; it is less so with the opposite sex. The nakedness of the superb figures of Greek sculpture no doubt is due to the absence of metaphysical awareness of sex in Greek society.

Conversely, too much sensitivity to the meaning of sexual polarization may paralyze erotic expression. A certain hardness in life is necessary for personal development. The overly sensitive fall by the wayside. One can also remember that erotic relationships fulfill two, not one. It is never immoral to be responsive erotically if the response reflects authentic feelings, even though it may occasion difficulties in one's personal circumstances.

However fulfilling are erotic experiences, man's state of sexual dividedness is never fully healed in this world. It can be soothed, mitigated, or understood, but always at the end of erotic fulfillment reappears the specter of sexual dividedness. Erotic expression helps one deal with his wound but only death eliminates it. It is well that this is so because man's erotic longings bring him in contact with his fellow humans. Otherwise mystical flights or materialist preoccupations would carry him into inhuman conditions of existence. This is the fate of those who deny themselves erotic expression at whatever stage of their life. In the human condition, sexually divided men and women need to personally relate themselves to a member of the opposite sex.

In time, the erotically fulfilled man comes to realize that the object of his desire is experienced not primarily as an individual personality, but as a symbol of his missing sexuality. In a metaphysical sense, erotic love is directed toward the sexual 'Form' in its Platonic meaning, not toward the other individual's concrete sexuality. Naturally, feelings of attachment and compassion emerge in erotic relationships. The most successful ones occur when the partners are alike in nonsexual aspects of their spirit, but opposite in sex. Yet always, expression of man's erotic impulses are basically directed toward a sexual symbol represented by the love object.

SLAVERY AND FREEDOM

> Autonomy is therefore the ground of the dignity of
> human nature and of every rational nature.
> –Kant, *Groundwork of the Metaphysic of Morals*

Freedom is the most important of all the conditions that provide the framework for human development. It is a basic assumption of civilized life that children have the right to develop their physical, intellectual, and spiritual potential. In one sense, there is always an element of the child in man, needing development throughout his life. The absence of development at critical growth stages may permanently damage the mind, as well as the body of human beings. Freedom is a metaphysical concept, not to be explained on a simple biological basis, but to be thought of as endowing the individual with unfathomed potentials for self-development. It represents the energies of animate existence brought to its highest level (cf. N. Berdyaev, *Slavery and Freedom*).

Without freedom, man is a passive creature, incapable of experiencing one of the most precious aspects of human life: the capacity for independent self-expression. An individual without freedom may appear to be self-directed, but the appearance is a fraud whose false nature is apparent to free men. Without freedom, man is at the mercy of his environment; determinism becomes the rule of his existence and his life becomes a series of reflex responses, albeit at a level of complexity beyond that seen in the rest of the animal world. It is one of the strange aspects of human life that men, acting through social institutions, have attempted to limit the personal freedom of their fellow men. Had not men's taste for freedom and dislike of personal fetters developed concomitantly with the evolution of society, it is likely that human life would now resemble ant society, differing only in details.

If one looks at the history of societies, great forward leaps coincide with the acquisition of certain forms of freedom. The flowering of Greek society in antiquity was based upon the appearance of certain forms of freedom for the individual that were foreign to the rest of the world at that time. In his famous funeral oration for slain Athenian soldiers, Pericles attributed the superiority of Athenian culture to the freedom of the citizens of Athens and admonished his countrymen not to relinquish their freedoms. Pericles' exhortation was not or could not be followed and with the loss of freedom of the Greek *polis*, Greek creativity faded away.

The phenomenon of Christianity is one of the most remarkable episodes in human history. It would have been impossible to anticipate the enormous consequence that flowed from the teachings of an obscure Jewish preacher in an obscure corner of the Roman Empire. An understanding of the power of Christianity requires a grasp of the freedom it offered to those laboring under the weight of the material world at that time. The spiritual message of Jesus acted to free men from that dominion. "And ye shall know the truth, and the truth shall make you free" (John 8:32). This is the astounding 'revelation' at the heart of the message of Jesus. Men are capable of the highest fortitude and heroism if they think it will lead to their freedom (as the United States discovered in the Vietnam war). The emphasis of the meaning of freedom is a recurrent theme of profound Christian thinkers (e. g. Nikolai Berdyaev, Paul Tillich); although, it must be said, this is not often transmitted in the activity of institutionalized Christian religion. The freedom in Christianity is the freedom arising out of any authentic spirituality; it is the freedom from bourgeois domination. Slavery to the power of external circumstances is the inevitable outcome of spiritless societies. Influences that add a spiritual element are experienced as liberating.

The European Renaissance provides an outstanding example of the awakening of creativity that follows a liberating development. In this case, it was obtaining freedom from the stultifying influence of institutional religion. Men became free to think in a way not previously possible. Access to the classical Greek writings was an important aspect of this development. One can look back to the Renaissance with a certain wistfulness since the personal freedom of those times seems not to be available in the present day with the latter's overwhelming complexity. Freedom seems to have been sacrificed for security and convenience. But past worlds have always seemed freer and simpler. It is easy to romanticize the past after its dangers and limitations have passed away.

The scientific progress of the nineteenth and twentieth century has led to a widespread (but not universal) freedom from material cares that would have appeared incredible to former societies. The new technologies have released a great deal of human energy that would have been previously required to assure physical survival. Yet along with this development has appeared a *dehumanization* of human life that may be regarded as a new form of barbarism. In his long essay entitled *The New Middle Ages*, Nikolai Berdyaev called attention to this new barbarism. It cannot be said that this has been reversed up to the present time. Still the relative freedom from economic pressures provides great opportunities to contemporary individuals.

It is to the enduring credit of Karl Marx and others like him that they awoke men to the meaning of the relentless pressures imposed by work slavery. It is ironic that the liberation from this form of slavery occurred to a much greater extent in capitalistic society than in the communist one. Like Freud at a later time, Marx refused to recognize a metaphysical basis of the desire for freedom. It was a tragic occurrence for humanity that the mature Marx and his followers lost themselves in the complexities of economic theory and the distractions of revolution (especially Lenin whom his contemporary Berdyaev diagnosed as being afflicted with 'rationalistic madness'). Again, curiously akin to Freud, Marx worshipped science and did not acknowledge the spiritual appeal of communism (a modern Jewish trait). In his great novel *The Possessed* or latterly translated into English as *The Demons,* Dostoevsky accurately foretold the outcome of the 'rationalistic madness' of communism.

In the Anglo-Saxon world and its outgrowths, the significance of freedom has always been greatly appreciated. The past successes of English-speaking nations in international life can be attributed to their sense of personal freedom. Many stock phrases illustrate this awareness—e.g., "a freeborn Englishman," "the land of the free," "let freedom ring," "the free world," and so on. Many famous quotes from English-speaking heroes refer to "liberty" as the quintessential ingredient for a fulfilling life.

The greatest expenditures of effort will be made by individuals to obtain their freedom. Numerous examples of this truism can easily come to mind. The forms of slavery have changed through history ranging from the brute force of physical enslavement to the more subtle varieties of social exploitation and thought control. The common denominator is the ever-present tendency to deny other human beings the right to express themselves freely, to make decisions about their own affairs, and to explore the world according to their own inclinations and abilities.

The justification for slavery is often on an altruistic basis, on the argument that a particular form of unfreedom is in the best interests of the enslaved or of the society in which they live. Even the cruelties of African slavery were justified on this basis. But slavery is always the forced infantilization of human beings. It is revealed in its deepest sense in Dostoevsky's Legend of the Grand Inquisitor (*The Brothers Karamazov*) in which the Inquisitor asserts to the returning Jesus that human beings are not ready for his message of freedom, that the forceful methods of the Roman Catholic Inquisition, relying on miracle, mystery, and authority, were necessary for the welfare of humanity.

The justification of any form of slavery on altruistic grounds is almost always a hypocritical stance on the part of the defender of the particular form of repression. Baser human motives are generally at work; these are envy, fear, and greed—the deadliest of human sins. The workings of greed are the most obvious; most defenders of slavery are nervous that they will lose money, property, or prerogatives as a result of extensions of freedom. Fear takes the form of apprehensiveness about the consequences of the unknown; men prefer the status quo to liberating changes, especially when they are benefitting from a current situation. New conditions require new efforts that are resisted by established, aging elements in society.

Envy is the emotion least recognized, but is a powerful force in human affairs. This observation was made by Melanie Klein, an influential psychoanalyst who emphasized the importance of childhood emotions carried over into adult life (*Envy and Gratitude*). Those who feel, usually unconsciously, that they have been deprived of certain gratifications in life tend to strenuously resist others obtaining them. H. L. Mencken once defined a Puritan as a person who lives in constant fear that someone, somewhere, somehow is enjoying himself. Medieval Christians assigned envy an important place in the pantheon of human sins. Jacob Boehme, that peculiar but insightful mystic, regarded envy as one of the chief assets of the devil through which man is led to damnation (*Six Theosophic Points*). Envy deserves more attention as a cause of personality distortion and as an antecedent to the slavery of man by man.

Great strides have been made in the past in the cause of human freedom, but slavery in all its manifold forms has definitely not been abolished from human societies. Each generation must make its own contribution to freedom. [My contribution is this essay—Au.] The problem is that forms of slavery vary greatly and individuals are often enslaved without knowing it. Those growing up in slavery have no knowledge of freedom; an exceptional effort is required of them to form new concepts and behaviors regarding free human existence. Once the concept is formed through the mysterious workings of the human spirit, slavery becomes intolerable and individuals will spare no sacrifice, including that of their lives, to achieve freedom.

Men tend to glory in the accomplishments of past eras as if somehow they can obtain credit for the efforts and sacrifices of their forebears. They will boast of political freedoms that were obtained with the blood of ancestors. They will be self-satisfied in their material wellbeing, rarely remembering that they have largely inherited it from daring and resourceful predecessors. They enjoy freedom of thought and religion that have been obtained by courageous individuals of past eras. Yet they neglect the moral requirement to obtain new freedoms in their own times.

Physical slavery and the slavery of extreme poverty have been largely abolished in the western world, even though they still exist in other areas of the planet. Religious and political freedoms have long since been acquired. But there are pervasive problems in western societies. More than in former times, when concerns for physical survival were preeminent, men expect fulfillment of their personality needs during their lifetime. Drug abuse, alcoholism, food overindulgence, and other self-destructive behaviors, with the consequences of mental disorder and violence, are found at all levels of society. It is the age of the psychotherapist, the one who is sought after to heal troubled souls. The prevalence of personality disorders can only mean that men are still subject to slaveries, to the absence of freedom for personality development.[*]

There is really no reason to believe that society should have reached the millennium and abolished all slavery from human life. It is far more likely that man has failed to recognize slaveries still operating in society that adversely affect the development of his personality. It is the thesis of this writing that there exists a deadly slavery interfering with the human personality at its highest level of function. I refer to the suppression of erotic expression through the institution of marriage.

---

[*] A remarkable statement by Henry Miller about self-liberation in life can be found in the first pages of *Tropic of Capricorn*. Miller often reveals his inclination toward existential philosophy in his novels.

FETTERS ON EROTIC LOVE

> And he said to them the Pharisees, The Sabbath was made for man, and not man for the Sabbath.
> —The Gospel According to Mark 2:27

> The Human Spirit is in prison.
> —Berdyaev, *The Meaning of the Creative Act*

> What use is a man who has spent all his time philosophizing without ever troubling anyone? (said of Plato)
> —Diogenes of Sinope, *Les Cyniques Grecs* (L. Paquet)

History has conspired against free erotic expression. Plato himself set the example for the devaluation of heterosexual erotic love because of the homosexual proclivities of his society. The ancient Judaic world looked with suspicion on *Eros* possibly because of its long struggle against phallic cultism. Old Testament morality only recognized demeaning sexual lust and harlotry in erotic relationships outside of marriage. (The eroticism of the *Song of Solomon* is an isolated exception.) Jesus himself, while never expressly condemning erotic expression, did not seem to think highly of its importance. It finally remained for the apostle Paul, founder of the Christian religion, to set the tone for ethical and spiritual attitudes of Christianity toward sexuality: "It is good for a man not to touch a woman" (1 Corinthians 7:1). Erotic life in the Christian world has never recovered from this soul-killing dictum. Compromises, adaptations, rationalizations have not served to revive its existence in the Christian conception of the spiritual life. It remains a suspect phenomenon, suitable perhaps temporarily in the life of the young, dangerous for the irreligious, and acceptable only when safely confined to the structured institution of marriage.

Philosophers who might have discovered the meaning of heterosexual erotic love have been ill suited to do so. The philosopher in western society has been a scholar, a systematizer, even at times a visionary, but rarely a fully developed personality. Immanuel Kant, generally regarded as the greatest philosopher after Plato and Aristotle, is believed to have died celibate at age 80 years. Kant set a tradition for German philosophy, orienting its practitioners toward de-eroticized attitudes and toward the scholarly systematizing of their philosophies. Even the eccentric and rebellious Kierkegaard feared erotic involvement although he continually obsessed over it in his writings. Nietzsche, who had freed himself of the constraints of Christianity, appears to have been traumatized by his failures at erotic expression.[*]

No matter how brilliant an individual may be, he cannot perceive meaning in an area of life in which he has no experience. The significance of erotic life can only be grasped through personal experience. The metaphysical meaning of *Eros,* more than any other form of human understanding, must be grasped in the context of the life of the philosopher. This is a large part of the dictum that philosophy is not dreaming, but action.

The connection of erotic expression to the time-honored institution of marriage receives much sanctimonious attention from those who would like to fuse the two behaviors. A great deal of nonsense and hypocrisy has been set forth on this subject. It is noteworthy, however, that virtually always those who write seriously about erotic feelings have little or nothing to say on the topic of marriage. Marriage and *Eros* exist on different levels of

---

[*] Nietzsche is known only to have had one erotic relationship of any consequence, which probably was never consummated. This was with Lou Salomé, a young avant-garde woman who soon lost interest in Nietzsche. The remainder of his creative life was largely spent alone. Nietzsche's life was a sad one, his genius for philosophical expression turning into querulousness and final insanity. Had he achieved fulfilling erotic relationships, his life might have taken a different direction.

human life; pious platitudes will not alter the reality of this difference.

Marriage is a social institution based on a vow and a commitment. It is a vast undertaking, an assumption of responsibility, and an acceptance of a mission in life. Marriage is one of the most remarkable acts of intentionality of human beings, often undertaken with no appreciation of its true nature. Success in marriage is based upon character traits that have nothing to do with erotic life. Within the family emerging from the marital act are developed the qualities of devotion, responsibility, and compassion that constitute much of the substance of the human personality. In the carrying out of their life's work, two individuals join hands to confront an uncaring, often hostile world.

Beyond the requirements of character, the marital experience can be affectionate and supportive. Individuals find the strength to stand up to life's vicissitudes within the context of supportive family life. Marriage can be a great consolation to man; this is why he may tenaciously hold on to it amidst the many stresses on the institution.

Foremost among the values of marriage is its role in the nurturance of children. It seems to be one of man's deepest feelings to wish to create progeny. The new person develops within the family structure because the presence of two parents is one of nature's ways of protecting development. As a generality, reduplication in nature is insurance against the risks of single entities. This is true in physiology as well as in societal life as most essential body organs are duplicated. The double parent situation is a valuable asset in the difficult task of rearing children.[*]

There is a sustained purpose in family life that can hardly be found in any other human activity. The formation of a family is one of the great creative acts in human life, perhaps the only one in the lives of most. Loathe to find spirituality in erotic life, man has freely assigned it to family life, so much so that it often appears as if the family has totally preempted the spiritual strivings of men and women. It is not surprising, therefore, that society wishes to

---

[*] Even two parents are often felt to be not enough in the world. The institution of godparents was developed as further protection against the loss or inadequacy of natural parents.

protect this institution and honors it greatly in its values for human life.

Yet in spite of all these virtues, the institution of marriage and the family are decaying in our time. It is disconcerting to find that the evidence of decay is most evident in the most advanced and productive elements of society. Discussions of the demise of the family are in the air, and alternative approaches to social life are undergoing consideration. Divorce is endemic with its calamitous effect on the raising of children. Nevertheless, it must be recognized that divorce is only the tip of the iceberg of marital discontent. It is often only the brave who risk the traumas of divorce, traumas that are magnified by the soulless legal system. The passive or fearful remain in erotic unfulfillment, suppressing their disappointment and anger to the detriment of themselves and those close to them.

The decay of the marital institution, in the opinion of this writer, can be largely traced to its repressive effect on erotic expression. The essence of erotic life survives only in an atmosphere of freedom, while the essence of marriage requires controlled stability. Marriage is a controlling influence brought to human relationships. But the erotic impulse cannot be controlled and no amount of "technology of sex" will ever change the need for freedom in erotic life. Chaucer, with his poet's sensitivity to erotic expression, wrote these lines of great insight and poetic beauty:

> Love wol nat been constreyned by maistrye.
> [mastery]
> When maistrye cometh, the God of Love anon
> beteth his wyngs, and farewel, he is gon!
> Love is a thyng as any spirit free.
> Women, of kynde [nature], desiren libertee,
> and not to be constreyned as a thrall;
> and so doon men, if I sooth seyen shal.
> The Franklin's Tale, *Canterbury Tales*

Chaucer's spelling is unfamiliar to the modern reader but his sentiments should not be. Germaine Greer said the same idea more succinctly, if less poetically: "A lover who comes to your bed of his own accord is more likely to sleep with his arms around you than a lover who has nowhere else to sleep" (*The Female Eunuch*).

Because of this inherent contradiction, marriage has often been the graveyard of erotic life. It is a living burial because the erotic impulse is never extinguished completely in the mind of man, whatever his age. But it can go underground and exhibit its influence in devious harmful ways. Freud's experience as a psychiatrist permitted him to fully gauge the effects of suppression of the erotic impulse as a result of exclusive marital relationships. In his monograph where he elaborated his final view on western civilization, he graphically portrayed the inhibiting effects of societal marriage on sexual life (*Civilization and its Discontents*). Freud wondered if human society could survive the trauma of such repression. But Freud's own personality was not suited for finding solutions to this dilemma.

Some of the greatest tragedies in human existence have come about because of the conflict between erotic desires and family life. Yet, unlike sexual dividedness, the conflict is not insoluble but is one that is imposed by societal attitudes. It has been greatly exacerbated by tyrannical and self-serving constraints of organized religions. Dependent upon bourgeois family life for financial support, there is a hidden venal motive of churches to avoid threats to the family regardless of the well being of its members. The Roman Catholic Church openly forbids divorce. (Jesus' admonition that a man's foes may be of his own household has been long forgotten.) This motive operates equally for those whose own needs rely upon a stable marital relationship and who utilize theologically based values to justify monogamy. However, the strongest justification for maintaining the stability of family life is in the nurturance of children, not in lifelong marital security for adults.

The termination of a marriage is a serious defeat in life and should be performed only as a necessary measure to preserve personality. In the presence of children, one may consider whether elements of the personality should be sacrificed for their sake. Yet in last analysis, if the core of one's own personality cannot be maintained in marriage, separation is an obligation to self as well as others who may be harmed by the personality disturbances of an individual. It is tragically true that a man may have to leave wife and children to find himself (Luke 18: 29-30). Jesus was not always consistent on this matter indicating that he too as a human being had his limitations. It is even more tragic when such a circumstance involves a person in an adversary relationship with those of his former household.

Separation from a marital partner is often sought under the illusion that a new mate will solve the contradictions inherent in the institution of monogamy. The modern romantic has absorbed the idea that the marital relationship cannot be dispensed with in erotic love, that "love (erotic) and marriage" are inseparable as a popular song stated and that the absence of one reduces the other to a sham and mockery. He or she thinks to solve the problem of erotic life by confining erotic gratification to rigidly monogamous relationships.[*] However, disappointment and depression is the fate of the extreme marital romantic since his worldview is not consonant with the reality of erotic love. On the other hand, the life of a compulsive Don Juan does not permit the existence of marriage. While romantic attitudes are an essential element in the growth of the human personality, fanatical romanticism is a destructive tendency that ultimately destroys one's personality.

As in all forms of tyranny, domination of the life of an individual is made possible through ignorance: in this case, ignorance of the significance of the erotic impulse for personality development. Societal culture has failed to appreciate the importance of erotic relationships and has permitted their repression through exclusive idealization of the family. In

---

[*] This was not the case in the medieval conception of romantic love. The great medieval love stories were always outside of marriage, albeit only in the upper classes of society. The compendium of the practices of 'courtly' love published by Andreas Capellanus specifically denies the possibility of love of sexes within marriage on the grounds that true love cannot exist where there is an *obligation* of marital partners to each other (*The Art of Courtly Love*; cf. Chaucer quoted above). *The Allegory of Love* is an early work of C. S. Lewis that gives an interesting account of the antecedents of the romantic concept of marriage. Lewis himself is a good example of the type of Christian apologist who has set Christian attitudes toward erotic love and marriage.

marriage, men and women often thoughtlessly give up their birthright of free erotic expression without considering the meaning of their act of self-renunciation.

However, western societies have recognized that slavery is incompatible with the dignity of the human personality. Frank slavery has been long since abandoned. It is not permissible that a man may renounce his freedom, even for a limited time period. The custom of indentured servants has passed into history. No vow can bind a person to servitude if he no longer wishes to honor it. The same is extended to mental life; enlightened societies permit every man to change his mind and adopt new beliefs no matter how fervent his past allegiances may have been.

For some reason, society has not extended this same high ideal of human freedom to erotic life. Punishment is meted out for free erotic life after a person has entered into marriage. In former times, the punishment may have been death or mutilation. Adultery is still punished by stoning unto death in parts of the Islamic world. In western contemporary society it can be the cruel and unusual punishment of loss of family. Men and women have been conditioned to accept the rightfulness of the suppression of their erotic life and out of envy or wounded pride vengefully insist on punishment for those who seek freedom. Even self-hatred may arise from the guilt induced by 'illicit' erotic expression. Abelard believed that his castration at the hands of Heloise's vengeful kinsmen was just retribution for his sin. It is astonishing to see how intelligent individuals can be taught to believe in the justice of these attitudes. Individuals are insufficiently suspicious of the social institutions in which they live; being childishly trustful, they often accept societal attitudes that involve them in self-destructive behaviors.

The apologists for the renunciation of *Eros* after marriage regard it as appropriate only at the initiation of a relationship between an unmarried man and an unmarried woman. Kierkegaard waxed eloquently of the one erotic experience permitted to a Christian. Soloviev conceived of its transformation into marital fidelity as a moral achievement. It is as though the erotic expression of an individual is analogous to the winged male ant that falls to earth to die after insemination of a female.[*] Erotic life is to be transmuted into the totally different nature of marital existence. Yet how can one expect that the erotic impulse would disappear upon acceptance of the marriage vow? If there is a metaphysical meaning to human sexuality, it must flow from the spirit of the individuals involved and not conform to a social institution. If an erotic relationship exists with a spouse, it is in spite of marriage, not because of it. When erotic feelings survive marriage, it means that metaphysical consciousness has overcome the societal element of marriage.

There is a tragic quality about the disintegration of man's most significant social institution through its conflict with erotic impulses. Society seems to be retrogressing as a consequence of loss of family values. Erotic expression and marital stability seem to require separation for the survival of the family, and even more, for the survival of spiritually significant individuals. Such behaviors are not unknown in certain elements of society and need acceptance. The means of accomplishing separation requires all the intelligence, determination, and compassion possessed by men and women. [**] It is as if an ancient custom deeply imbedded in the fabric of society must be overturned because it has become harmful to the individuals in that society. Yet there is no alternative if individuals are to move on in their personality development.

A person has an absolute right to the privacy of his erotic life. A fundamental feature of *Eros* is privacy. The world has no right to intrude upon lovers since their intercourse involves no others. They are outside of the societal whirl; intrusion of society into erotic love is its death. One can only express erotic impulses

---

[*] A fascinating account of nature's ruthless approach to sexuality can be found in K. von Frisch's *The Dancing Bees* (1953), an altered English translation of *Aus dem Leben der Bienen.*

[**] A sensitive approach to this issue was discussed by the O'Neills in their book entitled *Open Marriage*. Although there is nothing metaphysical about their discussion of *eros*, they understood the meaning of freedom for erotic expression. Their ideas can serve as examples of guidelines for free erotic relationships.

in seclusion; the display of the erotic in public spectacles is a sign of societal degeneration. If erotic impulses are free, an individual will naturally adjust them to other aspects of his life. Kant observed that human beings always wish to be 'good', because it is in the nature of the human spirit to wish it. It is perverted influences and institutions that often transform man into something 'bad'.

A person is under no obligation to reveal his soul to a hostile society. "Give not that which is holy unto the dogs, neither cast ye your pearls before swine, lest they trample them under their feet and turn again to rend you (Matthew 7:6). Jesus himself fell silent when questioned by Pilate and was not condemned by him. These sayings and legends have great symbolic significance. Even in a court of law, statements made under duress have no legal authority. What duress could be greater than threats to the wellbeing of a person's family, to his career, or his position in society? There are times when a man cannot avail himself of the luxury of openness. Compulsive openness is a sign of a weak or immature personality.

It is naïve to believe that utter truthfulness is an infallible guide to the complexity of human circumstances. A man must consider, judge, and learn to contain himself. One may have to act in devious ways at times in order to reconcile different elements of his existence; deceptiveness may be required at times in one's life. Like punishment, deception would not be necessary in a perfect world. Like punishment, excessive deception is harmful both to the deceiver and the deceived. Habitual deceit tends to corrupt the personality, which is one reason why an intelligent individual hesitates to be a deceiver for he senses the injurious effects of deception. But truthfulness is not a categorical imperative. William Blake saw deeply into the human soul:

> A truth that's told with bad intent
> beats all the lies you can invent.
> *Auguries of Innocence*

What is Truth for one may be Death for another.

When all is said and done, a person must be always prepared to bear the consequences of his acts with dignity. If he is not, he should forego the desire for full personality development when it involves behavior contrary to societal standards. The Russian Social Revolutionaries and Anarchists, imbued with a moral fervor beyond that of Kant, justified their assassinations by their willingness to give up their own lives for their actions. This doctrine of terrorism led to the extermination of the flower of the Russian revolutionary movement and paved the way to power for the more opportunistic Bolsheviks. In light of history, it is impossible to justify their behavior. Yet the memory of the early Russian revolutionaries is respected because of their dignity and moral aspect of their lives.

Regarding the question of morality, there is a self-centeredness of two in marital exclusivity that is overlooked in the idealization of marriage. Traditional marriage erects an impassible spiritual barrier between each marital partner and other members of the opposite sex. This apartness has an element of 'immorality' to it; it is a form of 'apartheid' with all the evil consequences of this state of affairs. The time has come to move beyond the exclusivity of family-centered Old Testament morality in the matter of relationships of the sexes. On a social level, the time has come to speak of the immorality of traditional marriage. Jesus reminded his fellow Jews that the Sabbath was made for man, and not vice versa; in this thought extended to marriage will lie an enlightened understanding of marital 'morality'.

Morality is concerned with man; its judgments should be dependent on knowledge of man's nature and needs and on the awareness of his sexual dividedness. In this sense, the issue of exclusivity versus plurality has no dogmatic answers. Aimless promiscuity is debauching and leads to loss of coherence of the personality; rigid monogamy is narrow and stultifying, resulting in petrifying of the personality. Between the Scylla of debauchery and the Charybdis of rigidity, each human being must steer his own course guided by his sense of his own needs for personality development.

In no area of life is respect for personal individuality more important than in the area of erotic expression. In case this task should appear to be too difficult and a person be tempted to fall back into the security of time hallowed traditions, he should bring to mind the fearful vision of William Blake with its import for every individual:

> I cry, Love, Love: happy happy Love! free as the
> mountain wind!
> Can that be Love, that drinks another as sponge
> drinks water?
> That clouds with jealousy his nights, with weepings
> all the day?
> To spin a web of age around him, grey and hoary!
> Dark!
> Till his eyes sicken at the fruit that hangs before his
> sight.
> Such is self-love that envies all! a creeping skeleton
> with lamp-like eyes watching around the frozen
> marriage bed.
>
> *Visions of the Daughters of Albion*

EROS AND CREATIVITY

> The whole fullness of man's life must become a creative act.
>
> –Berdyaev, *The Meaning of the Creative Act*

The most injurious effect of suppression of one's erotic life is not in sexual disturbances but in the arrest of personality development.[*] Preoccupied by blocked erotic impulses or rebelling against resented societal controls, an individual is incapable of fostering the creative elements of his personality. Boredom and irritability are signs of erotic repression; they indicate failure to achieve self-expression. Strong personalities resist boredom through rebellion or self-assertive behavior. The legend of Don Juan is an example of extreme assertiveness of a vital personality. Weaker personalities lapse into the diminishment of spirit that is the outcome of a de-eroticized life.

The muse of erotic love and the muse of artistic creativity are closely related, if not identical (as many women have instinctively known). Suppression of one has an inevitable adverse effect on the other. Erotic love is an art form to be ranked with the other arts (cf. E. Fromm, *The Art of Loving*). Preoccupation with

---

[*] The eccentric psychoanalyst Wilhelm Reich recognized the pervasive noxious impact of sexual repression upon personality development. He referred to blocked sexuality as "The Emotional Plague" that grips contemporary humanity. Reich was not submissive as was Freud. However, Reich's meaningless sexual physics reveals what can come from an exclusively scientific-mechanical conception of human sexuality (W. Reich, *Reich Speaks of Freud*, 1952).

255

physical sex may be a form of sublimation of repressed erotic impulses. Freud thought that 'spiritual' feelings were a sublimation of sexual drives, but the reverse is more often true; obsessive physical sexuality is a sublimation of unfulfilled spiritual eroticism. This is the deeper meaning of the ancient maxim, *Omne animal post coitum triste est.* (All animals are sad after coitus) It is only when men's eroticism is liberated that obsession with coitus fades and higher aspirations emerge. Once more, Blake brought his uncanny poetic vision to human life:

> Love too long from Me has fled,
> Twas dark deceit to earn my bread
> Twas covet or twas custom or
> Some Trifle not worth caring for
> That they may call a shame and Sin
> Love's temple that God dwelleth in
> and hide in secret hidden Shrine
> the Naked Human Form divine
> and render that a Lawless thing
> On which the Soul Expands its wing.
> *The Everlasting Gospel,* 1818

The pathos of these lines is almost unbearable. One suspects that they were autobiographical in spite of the tendency of scholars to idealize Blake's marital life. Blake's fate has been to have his art and poetry extolled, while ignoring his thoughts.

It is in creative activity that man's greatest possibility of spiritual development exists. Through his expression of the meaning he intuits in the universe, an individual acquires the heightened consciousness that stamps him as human. Berdyaev regarded the creative act of philosophy as the supreme achievement of the human soul, the means by which he attains to a higher form of life. Materialist-minded thinkers call this mysticism, which is merely a label for concealing their intellectual limitations. Creativity enhances the personality of creative individuals even though society may not recognize their value and may ultimately make their life within the society impossible.

Beyond personal fulfillment, man wishes to offer his creative acts to the world at large out of gratitude for his participation in life processes. Gratitude is a uniquely human quality that has been recognized in the earliest stages of development (M. Klein, *Envy and Gratitude*). There is no reason to limit gratitude to the superficial experiences in life; as man's soul matures and his consciousness deepens, he will be grateful for his opportunities for life at all levels. *L'Chayim*–To Life! is the traditional Jewish toast based on this higher consciousness. An individual may express his gratitude by honoring his parents, by acts of altruism and, most significantly of all, by freely offering his creative efforts to the world (then *attrape qui peut*). Finally, there is the gratitude expressed by the lover to the loved one for the opportunity of healing the sexual wound. This is a most important form of gratitude often ignored by the intelligentsia of society. The feeling of gratitude requires freedom, for without the latter a human being is as any other animal, chained to the determinism of impersonal nature and the world of material objects. Without freedom, there is nothing to be grateful for in this life. One must be free to feel gratitude.

There are those who believe that one must choose between the experiences of living and the experiences of creativity. It is a common conception that the creative individual withdraws from his personal life in order to fully direct his energies into creative activity. Unconventional behavior may produce the appearance of mental illness, which may be believed to be the price demanded by creativity. Admirers of creative individuals assume that personal incapacities should be tolerated for the sake of their artwork. Incredibly, Otto Rank, a psychoanalyst who was deeply interested in the psychology of creativity, came to an opposite conclusion; he asserted that creative individuals should renounce their work for the sake of their personal relationships (*Art and Artist*).

Unconventional behavior is not necessarily indicative of mental illness. Quite the opposite, it may indicate superior personality development. Inappropriate psychologizing applied to creative individuals began in antiquity with the labeling of Heraclitus as a depressed individual. The practice has continued to this day. In fact, however, the continued development of personality is dependent upon formation of new behavior patterns involving conflict with society. Deterministic *status quo* thinking never supports creative life or, ultimately, personality development. But the emergence of new values comes out of the life experiences of a creative person and their fruitful effects upon his mind. Creativity can never long be separated from life's processes without its degeneration into meaninglessness.

It is a moral necessity to actively resist influences that impede personality development (i.e., spiritual growth). Kant asserted it to be a *categorical imperative* that every man act according to the conceptions he can will to be universal law (*Metaphysics of Morals*). An earlier and simpler expression of the same idea is the Scriptural injunction to do unto others as you would wish them to do unto you. It is not enough to concur in the recesses of one's mind as to the desirability of this or that idea about living. A man's whole life must stand for something; in the *creation* of his own life, an individual is expressing his highest human potential. Hypocrisy is the ultimate sin, as Jesus never tired of repeating. Pious platitudes without actions lead to spiritual deterioration.

Men should resist slavery as antithetical to the essence of the free human spirit. Slavery of the erotic aspects of spirit is no different in nature from slavery of the physical self or of the thinking mind. It is a humiliation and a disgrace. An individual will never fully respect himself or be truly creative until he has freed himself from the chains of erotic enslavement. No amount of self-assertion in other areas of life will remedy this humiliation and disgrace.

Yet, as can be seen in the history of resistance to other forms of slavery, it is ultimately self-destructive to abandon all other considerations in life for a single-minded purpose. A totally free life uninfluenced by other human feelings is an inhuman one, and he who loves too easily or too intensely may be exhibiting corrupt elements of his personality. Individuals must also be responsive to feelings of compassion, devotion, and obligation. It is in the individual's reconciliation of the forces in his life that the human drama exists. But reconciliation does not mean surrender to tyranny.

Excessive attachment to material possessions and societal success is the greatest enemy of human freedom. The Gospels are filled with this insight of Jesus. Human beings are prone to hide behind mountains of money and possessions. But object possession has no meaning for the human soul, which can grow in the soil of erotic interpersonal relationships. There is often a psychotic quality to the bourgeois obsession with object acquisitions and with good physical health. Fear is the inevitable consequence of these obsessions since no one can be assured of his possessions or of his health; the uncertain nature of human existence extends to all aspects of his life. Fear is certainly the most degrading of all emotions because it is the polar opposite of love and reduces men to the level of frightened animals. And the myth of hell may be regarded as based on a person's existence in a life of fear.

Out of societal rejection and hostility arise events of great import. Only the ability to accept periods of aloneness will permit a man to move beyond the stagnation of social institutions, an ability that gradually emerges from man's discovery of his own spiritual being (cf. E. Berdyaev, *Solitude and Society*). E. F. Schumacher in his radical yet highly influential departure from conventional economic thought stated that the major task of his generation was one of "metaphysical reconstruction" (*Small is Beautiful*). If this is true for economic affairs, how much more true it must be for erotic experience, which has virtually always been viewed by society from a materialist bourgeois or mindlessly romantic point of view. Until the erotic impulse in man is accepted for what it is—a manifestation of metaphysical need in man's nature—until it is liberated from the shackles of superannuated dogmas, men will continue to be shackled personalities, deprived of the opportunity for personal fulfillment.

FOURTH PART

CONCLUDING DIVAGATIONS

To begin with, I am a conscious independent existent at this instant. I have my share of reality, minimal though it may be. My relationship with others is tenuous and their reactions to me are uncertain. What I need is to protect my tiny share of reality from disintegration before its time. The past is over and the future uncertain. My sliver of the present reality is all that I have. I must not toss it away over useless messes of pottage.

The bit of life within me is precious. But precious for me only? For whom else? My answer: Precious for the 'ultimate reality' (God, Divinity), of which I am the metaphysical offspring. 'God' will sustain me even if nothing else will. I feel the Biblical *Psalms* to be the response of an anguished individual(s) to metaphysical isolation.

~ ~ ~

The awareness that I am part of Divinity reassures and calms me. My weaknesses can be forgiven by my metaphysical 'father' even if my natural father could not do so. I am not alone. Yet I wonder if there is any *reality* to this feeling? Is it merely a form of self-engendered reassurance? The feeling that I am part of an ultimate reality does not have the same clarity as my feeling that I exist as a soul or that I have a physical body. Still, it is a feeling that I choose to accept as valid. It fits into my sense of the scheme of things and does not offend my intellectual conscience.

260

I sense I am an offspring of God, not offspring in a natural sense but in a more meaningful metaphysical sense. My intellect does not reject this belief. It completes and fulfills me. I would like to cry "Hosanna; glory to the highest!" but something in me prevents me from doing so. I do not wish to be presumptuous. I do not need to engage in pious rituals, kill fatted calves, or to perform holy *mitsvot* to validate my feelings about my relationship to God. The thought is sufficient for me and, no doubt, for Him also. Religions are unnecessary impediments to my feeling about the ultimate reality and my connection to it. Henry David Thoreau advised to speak only to the Master of the house, not to any of His servants.

I believe that the poet Heinrich Heine was right to finally come to a realization that the Bible is the repository of the relevant ideas necessary to put one's life on a secure footing. One has only to find them amidst the mess of its primitive and dogmatic verbiage.

Time for me to meditate on what I have just written and think through their consequences.

~ ~ ~

Some important thoughts in the Bible:

- ➤ There exists an ultimate creative reality (God) to whom human beings are connected – *Genesis*
- ➤ God created man in his image – *Genesis*
- ➤ God stands with an individual – *Psalms*
- ➤ An individual can be born again in spirit – *Gospels*
- ➤ One must love God intensely – *Deuteronomy*
- ➤ Don't try to understand all aspects of reality – *Job*

Of course, one must approach the Bible with a discerning philosophical eye and not in search of religious authority (as do Talmudists and fundamentalists).

~ ~ ~

Important idea: *Myself* developing is a metaphysical phenomenon; my feelings, intuitions, emotions, desires and *thoughts* are all metaphysical phenomena. My metaphysical existence occurs in a different dimension from that of material existence.

Important idea: *Human death* is a crossing over of the spiritual self to somewhere else. How, why, or wherefore this occurs is impossible to know or even imagine (Heraclitus). In the end, one must accept this limitation of one's consciousness.

Important idea: In the beginning is *desire*; the soul forms later and develops itself in order to add to God, the ultimate reality.

~ ~ ~

I wear masks wherever I go so it doesn't make much difference where I live. My principal activity is creating philosophical artwork; writing out my thoughts, feelings, and intuitions. I have been searching for a stable worldview (faith) but haven't found it so far. Perhaps it will come in time but I am already well into old age. I do think faith in 'myself alone' (the IRA motto) is not enough.

   Amor intellectualis Dei (Spinoza's intellectual love of God) is one answer. "Love God with all your heart, all your soul, all your mind" (Deuteronomy) is perhaps a better answer. But I think the Russian-Jewish philosopher Lev Shestov was wrong in opposing Jerusalem to Athens (*Athens and Jerusalem*). Both are needed for an effective faith: Athens – mind and Jerusalem – heart. One without the other leads to a dead end.

   God is not dead; only the Judeo-Christian God Jehovah is dead. In its place must come the God of Spinoza fused with the God of Jesus.

   Expressing these thoughts goes a long way to establishing their truth for me—creating *facts in my mind, realities in my soul.*

~ ~ ~

Concept: Man is a thinking animal who inevitably must come to worship Deity. But first he must establish a meaningful concept of Deity; otherwise worship quickly becomes stupid superstition or fanaticism.

I don't need a prayer shawl, a *minyan*, a church or synagogue to worship God. My mind suffices for the purpose. It, not my body, is my temple.

~ ~ ~

Does 'God' exist outside of my mind? From whence comes the strange pull toward a greater being that I often feel? The feeling is strongest when I first awake in the morning and the world has not yet imposed itself upon me. I am not given to pursuing chimeras. Why would recognizing Him be such a compelling feeling for an intellectual like myself if He did not exist? This being must exist in some way incomprehensible to me. Here is where faith in my powers of discernment enters. He must exist.

~ ~ ~

Looking at and becoming conscious of the vastness of the Mediterranean Sea from my hotel room in Menton, France is a potent stimulus to my soul. But hearing all the motorized traffic rushing along in the street below is a reminder of the civilization in which I live.

"Eternity come to me—I have need of you!"

~ ~ ~

If I wrote in French or German, I think I would have some readers. But writing in English, I write for myself. I have gotten used to this state of affairs. I am like an old bachelor who can no longer live with anyone. I don't think I could tolerate a strange reader peering into my writings, and even worse yet, a literary critic passing judgment on them. It is best for me to remain unknown.

~ ~ ~

I have abandoned the idea of a personal God as a childish one. An ultimate reality must be suprapersonal. If I ultimately merge with it, I also will be suprapersonal. The old me will be transformed like the caterpillar that becomes a butterfly. This is what I understand to be the meaning of the term 'transfiguration'. My mounting bodily infirmities are signs that this event cannot be far off. Why bemoan the former when the latter will be such an interesting happening. The more my physical abilities diminish, the more my consciousness increases. I truly believe my soul is going somewhere after my physical death.

~ ~ ~

I respect the idea of 'born again' individuals. I feel that I am a born again philosopher. I am not born again in Christ but that is a minor detail. Being born again *spiritually* is what is important. As long as born again Christians are not fanatical or intolerant, I greatly prefer them to materialistic, over-intellectualized bourgeois.

~ ~ ~

There is hardly any greater pleasure for me then sitting on the *Promenade du Soleil* of Menton gazing at the azure Mediterranean with its distant horizon sharply in view. I envision this to be a stepping-stone to heaven. It is easier to imagine eternity looking straight ahead at the sea's horizon then straining one's neck upward toward the sky.

~ ~ ~

In a decadent and spiritually degenerating society, one's attitude toward God is crucial. It serves as a shield for one's soul.

I could be a Christian if I did not have to be baptized, accept Christ as my savior, or engage in similar inane activities. My attitude toward Jesus of Nazareth is similar to that held by his disciples: awe, reverence, affection. They saw him to be a superior personality. I see all the ponderous theological superstructures subsequently erected by the Christian institutions to be a lessening of his *human* importance, a transforming of his superior nature into an object of idol worship. Beware of clerics bearing prayers and preaching love!

~ ~ ~

For me, Menton is spiritual while Paris is intellectual. More and more, I prefer the former. Here in Menton, I can sit on a rock, gaze at the horizon, and concentrate on the development of my soul.

~ ~ ~

The contemporary American literary industry has no regard for me as a writer or philosopher. This situation is quite proper, as I have no regard for it either; neither intellectually, culturally or spiritually. The American literary world is dominated by a market-obsessed industry and by self-serving academic cliques. As a consequence, there is no serious interest in the human spirit; only in the interminable striving for profits and prestige. No self-respecting individual of any depth of mind should wish to be part of this decadent scene.

I ought to be ashamed of my involvement with it, miniscule though it may be. But I have no complaints. There is no entitlement for me to be recognized by the American culture industry. If it did, I would probably be unhappy, feeling that I should stand apart from it. If I lived in France and wrote in French, I would be even more alienated from the hypertrophied intellectualism of French philosophers that I also perceive as decadent. I find repulsive those who are ever ready to capitalize on the harshness of the world to their own advantage. No, I am fortunate to be where I am, relatively secure in my circumstances and free from oppression. I can develop and speak my mind as I wish. If no one in society notices, *peu importe*; my writing is self-instruction. However, against all the material evidence, I sense that a 'reality' beyond my society does notice. *Amor fati* is the right attitude for me.

~ ~ ~

As an independent philosopher, without a university affiliation or celebrity status, I am of little interest to academicians or litterateurs. They do not see any advantage to themselves in cultivating a relationship with me just on the basis of philosophical intercourse. It is better for me to avoid these kinds of people.

At my age and circumstances, I cannot expect market-oriented publishers to be interested in my writings. Like Kierkegaard and Nietzsche, I must rely on my own resources to bring what I write into objective form.

~ ~ ~

I have now reached an advanced age and am still apparently going strong physically and mentally. I don't know why I am lasting so long when my contemporaries are rapidly disappearing. However, there is no point in looking in the mouth of a gift horse. "Live till you die" is my motto.

~ ~ ~

Nikolai Berdyaev's emphasis on creativity, which necessarily means a life of striving, is more valuable than Lev Shestov's emphasis on faith. One must *create*; simply worshipping God is insufficient. If human beings have been created in God's image, they must be creative themselves. Creative artists, in the widest sense of the term, are God's favored people. They are usually crucified by the world in which they live; rarely, Lady Luck spares a few from such a fate. But if they become 'successful', they will pay a steep price for their success.

~ ~ ~

I am increasingly aware of the absolute solitude in which I exist as a philosopher. I have been cognizant of this circumstance for many years but only now am I becoming aware of its full significance and impact upon me. If I don't love God with all my heart and soul, I will be lost in a spiritual sense. Finding Him intellectually is not enough. In my opinion, Spinoza committed suicide because 'the intellectual love of God' was not sufficient to sustain him. The details of his death support my opinion.

Now I turn to the *Psalms* of the Old Testament for support. If the Psalmist could feel as he (they) did, I can also. His enemies are my enemies; his support can be my support. Sadly, the psalms have come to be used for liturgical purposes in churches and synagogues, rendering them meaningless for the individual.

God is within me; this is the truth I must constantly hammer home in my mind. To imagine he exists outside of me is the error that destroys my religious feelings. God dwells within my soul—or better yet, my soul is part of the ultimate reality called God.

My thought may be regarded as a passionate Spinozism: the intellectual love of God plus loving Him with all one's powers. Both are necessary for personal fulfillment.

Unlike Spinoza, I do not think that everything is a manifestation of God; I am not a pantheist. I think only *life* is a manifestation of God and that human life is its highest form. But this is a theo-ontological issue that I do not care to pursue. Whether there is life outside our planet is also an issue I have no opinion about. Life on earth is enough of a problem for me. The main thing is to cultivate my awareness of God.

~ ~ ~

For me, 'evil' individuals are like violent acts of nature; they may represent inexplicable assaults on human beings. Here one should have recourse to the wisdom of Shakespeare expressed by Hamlet, "There are more things between heaven and earth, Horatio, that are found in your philosophy." Morality, good and evil are human concepts, not those of God. Kant's categorical imperatives are not those of God. Nietzsche has discussed all this in his trail-blazing essay, *Truth and Falseness in an Extramoral Sense*.

~ ~ ~

Academic philosophers put their energies into writings and discussions that will further their careers. Private dialogues with individuals that do not serve this purpose are seen by them as a waste of time and energy. The world in the guise of academic success is always with them. Poor fools! They sell their humanity for messes of academic pottage.

~ ~ ~

Should I ever obtain calling cards they will say:

Richard Schain
Independent Philosopher
Man of God

~ ~ ~

Having written down all the wisdom I can think of, it remains for me to incorporate it into my soul—a task much harder than writing it down. Writing out one's thoughts is only the first small step toward acquiring wisdom. Assimilation into my psyche of what I have written is now needed.

I have always resisted committing myself to groups, institutions, or organizations of any type. I have not realized, however, that I need to commit myself to God—the ultimate reality. No group, institution, or organization can do this for me.

~ ~ ~

I remember previously saying that spiritually born again Christians are greatly to be preferred over mentally superficial intellectuals. But the former need to refine and purify their awareness of God. Idol worship or blind obedience to the Judeo-Christian Bible or other authority figures will not do.

~ ~ ~

Philosophy is a means to arrive at personal fulfillment, but is itself not that fulfillment; just as education is a means of acquiring wisdom, but is itself not wisdom. One must distinguish means from ends.

The dichotomy between reason and faith is a false one because of a confusion of means and ends. Reason is required to finally arrive at the fulfillment conferred by faith. If the former is dispensed with, one arrives at superstition, not faith. The Scholastics were wrong; one must start with reason and not with faith. They put the cart before the horse.

In this regard, the example of Augustine is instructive. This brilliant individual spent the first half of his life experiencing and thinking about the world. Only after much mental effort did he come to his faith. But the Abrahamic monotheisms do not recommend Augustine's path. Being saddled with a religion from childhood is a handicap that must be overcome through drastic measures and there is no guarantee that this handicap will ever be overcome.

~ ~ ~

I do not ever intend to abandon the drive toward personal development, toward the *augmentation of my being* that has been my goal throughout my life. It is the essential part of my personality. But I would like to complement it with an awareness of my role contributing to an ultimate metaphysical reality. Acquiring consciousness of this event can be referred to as being born again. I feel I have something to contribute to God and am not merely a passive worshipper.

Anyone who wishes to call metaphysical awareness 'mysticism' may do so but name-calling does not bother me. As far as I am concerned, all true progress in knowledge of the human condition from Heraclitus and Parmenides to Bergson and Berdyaev has been the result of mystical thinking. Scientific thought is for scientists who want to master nature, but philosophy is the province of metaphysically-minded thinkers. Out with all those who want to make philosophy a miserable stepchild of science!

~ ~ ~

Identification of a human individual with abstract categories is an erroneous act and leads to mistaken judgments. I am not merely an American, a doctor, a philosopher, a Jew, an expatriate, and so on. I am an individual human being. Attempts to identify me with any abstract category are doomed to failure. These categories serve the purposes of others whose agendas are different from mine, which is to fulfill myself as a spiritual human being.

I know that I am part of the ongoing current of life. I am a part of the animal kingdom with special rational abilities. I have various superficial connections, but additionally, and most importantly, my soul is part of the ultimate metaphysical reality whose name is God. My personality contributes to Him and I think He would be less without me. My unique individual perception of reality is my contribution to God. He may be an infinite force moving in ways beyond my ken, but he benefits by my contribution to Him.

Worldly or bodily catastrophes might overwhelm me (e.g., the horrors of a holocaust or the occurrence of cancer, stroke, etc.). One has to deal with fate as best one can. Living one's life until its natural end is not an entitlement of existence in this world. However, consciousness of one's *metaphysical destiny* must not be relinquished—not by me anyway.

~ ~ ~

I would like to fully break out of the shell of my rigid rationality. Yet I seem often to be incapable of doing so. I need a hammer to break the shell. Nietzsche broke out of his shell by going mad but his fate does not appeal to me. I need to fully accept my participation in the reality of God through rational *faith*.

~ ~ ~

My deeper yearnings are the most important element in my life. Never mind that they represent mystical leanings. They are signs of my participation in the reality of existence. But where do they come from? What do they signify? What is it that I want? I struggle to find the answers to these questions. Religion and Neurology have contributed nothing to my understanding of them. I have the feeling that God has the answers, but I am still uncertain and do not know how to communicate with Him.

~ ~ ~

The artist Marc Chagall and the writer Heinrich Heine thought the Bible was the great source of wisdom in human life. Many have agreed with them and I have come to agree also. However, the Bible needs to be supplemented with other philosophical works embodying spiritual visions such as those by Antero de Quental, Nicolai Berdyaev. Teilhard de Chardin, and—my own writings. No sense in assuming a false modesty!

The prose writings of Antero de Quental, the important Portuguese poet-philosopher, have been largely ignored outside of Portugal because few philosophers read Portuguese. But a French translation of his main philosophical work, *General Tendencies of Philosophy in the Second Half of the Nineteenth Century*[*] (a most inapt title), has become available, which ought to increase his influence among metaphysically-minded readers. An English translation is needed.

~ ~ ~

I have been trying for a number of years to grasp the thoughts of Lev Shestov, a Russian-Jewish philosopher little known to the Anglophone world, but prominent among devotees of Russian philosophy. He lived the last twenty years of his life in exile, as did so many Russian philosophers who were unfortunate enough to have lived at the time of the Bolshevik takeover of Russia. I say unfortunate, but this may be a misstatement because it may well be that their experience of exile, especially in France, stimulated them to a broadening of their intellectual horizons.

Shestov is a special case. He possessed a vast philosophic erudition, but he conducted a relentless campaign against the role of 'reason' in human development. His prolific writings are backed up by his exceptional knowledge of the history of thought. They consist of original analyses of the foremost figures of western religion and philosophy. Shestov's writings can be regarded as

---

[*]*Tendances Générales De La Philosophie Dans La Second Moitié Du XIXe Siècle*; Éditions de la Différence.

outstanding examples of the fine European tradition of the 'feuilleton'.

Most considerations of Shestov concentrate on his espousal of 'faith' as contrasted with 'reason.' It is assumed that the faith he means is faith in the Judeo-Christian God. He quotes often from the Hebrew and Greek scriptures contrasting their viewpoints with those of classical Greek philosophers, much to the disadvantage of the latter. One is hard-pressed to classify his religious preference as Jew or Christian. Probably the best attitude is to view him as a spiritual Jew who looks with favor on the New Testament. However, he never converted to Christianity.

Having read most of his books, including his *magnum opus*, *Athens and Jerusalem*, I find most of what he writes is withering criticism of the role of reason (Athens) in western philosophy. Shestov is very metaphysically minded. But he has little specific to say on the subject of faith (Jerusalem), other than it represents a higher condition of mind than that of rationality. One cannot say that he is an 'inspired' writer. He is rather a *littérateur* who provides new approaches to western philosophy.

However, in the last few pages of *Athens and Jerusalem*, his last book, I think he finally reveals his true viewpoint. He discusses the attitudes of Socrates, the virtuous father of western philosophy and Alcibiades, a larger than life figure in Athenian history, contemporaneous with Socrates. Shestov feels it is proper for these two very different personalities to be guided by their own *daemon*. Not to be guided by one's own *daemon* is to have a slave morality. He quotes Nietzsche's insight on the morality of slaves, saying that here Nietzsche was much closer to Christianity than his critics imagined. Finally, the last sentences of his book joins Nietzsche's concept of 'will to power' with the teachings of Plato and Plotinus. "Philosophy must go forward fearlessly, without taking account of anything whatever..." Without *Besinnung* (the cardinal error of philosophers), without reflection or reasoning. Reasoning or *Bisinnung* is for obedient weaklings, which is how Shestov regarded most philosophers' intellectual attitudes.

The faith Shestov really proposes is faith in the intuitive self of the individual. If an individual develops faith in God, he should trust his faith; if he has faith in his inner self, he should trust that as well. In Shestov's profoundly metaphysical mind, the two forms of faith ultimately merge together. Faith is the key idea but Shestov does not concern himself much with specific objects of faith. Rather he seems to fully embrace the Nietzschean dictum of 'reverence for oneself', meaning one's own believing, willing, yearning soul. One could think Shestov should have entitled his last book 'Socrates or Nietzsche'. As for myself, I think more highly of Shestov, now that I understand his concealed personalism.

~ ~ ~

I believe the meaning of human life is to be found in the consciousness of one's *metaphysical self.* From that awareness spring all the important metaphysical issues; God, the soul, freedom, creativity, even the forms of immortality. The Biblical commandment: "love God with all your soul, with all your heart, with all your strength" (Deut. 6:5) in my view is meant to apply to one's metaphysical consciousness merging with an ultimate reality. It was repeated by Jesus as the greatest commandment; encompassing all the law and the prophets (Mt. 22:37).

ORACLES

- The dubious faith of the philosopher is that what he feels, all can feel.

- Dogmatic religion is not opium for the people, it is honey laced with cyanide.

- "It is finished," said Jesus as he gave up his ghost, but unhappily he was not taken at his word.

- "I searched out myself" (Heraclitus)—the alpha and omega of human existence.

- What I like best is reality,
  The impetuous flow of my thought.

- The Threefold Path to an American dead end: Career, Marriage, and the Family.

- Eternity is the dear friend with whom one must never lose touch.

- Energies that go into religion inevitably are at the expense of the creative self.

- Until one wrings out the childishness in oneself, he is not fit to know reality.

- Without higher consciousness, it is hardly worth the effort to maintain space in a congested planet.

- If you don't comprehend, wait a while; something may happen.

- The only peak experiences I know are erotic fulfillment and creative activity. The rest are tasteless icings.

- If love is the most overindulged emotion, gratitude is the one most in need of cultivation.

- 'But what does true love mean, mother?'
  It means goodbye to your soul, child.'

- Christianity is a bone chewed by starved dogs.
  Higher Education refers to learning Greek.
  Fame is the ignoble refuge of the literati.
  The scholar is the hyena figure of literature.
  Love me; love my thoughts.

- One must deal with the desire for fame as one deals with an insane passion; wait until the feeling passes.

- 'The one thing needful is to know reality" sayeth this preacher.

- Just as with one's family, children are the natural enemy of consciousness. This is an area where Jesus was misinformed.

- The antique Pillars of Consciousness were experience and expression.

- Søren Kierkegaard was poisoned by his father—a common Christian practice.

- The most consuming passion is the passion for reality. This insight was Sophocles' contribution to culture.

- One who cannot suffer, cannot learn about reality. Παθει μαθος.

- If ignorance is absence of consciousness, sin is the rejection of same.

- Welcome erotic love, fear endless love.

- I have found my maturity to lie in the progressive intensification of radical thought.

- Before you die, make at least one pilgrimage—even if it is to nowhere.

- It is destiny to lose a life, but it is tragedy not to gain a soul.

- Plato was the first authentic litterateur; his breed has absconded with philosophy.

- Rhythm, rhyme, and subtle meters
are Santa's reindeer
that pull weak readers.

- Writing a long book is the peculiar death dance of literati.

- The bourgeois is a person who has sold his soul for societal rewards—usually at far too high a price for value obtained.

- My mind has been riven in two by a thunderbolt called bourgeois life.

- Those who do not support euthanasia usually do not believe in the human soul.

- To love another too much or too long is a form of self-mutilation.

- Without direction, energy dissipates,
without consciousness, there is no direction,
without anger, there is no consciousness.

- Learning to earn money is like learning to walk; it is a knack one hopes will lead somewhere—but it rarely does.

- The United States has produced a special pathological type: the compulsive moneygrubber.

- Unraveling the mysterious energy of existence is what art has always been all about.

- It is essential to grasp the dementia prevalent in one's society.

- To be 'successful' in a demented society…

- The National Publishing Scene: *Exhibition of the Successful.*

- The world could be heated for a hundred years with books that need trashing.

- When I look at my compatriots, I usually see only mouths and fingers.

- The continuous smile is the pathognomonic stigmata of bourgeois dementia. No blood test is needed.

- I impatiently advise my fellow bourgeois: "Lift your head out of the trough so that you can see something!"

- Technology is like a cancer attached to the skin; the outlook for cure is not too bad.

- To be a professional scientist is like being a silver miner— the metal rarely gives any heat and the vein soon gives out.

- I have been a research worker so I know what it is to copulate with witches and prostitutes.

- Saintliness is consciousness without contempt.

- Nietzsche understood German culture but it drove him insane anyway.

- *Amor fati!* I love my fate to its very core and rind.

EPILOGUE

It would not be incorrect to say the term 'philosophy' as it is utilized in this book is often synonymous with the term 'mysticism'. I entirely reject all the negative connotations of the latter word. One of the definitions of mysticism given in the *American Heritage Dictionary of the English Language* is as follows: "any belief in the existence of realities beyond perceptual or intellectual apprehension but central to being and directly accessible to intuition." This definition can easily be applied to the concept of philosophy that originated and developed in Greek antiquity, and currently has been abandoned in favor of 'scientific' thinking. This to me has been a serious error in western cultural development.

The term mysticism has also been applied to the beliefs of those who feel within themselves a direct contact with 'Divinity'. This has been the path of Christian and Jewish mysticism. Religious mysticism is to be distinguished from existential mysticism, which rests entirely upon the interior state of individuals. In last analysis, this distinction may be difficult to maintain for who can discern the origin of intuitions? I think it better, however, not to have recourse to Divinity to describe one's own beliefs. A mature person should be able to stand on his own two feet and utilize his own functioning mind to justify his feelings about ultimate realities.

There have been only a few philosophers in the twentieth century whose mystical thinking has achieved widespread recognition. Among these are *Henri Bergson,* who relied heavily on biological sciences to support his mystical idea of an *élan vital* underlying life; *Carl Jung*, who developed his mystical idea of *archetypes* within a psychoanalytic framework; and *Nikolai Berdyaev*, whose mystical ideas about freedom, creativity, and the spirit are based on a Christian foundation. *Père Teilhard de Chardin* had recourse to all the sciences plus his own background in Christian faith to develop a mystical philosophy about the human phenomenon.

In my judgment, what is needed in philosophy today is an independent *existential mysticism*, firmly based on intuitions that derive from an individual's life experiences (conceived in the broadest sense). Ideas based on imaginative mental activity are more appropriate for the art forms of literary fiction. Rigor is needed in intuitional philosophy as much as in scientific thought. The temptations of esotericism or Gnosticism are to be avoided. Existential philosophy is the highest form of expressive art and the most spiritual of all human activities. It is too important to an individual to be left to sectarians or to professional scholars. No one should fear boldly following the path of existential thought into the realities of his own life. Simple introspection is not enough. What comes later, as the far-seeing Heraclitus said, no one can know or even imagine.

Glen Ellen, Alamos, Sonoita, Paris, Menton
2008-2017

THE END

ADAM'S LOVE SONG

After a long while, I opened my eyes,
stretched my limbs,
suddenly, without warning,
things happened.

"Come my lovely, let us rise together,
we have slept but now we shall awaken,
let us take a magic journey
and you shall hear a magic story;
Yes, let us go together swiftly.

We two shall row upon this eerie river,
it is an unsafe place.
Do not forget
Creatures lurk below the surface
lashing armored tails
that can hurt us.
Be vigilant my sweet,
the creatures strike quickly
when provoked.

We shall steer our silent vessel
through marshes black, midst soaking drizzle
looking, searching for the light
that will illuminate the night,
who can say in what waterway
we shall find our heart's desire?

though in this leaky vessel of ours
     sits tyrant Fear
     a Presence
     saying nothing."

Early in my life I learned obedience,
order was my liege, the lord of all,
I have lived my days and evenings
with measured tread on narrow pathways.
I have sat at one thousand tables,
I have measured word and deed
by careful formulae.

"That is an appropriate statement, yes, right on target,
I suggest, however, that we modify the phraseology
in order that the subcommittee recommendations
for long term support be facilitated."
     The rhythm moves on
     like a dull tom-tom,
     bam-bam, boom-boom
     goes the tom-tom
     in my weakening mind.

"What is it? What is it, my beloved?"
you ask,
I cannot say,
I wipe away the glistening tears.

"Yes son, I know it's difficult,
you mustn't expect too much
of your teachers;
they're underpaid, you know,
for that matter, don't
expect too much of your mother
or of me;
we too
are underpaid
and over controlled."
 (I would like to say I have special feelings for you

but I don't know how to put it;
the language fails me.)

I shall not fail you, my dear ones!
You are my sacred treasure,
you are my special solace,
you are what all men wish for,
By God! I shall not fail you!
I shall defend you....
A man who can't defend his family
isn't worth very much.

A sadness creeps over me,
all clothed in gray,
a sadness is my mistress,
with withered arms
she presses my trembling form
to her barren breasts.
"Oh my beloved, I am so tormented!"

I have searched for compensating power,
a tiger am I, stalking its prey
camouflaged, I blend into the scenery,
I wait, I watch, I spring—aha!, aha!
I am not to be trifled with,
I am surrounded by victims,
I live in a savage land,
that's the way it is.

"Laurence, it is important that we discover—and correct
the origin of this discrepancy of values.
Contradictory results
suggest unreliability of our entire program.
Let us review the data,
especially concentrating on the lower portion
of the spectral frequencies.
Let's straighten this problem out!

Reality—the only question,

where does it dwell?
Perhaps it is only a figment
of my overwrought imagination.

Coming and going, I spend my days,
the truth emerges;
I am the comic 'I',
somewhere, I feel,
I am amusing someone.

Looking in the mirror,
I see the familiar face, unruly hair
growing blacker with age (a demonic sign),
behind the mirror
I see another face,
this face is marked
with the grisly signs of illness,
a ruined nose, contorted
by a golden ring of bondage,
gray bloodless lips
tightly sewn together
with silver thread.
Away leper!—sick doomed thing
Away leper!—lost soul,
lost to love's sweet intercourse.

I move through the Valley of Death,
In the dim recesses of my soul
dwells an angry demon.
I live on the edge of a razor blade
balanced on a shaky basin.
"Beloved, stand by me!"

Destiny is position,
My destiny is a folded card perched on a yellow napkin,
telling me of my evening's recreation.
"How are you, Rena? It's nice to see you
this evening. What have you been up to lately?
You look so tan and fit.

Ah yes, the Holly Linda tennis-go-round...
No, I hardly play at all."
Rena, what kind of thoughts are within your head?
Are you alive or are you dead?
Or is my suspicion at all correct
That you're a folded card from an absurd deck?
Are you like me or do you like tea?
Are you a tanned shred of insanity?
"Good night, Rena, good night,
see you again soon."

I cannot Howl, the problem is Me,
I know this world is Mine, only Me
Me and Mine is what I must see,
I must dig deeply, must feel it all,
Must merge it all, yes all.
but if I Howl and Weep and Cry
I shall turn into a butterfly.

"My beloved, into this uncharted land,
we shall move forth together,
let us not shrink from love,
let us not be the vassal
of humiliating fear."

"Ah my dear one, in your bright eyes
I see a shining, flaming prize,
this moment your sweet self I must have,
your love for me my wound will salve,
Yes! Yes! I shall be your eternal lover,
my passion for you has endless power."

"Boogie with me, baby!
Don't be frightened."

"Oh let us depart from time and space,
let us fly to that joyous place
and live as one for eternity,
there must be something more

beyond this jagged rocky shore,
so full of evil things."

"Be my lover, I shall be yours
and we will fly aloft on wings,
satin lined with airy folds,
dream on, dream on, my beloved one,
fear not the sun scorched deserts
and we shall live together
in love's kind embraces."

The alchemy of language seizes my imagination,
my smooth and limpid speech musically records
the gay and gloomy history of my yearnings;
full of libido, I caress the words
with paroxysms of desirous longing.
I am entranced by my torrent of words.
In the Beginning was the Word!

By the ocean shore
The roaring surf pounds the silent sands,
Seabirds scream, blackened hulks
Rear jagged timbers into the evening mists.
Wissen wir's, Freunde, wissen wir's nicht
in dem menschlichen Angesicht?
That night, Esmeralda and I
swam in the storm tossed sea,
the carved dolphin fell adrift, she gave me hyacinths,
we breakfasted on scones and sarsaparilla.
Who knows the man with the Blue Guitar?
Or the lad with the Pink Oboe?
Plato knows....

"Well, I think the old guy's right,
ban the buggers before they bore us to death.
No, not you....silly!"

I hesitate, I vacillate, I ponder,
In the Beginning was there the Word?

No, it can't be so,
A spirit guides me,
now I know
Im Anfang war die Tat.

"*Die Tat?*—well, it means the Act…
What Act? What a foolish question!
Are you some kind of intellectual, my sweet?
Why the Act of Love, of course!"

Dinner is served at seven,
night after night, there is dinner at seven,
I have lived a life of dinners at seven,
Dinner at seven is the path to heaven,
someone must have believed that I can thrive
by having dinner at seven for the rest of my life.

"Yes, the value of our home has increased remarkably,
I don't think there is anything wrong with that.
A fine home adds a lot to one's life.
Don't you find that to be true, Adam?
I don't know how Henry and I would manage without air-
conditioning,
It would be just a nightmare to swelter in the summer."

The tragic pattern has been set,
I have been baptized in the waters of what must be.
Father Custom, my parent, guides the tempo of my life,
He expects much of me, he is master,
He rewards me with margaritas and a Lexus
and with strength for the hunting,
he punishes my transgressions,
with Him, I know just where I stand.

I have long resented this unjust predicament,
I have often thought away the cruel impediment,
I have soared toward the heavens far above the land,
I have dived deep into the ocean's murky embrace,
all have I given for you and I,

but at the end of the Odyssey,
the harp is muted, the song is stilled,
remains the ancient hallowed vise
that clamps the body with holy ties.

There is something strange about my poetry,
it always ends with the same old tired turkey.
"My dear, shall we have turkey for dinner?"

If I can't act, I can always analyze,
find consolation in contempt
seek mastery, tell lies....
a tragic comedown, though.

Where is the little boy
who played here yesterday?
"Gone, they had to move away,
he cried but there was no help for it.
No, his father lives in Kansas City.
He left one wheel of his bicycle,
it fell off, I suppose,
he couldn't reattach it.
I couldn't either,
no one could."

There are no easy riders
among my little partners.

I have known slavery well,
it has been the only evil I have ever known
in my life. I know no other,
I hate it, its ugly face,
its brazen chains, forcing me
to kneel abjectly, destroying
my sensitivities, tormenting
my proud spirit, humiliating
my gentle self, crushing
the best within me.
Love is freedom's gift,

For the sake of love
I shall be free!

This land is made for you and I. . . .
This life is lived by you and I. . . .

Do I dare? Have I the wisdom?
To alter an archaic outmoded system.
And what will come into its place?
perhaps some creature from outer space.

How exciting!!!

Oh sunflower child, so gay and so free,
Your star-crossed self appeals to me,
take care, take care, fragile thing,
a tiger lies hidden, ready to spring,
learn how to live independently,
the mistress of your life.

My boat is breaking up, the timbers do not hold,
I sink, I cannot find the line of life,
Reality, my lost parent, is a flickering memory.
Mother, I need you
now!

I know the worm of fear that dwells within my heart,
I know the ambiguities of life that waste my powers,
yet without equivocation, in full possession of my faculties,
having experienced all life's gratifications and disappointments,
I assert that the love of sexes,
given freely, given fully,
gives life its highest value, the tender healing value,
all the rest is birth dues, housekeeping and the like,
and fame?—fame is what I seek when love's warm rays
have passed away.

What do I fear?
pain, ridicule, privation?

Yes, all these too,
but most of all,
I fear my soul's rejection.
I must learn more about rejection.

It is said that a harp made responsive to the fingers
          gives music to many winds,
patiently, I wait for the moment of responsiveness
          though time is not my friend,
I await the season of the harvest
          though the world's gardens are rocky places.
I know love by its erotic energy
          though its stinging rain is deadly,
the world smiles at the virgin lovers
          but to love all ages owe submission,
the Celestial Rose is a vision of love
          but my vision is not of heaven.

Dante, you odd Italian,
eat your mystic heart out!

                    The poem is the thing
say some
          who prefer
                    the thing
                              to the thought.
to the living
          it may be
                    this poem
                              is a thing
(a deformed thing?)
          but it is
                    wearing out
                              growing old
                                        it is becoming
a curious toad
          so I think
                    that I shall
                              terminate it

in a moment.

Das Ewig-Weibliche noch zieht mich hinan. . . .
that old Black Magic still weaves its spell. . . .
you know, I must spread my wings and fly
when the wind blows.

I don't know about advancing the language,
but I do like to sing to my friends.

THE LAST TRANSPORT

Early in my life I learned to bow my head,
to cringe, to creep, to slither on my belly
and to worship all the powers of the world.
How I learned such worship, I scarcely can recall,
but through a thousand secret channels,
and through a thousand hidden entries,
the worship seeped into my child's mind
like streams of molten lava congealing the life below.

The lava cracked, in time green shoots of life thrust through,
I breathed, I felt, I noticed all about
Life gaily fluttering in the breezes,
Ah, how good it was to notice life!

I redirected long felt fears,
must I fear Want? Loneliness? Rejection?
those ancient hobgoblins of a bitter world?
have I not known them all?
Shall not Death, the rescuer, possess me in the end?
The subtle swaying rhythms of life
are gifts to be firmly grasped
with untrembling hands.

I learned to fear unconscious slavery,
I learned to notice slavery is to begin its conquest,
unseen bondage poisons furtively,
as an assassin doing his deeds by night.

I saw the cruel obsession with daylong labor,
The great escape from self, the unperceived addiction.
Oh my poor brothers! yourselves devoured,
dehumanized, emptied of your inner selves,
servants to a monstrous habit,
the way of the soulless,
the way of the bee-hive.

My eyes grew sharper,
I found the secret vice of societal marriage,
an incestuous passion that dwells in its depths,
the mother-passion arising from the ashes of erotic love,
the passion of the wife-mother
coiled as a chain about the necks of man and woman,
transforming the amorous Dalliance of the Eagles
into a sheltering nest for that great infant,
the married man.

I struggled against the narcissistic frenzy,
the compulsion to merge self with the world's stuff,
I yearned to stand alone,
to arise from that glittering pool of illusion,
Great Spirit! Teach me to stand alone!

I have known the thrill of transport out of self
into achievement, into power, into societal adulation,
I have known the family transport,
the feeling of the extended self,
and I have known the surge of sex, the fiercest transport,
engulfed by Eros, I have soared into the burning beyond.

Transport—a mysterious plank over the sea of life,
boldly I have stepped forth on that plank,
then have I plunged into that foaming sea,
madly seeking oblivion.

Marooned, abandoned, I have been cast adrift
On an immense uncharted sea,
A lonely sailor am I,

finding my way by dim stars,
and by the glimmerings of distant lighthouses
perched on fogbound cliffs.

My poem is a psalm to my searching self,
I am the single Me, the only truth I know,
I am the mission, the sacred task,
silently, I consider myself,
I have a strange beauty!

I have made the vow of freedom
the vow never to be broken,
again, I set free the mystic vessel of my life,
again, the moorings are released.
Vigilantly, watching the treacherous reefs,
I move toward the open sea,
I make my way into deep waters,
my spirit calmly scanning the distant horizon,
searching for an unseen destination.

ALSO BY RICHARD SCHAIN

Affirmations of Reality, 1982

Philosophic Artwork, 1983

Fanatic of the Mind, 1987

Souls Exist, 1988

The Legend of Nietzsche's Syphilis, 2001

Reverence for the Soul, 2001

Radical Metaphysics, 2003

In Love With Eternity, Philosophical Essays and Fragments, 2005

Behold the Philosopher, A Memoir, 2007

Sculpting Sententiae, An Art Form of Independent Philosophy, 2010

Interior Lights in a Dark Universe, 2012

Souls Exist, 2nd ed., 2013

Spiritual Pathways: Existential Reflections on God and the Soul, 2014

Toward an Existential Philosophy of the Soul, 2014

Landesman's Journal, Meditations of a Forest Philosopher, 2016

The Anarchist Banker of Fernando Pessoa, in press

A Contemporary Logos, Sententiae, Sentences in Small Spaces, Pamphlets containing Aphorisms, 1984-85.

The author is an independent philosopher living in Alamos, Mexico and Sonoita, Arizona. His many publications reflect the predicament of a metaphysical self existing in a materialist age of science.

www.ingramcontent.com/pod-product-compliance
Lightning Source LLC
Chambersburg PA
CBHW052031090426
42739CB00010B/1862